Paupers' Paris

Miles Turner is an impoverished American, living in Oregon. He spent his fourteenth birthday in Paris and never recovered from the experience. Over the years he has spent vacations there whenever possible, living cheaply, exploring the city, and researching his book. He has made numerous Parisian friends and contacts, whom he has persuaded to reveal hints and well-kept secrets for the penniless traveller.

Paupers' Paris

MILES TURNER

PAN BOOKS

First published 1982 by Pan Books
This revised edition published 1997 by Pan Books

an imprint of Macmillan Publishers Ltd
25 Eccleston Place, London SW1W 9NF
and Basingstoke

Associated companies throughout the world

Revised 1983, 1984, 1986, 1988, 1990, 1992

ISBN 0 330 35022 6

Copyright © Miles Turner 1982, 1983, 1984, 1986, 1988, 1990, 1992, 1997

The right of Miles Turner to be identified as the
author of this work has been asserted by him in accordance
with the Copyright, Designs and Patents Act 1988.

This 1997 edition revised by Fiona Lazareff.

9 8 7 6 5 4 3 2 1

A CIP catalogue record for this book is available from
the British Library

Typeset by CentraCet, Saffron Walden
Printed and bound in Great Britain by
Mackays of Chatham plc, Chatham, Kent

Contents

Introduction

This book is for paupers – or if not paupers, cheapskates – who would love to spend some time in Paris, but would prefer not to spend much money. It sets out to prove that, while Paris has justly earned its reputation as one of the world's more outrageously expensive places, there are hundreds of ways to avoid the city's grasping hands and still share in its pleasures.

If we have a single motto, it's 'Sleep cheap and eat well'. It turns out that you can sleep *and* eat for next to nothing, and do both rather well if you set your mind to it. There are cheap routes to Paris; there is limitless cheap transportation all over the city; there are hundreds of low-budget hotels that are clean and friendly and charming; there are incredible meals to be had in the humblest restaurants; there are more free spectacles, sights and attractions per square block than anywhere else we can think of. We've tried to fill this book with specifics – a mere scratching of the surface – of all these subjects, and with some pointers on how to use the information.

To make maximum use of our information, you'll need at least some of the following:

- *A sense of adventure:* If tripe is half the price of steak on a menu, and you've never had tripe before but have a queasy idea of what it is, still you're *driven* to order tripe.

- *A low entertainment threshold:* That quality which makes a person a cheap date. In Paris it means that the clientele of the nearest brasserie is as interesting and amusing and exciting to you as the entire cast of Covent Garden.

- *Unqualified adoration for the city:* Everyone loves Paris in theory. To relish that slightly gorgonzola-like aroma in the lower depths of the Métro is a measure of true love.

- *A sense of self-mockery:* If you can't enjoy the spectacle of yourself as a total imbecile when it comes to haggling (or saying *bonjour*, for that matter), then you should go to Denmark where they speak English.

- *A tourist's loathing of other tourists:* The best thing that can happen to you is when a Parisian asks *you* for directions.

- *More taste than money:* While you can't bring back a Cézanne, or the contents of Lanvin's windows, at least you will have paid them a visit.

- *A good deal of low cunning:* The ability to wash (and dry) your entire wardrobe in a hotel basin without leaving a trail of evidence for the chambermaid.

We suggest that you take with you at least a few words of French – even if they're all in a pocket phrase book. Parisians are rather proud of their language, and on their own turf would rather converse in French than try their English out on you. If you need help, or just crave human contact, remember that the French help those who help themselves. The ice begins to break when you make the effort to communicate, but it's up to you.

It's this lack of linguistic hospitality – and also some misunderstandings about customs and manners – that has given the French a reputation for rudeness among travellers. *La politesse* is central to all transactions in France. The French are formal: they'll preface every question with '*Pardon, Monsieur ...*' or '*S'il vous plaît, Madame ...*' They'll consider *you* rude if you don't do the same.

Remember also that Parisians who habitually deal with apparently ill-mannered American, German and English tourists – who may in fact be less callous than tongue-tied – develop their own callousness for dealing with foreigners. If you stay off the beaten track (and with the help of this book you can), you'll avoid these unfortunates and come into contact with a friendly, garrulous, buoyant race of Parisians you've never met or heard of before.

You will note that certain *arrondissements* – the 5e, 7e, 8e, 11e, parts of the 19e and 20e – have been given fairly lengthy descriptions in the Footwork section (page 45), while others, better known apparently, have been slighted. This is highly personal; the ones that are in are there because they are places we have enjoyed which may have been missed out in other publications. The 6e, especially around St-Germain-des-Prés, has been written about everywhere; visited by everyone. As a consequence, waiters can be rude, hotels overcrowded and overpriced, meals in the main to be avoided. You'll go there anyway, and find your own pleasures without help from us, so there's no general talk about it here. But it would be a pity to miss, for example, the less-known areas such as the *Batignolles* (page 45), the hidden and charming parts of the haughty 7e *arrondissement*, and the pleasant, rather domestic bits of the forbiddingly elegant 8e. Two neighbourhoods which are changing so fast that it's impossible to include them with complete accuracy in this edition are the 11e around the *Bastille*, and the 13e near the rue de Tolbiac – Asia in Paris. You'll have the delight of discovering them yourselves.

Paupers' Paris is the result of the labour and support of all my friends and relatives: many contributions from people I've never met but am most grateful to. Lena Skadegård took over the task of editing and coordinating information, and putting it all on disc for this new edition. A crew of young Paris residents ate their way through the restaurants, and in the process turned up many new ones. I still owe thanks to my mother Martha Lomask, who researched and rewrote entire sections of the original editions, and my father Milton, who covered art galleries, museums and music as well as verifying dozens of addresses. Leonard Yoon helped me plot the book over countless bottles of wine, and Charlie White closed his eyes to my long absences from work. M. Patrick Goyet of the French Government Tourist Office in London has helped with letters of introduction, and Marc Humphries answered our last-minute questions. The Bureau de Tourisme in Paris has been generous with advice and information. And to the kind readers who have contributed useful tips and corrected egregious errors in previous editions of *Paupers' Paris*, many, many thanks. I hope the city will always treat them as well as they have treated me.

It should be noted that prices in this book were correct in spring/summer 1996. We hope they'll still be as accurate as possible when you read these pages, but costs do have a habit of creeping upward when your back is turned. Still, Paris continues to offer, at very good value, hundreds of good hotels, charming restaurants, and its own distinctive attractions for those who know where, and how, to look.

Miles Turner

Allons-y (Preliminaries)

WHO?

Before anything else you must decide – who's going? Just you, your nearest and dearest, your bridge club? A few pros and cons:

Travelling alone is the best way to see and do exactly what you want. If you get lost or bungle seriously in a restaurant, feel like sleeping until noon, or decide to spend the rest of your life in Paris, the decisions (and the responsibility) are all yours. If you make mistakes, nobody else gets blamed. You don't have to adjust to anyone else's diet, or standards of hygiene, or attention span. If you can handle being on your own, it's the best way to go.

But, if your gregariousness and your French aren't up to it, you can die of loneliness. You'll have to survive on a few encounters a day – in cafés, restaurants and shops. You'll always be treated well, if you make the effort to make yourself understood, but it's unlikely that anyone will adopt you.

Travelling in company guarantees that you'll have someone with whom to share the experience, and a helping hand if things get dicey. The drawback is that your tastes will differ. *You* will want to spend eight hours in one room of the Louvre *she* will choose to spend the day playing pinball in a café behind the Bastille.

Our solution for days when your energy and interests don't coincide is to split up: plan to meet for lunch, and plan to meet again for dinner. (Agree in advance on the restaurants. No last minute searches on an empty stomach.) If one person doesn't show up within fifteen minutes, the other forges ahead with the meal. We've found this to be a good way to avoid getting bored with each other. Travelling in company can have an odd, isolating effect. You can get on each other's nerves. And it's bad for your French.

Small groups can be worked in the same way: you can pack the kids off to the Bois, send Granny to the flea market, and you're on your own. The one thing you must not do is travel in packs. Even a benign dictatorship can end up in communal misery.

WHEN TO GO?

Of course it's best to go when the spirit moves you. When you can't stand the grind a minute more. When your boss *lets* you go. But if it's not purely a matter of impulse, desperation, budget, or tight scheduling, there are a few matters about timing to consider.

HIGH SEASON, NORMAL SEASON, LOW SEASON

Naturally, this affects airline or Eurostar fares: get a good travel agent, or do a real study yourself of what the flying people are up to at any given moment. Equally important: there are certain times of the year when it's all but impossible to find a room in central Paris or anywhere near it at short notice. The Bureau de Tourisme in Paris has this advice:

MOST HEAVILY BOOKED PERIODS:
April: 5–7
May: 16–18 and 24–30
June: 1–9
September: 6–9 and 18–21
October: 3–13 and 20–24
November: 12–16
December: 26–31

Do not arrive on these dates without a firm booking.

The most heavily booked periods in Paris are almost always the same, year to year, with the exception of special events. The determined periods are based on trade shows and holidays. During 1997, special events are as follows: an air show and a visit from the Pope in June; in November a tentatively scheduled trade show for the

International Textile Machine Association; and in 1998 the Football World Championship will take place in France.

NORMAL PERIODS:
The two middle weeks of January, March, most of April (avoid Easter weekend), some of May and September and the second half of October.

LOW SEASON:
Surprisingly, July, August, early January, and most of February are times when you can almost always find a room somewhere, even on short notice. However, it may be a good precaution to have a firm booking for the first few days if arriving in July or August. For real Paris-lovers, the first weeks of both December and January (when the wonderful sales are on) can be the choicest time to be there; Paris is at its silvery best then, with the light shining through its bare trees and the life of the city vibrating all around.

We once found ourselves, through ridiculously bad timing, in Paris in the first week of March during two major trade fairs and the opening of an important art show. We managed to get a room in a very good, low-priced hotel, in a great neighbourhood we'd never stayed in before, which immediately became our second home. This was done by exerting ourselves somewhat, visiting a number of hotels until we found one that would have us for one night, which stretched to six. We wouldn't care to do this if arriving at midnight after a long flight, tired, drunk, or travelling with small children or an elderly companion.

CLIMATE
The weather can influence your plans and will certainly determine your wardrobe. To give you a rough idea – the mean temperature in February is 36.5°F (2.5°C), in July 65.5°F (18.5°C). East and north-west winds keep Paris cool and fairly dry in winter and spring; there can be stretches in December and January when bitter winds come shrieking across North Europe from, apparently, Siberia, and you'll be glad of woollies and a warm coat. Prevailing south-west winds bring the heaviest rains in summer and autumn, so pack a folding umbrella and a light, waterproof coat.

WHAT TO TAKE

Your wardrobe naturally depends on what you have, and how much you are willing to lug around. 'Travelling light' is a phrase that has an adventurous ring to it – people who drag along only one steamer trunk rather than three probably consider themselves light travellers – it's a relative term, but a worthwhile goal. We figure you can live comfortably, and indefinitely, on about 14 kilos of luggage; more if you are strong of arm or not averse to porters; less if you're a wimp, anti-porter, or have read the following list and know how to pack intelligently. In either case, here are a few suggestions:

1   Dress in layers – for all climates and most seasons. Everything should be easily washable or dry-cleanable and easily folded (or preferably rolled, which cuts down on creasing). Think twice about heavy items. If your overcoat is going to be a millstone, don't take it. In all but the dead of winter, rely on piling one sweater on top of another under that light waterproof wind-cheater.

2   Take nothing you haven't worn before, and nothing that you don't love. Take nothing you can't walk or climb in.

3   Take a couple of pairs of durable, comfortable, well-broken-in shoes; for women, they should be of different heel heights. Armies may travel on their stomachs, *you* travel on your feet.

4   *Indispensables*
    *   A cotton kimono
    *   A pair of rubber flip-flops (thongs, *zoris*, or whatever those Taiwanese sandals are called)
    *   For cold weather, a really warm, soft scarf – lambswool for preference. And two identical pairs of gloves, because you're going to lose one glove the day you arrive
    *   A telescopic umbrella – one that fits easily into the suitcase
    *   A good plush hand-towel – not too small – which will help pad breakables and will supplement the sometimes meagre one common in Paris hotels
    *   Soap in a plastic box

* Blow dryer, heated rollers, electric razor (see Electricity, page 225)

* A plastic carrier bag for unwashed clothes. A few plastic bags and twist ties. A featherweight bag that folds into your luggage and can double as an overnight case or carry home all the extras you will buy

* Nail scissors and, even more important, toenail clippers – real agony savers

* If you wear glasses or contacts, take an extra pair and/or a recent prescription

* If you can't sleep with the French bolster, your own inflatable pillow

* Medicines: an adequate supply, and a refillable prescription

* Indispensable for picnics, hotel, and otherwise: a cup and an immersion heater if you *must* have tea (see Electricity, page 225)

* A saucer-sized plate, a small sharp knife, a fork, a spoon. Be as ingenious as you want about this

* Clip-on reading light (220 volts) if you can't live without it and don't trust hotel lighting

* Three or four lightweight plastic hangers for drip-drying. A few clip-type clothes pegs. A little detergent in a plastic squeeze bottle (see Hotels, page 59)

* A corkscrew

* And, not to labour the obvious, don't forget your toothbrush.

MONEY QUESTIONS

(For denominations, mechanics and equivalents, see Money, page 236)

How much to take? Some advance decisions are going to be necessary here. You'll have to decide after considerable thought what's important to *you*, not to us or your next-door neighbour. Budget for your extravagance, and save somewhere else. Do you feel best in a room big enough to spread out wet coats, luggage, bottles, flowers, newspapers? That's what you should budget for. Can't live without *petit déjeuner* served in your room, or your own shower, a private loo, a lift? A hotel within an arm's length of the Louvre, or a quieter, cheaper, possibly more spacious place ten minutes away on the Métro? Budget for it. Save on museum entrance fees by going on Sundays (free or half-price) or have a week of picnic lunches instead of eating in restaurants.

TRANSPORT TO AND FROM PARIS
Maximum: £205: will buy you airfare, London-Paris and back, open-dated ticket and ultimate convenience.

Minimum: £49: provides the cheapest bus/boat/bus service and a modicum of discomfort.
   See page 15 for details.

HOTEL PER NIGHT
Maximum 350F: a nice, bourgeois hotel in a 'good', close-in district, all facilities including shower and loo.

Minimum 150F: cheap, clean, away from it all, no frills.
   See page 61 for details.

FOOD PER DAY
Maximum 250F: breakfast in bed, a lunch that will take up half the afternoon, and dinner half the night.

Minimum 125F: coffee at the *zinc* of the local café, a picnic lunch indoors or out, a modest but satisfying dinner.
   See page 96 for details.

GETTING AROUND
Maximum 200F: includes a few taxis for quick getaways to stations or after a late night out. (28F per day)

Minimum 67F: unlimited Métro/RER/bus travel for seven days.
   See page 31 for details.

THE SIGHTS
Maximum 130F: full price museum admissions; a movie; innumerable cups of coffee, seated.

Minimum 45F: everything gratis, or very, very cheap.

THE SHOPS
Maximum ?F: a matter of taste and income.

Minimum 0F: don't buy *anything*.

NECESSITIES
Maximum 250F: enough to get your hair cut, your laundry done, your baby sat, your post sent and your pockets full of change.

Minimum 45F: an afternoon in the laundrette, one cup of coffee, a visit to the lavatory and one postcard and a stamp.

EMERGENCIES
Maximum and minimum depend entirely on you. If you're accident-prone, provide extra money for crises. If you have an invisible plastic shield, or a lot of sensible insurance, take less. But always keep some 'mad money' in reserve.

See page 255 for details.

HOW TO CARRY MONEY

CASH
You'll need some within five minutes of your arrival in Paris: enough to get you your *Carte Paris Visite* or *Carte Orange* (see page 36); enough to get a bite to eat and transport to your hotel; a few more francs for a left-luggage locker; possibly a phone call home, or to pay the *Hôtesses de Paris* for locating a room for you (see page 26). Arm yourself before you leave with at least 200F in cash to get you into town. Change pounds or dollars before you leave home, at a bank or *bureau de change* where you know you'll get a good rate.

TRAVELLER'S CHEQUES
Your own bank or building society may offer them as a free service (but avoid the lesser-known brands which can be difficult to cash in some Paris banks or bureaux). Size of denominations depends on how often you want to sign your name, and how careless you get when you've cashed a big one.

PERSONAL CHEQUES

Fortified with a cheque-cashing card from your bank, it is possible to cash personal cheques – Barclays lets you cash up to £250 per day, but charges 250F (or £30) and requires a time-consuming process.

EUROCHEQUES

Maximum amount per cheque is 1400F and up to three cheques can be cashed at a time (see page 240).

VISA, ACCESS, MASTERCARD, EUROCARD AND SUCH

Using your bank card directly to withdraw money takes about one minute and the charge is approximately 4 per cent of the amount withdrawn. You can use your credit card to get cash advances from banks showing the appropriate sign, or from an automatic cash dispenser out of hours. (The ACD is nicknamed 'the Harvey Wallbanger' by certain West Coast Americans.) The maximum withdrawal amounts are 2000F over a seven-day period and 5000F over a fourteen-day period with a Visa card.

Credit cards used abroad may not protect you against fraud, undelivered merchandise, or defective goods, as they do in this country (for purchases over £100). Therefore, only use credit cards for smallish purchases, for meals, petrol, etc., in other words, something you can eat, wear, use up, take home or discard. Even in France, it's dicey to buy something on a credit card (or with cash, for that matter) to be shipped to you later, unless you know the merchant is long-established and reputable. Big buys which go bad can leave you exposed to fraud, and the UK bank which issued your card can do nothing to alter this.

In France some shops will accept credit cards only for purchases over a certain amount (usually 100F), but they must display a notice to that effect either in the window or at the cash desk. This is true in *Gibert Jeune* bookshops in Paris; some restaurants will refuse to accept credit cards for inexpensive meals (such as a 55F set lunch menu) and must make this plain on the menu card.

Many small hotels, shops and restaurants cannot afford to pay the credit card companies a commission, so they may not accept your plastic; however, a surprising number of them will now take major credit cards, and it's certainly a great convenience to keep your cash in your pocket and let the card do the work. You can use your plastic to buy the *Carte Orange*, a *carnet*, or a two-, three- or five-day *Paris Visite* pass at ticket windows in the Métro, and often, with your PIN number, from automatic machines in the Métro station.

BOOKING HOTELS IN ADVANCE

If you know more or less what you want, where you want to be and how much you want to pay (see 'Au lit', page 55), it's a good idea to reserve in advance. It's not in the least difficult if you have a little time to work it out. It can save you energy and anxiety at the moment of your lowest ebb – your arrival in the chaos and confusion of the Paris airport, terminal or railway station.

Once you've picked a hotel, write a letter to the management. In French. Use, if you like, the form letter – a service of the Bureau de Tourisme – reproduced below. Specify the dates and time of arrival (especially if it will be after 6:00 p.m.), the date of departure (if you can), number of people and your requirements – with or without a loo or *salle de bain*, single or double room, breakfast and so on. In some cases you might be obliged to send an advance deposit in order to confirm a reservation.

Form letter to hotels (freely adapted from that used by the Paris Bureau de Tourisme):

Le Directeur
Hôtel   .. ..
Address   .. ..

Monsieur le Directeur,

Je vous serais obligé de me communiquer vos conditions
(I would be grateful if you would let me know your terms)
et tarifs pour un séjour de .. .. .. nuits, commençant le .. .. ..
(and prices for a stay of .. .. .. nights, beginning .. .. ..)
à .. .. .. heures, et se terminant le .. .. .. à .. .. .. heures.*
(at .. .. .. o'clock, and ending .. .. .. at .. .. .. o'clock.)

Nous souhaiterions réserver .. .. .. chambres àun lit
(We would like to reserve .. .. .. (single rooms))

(chambres à grand lit) (chambres à deux lits) (avec WC/bain/douche).
(double rooms) (twin-bedded rooms) (with WC/bath/shower).

Avec mes sincères remerciements,

*Use the 24-hour clock

USE AN INTERNATIONAL REPLY COUPON

Whether you're reserving a room or just asking for information from any French source (other than a government tourist agency), the hotel, shop or agency can exchange the coupon for return postage. Many of these operations are running on a tight margin, and cannot afford to send free information to rich tourists. The courtesy will be appreciated. A self-addressed airmail envelope is another form of good manners, and can help ensure that you do get a reply.

IRCs can be purchased at post offices in Britain.

POSTSCRIPTS TO PRELIMINARIES

Life-saving tips from the most experienced travelling paupers we know:

1   Never travel without a good supply of soft toilet paper (not just for obvious purposes, but for blowing noses, mopping brows and even as napkins for picnics).

2   Never travel with more luggage than you yourself can carry in comfort, without porter or taxi.

3   For dire emergencies, never travel without a little bit of cognac in a flask.

En route (Getting there)

Your choice of routes to Paris will depend on your finances and need for comfort, how much you will want to spend *en route*, how long you want to stay and what time of year (or time of day) gives you the best deal.

LONDON TO PARIS AND BACK

Myriad possibilities, listed from the cheapest to the dearest.

EUROLINES
National Express, the giant spiderweb that links all of the UK to London, can take you to Paris – and beyond – with its Euroline coaches. They leave from Victoria Coach Station, and run two daytime trips and one overnight.

	Return: day	Return: night	One way: day/night
ADULT	£44	£49	£36
STUDENTS under 26	£29	£44	£33
CHILDREN between 4–12 years	£33	£37	£29

Children under 4 travel free, if they sit on their parent's lap. Here's how you travel:

COACH/BOAT/COACH: Day trips are about nine hours, depending on road conditions, night trips as comfortable as can be expected – and you do save a night's hotel bill. But you'll roll into Paris with the dawn, and the first day can seem endless, as most hotels won't book you in until noon. The buses are equipped with reclining seats and all the usual facilities, and ventilation is reasonably good. Departure: Victoria Coach Station. Arrival: Eurolines Coach Station, avenue du Général de Gaulle in Bagnolet (east Paris, Métro Gallieni).

Book through any National Express office in the UK. In Paris, at the Eurolines Coach Station in Bagnolet, tel: 01 49 72 51 51 and their ticket office at 55 rue St-Jacques, 5e *arrondissement*, tel: 01 43 54 11 99; or at SNCF (French Railways): 01 45 82 50 50.

OTHER COACH SERVICES: Have a look at *Time Out* or the free sheets distributed on the street, mainly for young Aussies and New Zealanders, for details of other cheapos ... we have varying reports which range from 'not too bad considering the rock bottom fares', to 'beer-drinking all night long, smoke you could cut with a knife, and a coach driver who hadn't had a licence for long'. You make up your own mind.

HOVERSPEED

CITY SPRINT: Faster but more expensive than the above. Clean, comfortable coaches which take you from Victoria Coach Station in London and Dover and across on Hovercraft, then on the Autoroute into Paris. About seven hours' travelling time.

Departures vary with the seasons. In spring, there are two or three departures a day; from mid-June, three departures a day and one a night, dropping back to two or three in September. The first bus leaves London at 8:30 a.m., the last at 7:30 p.m. (in summer). Returning, you leave Paris on the first bus at 9:15 a.m., last bus at 11:00 p.m. (in summer). A useful way to travel if you are going on other European stops, as you can buy one-way or round-trip tickets and it's pretty cheap.

	One way	Return
ADULT	£36	£44
YOUNG PERSONS (16–25)	£33	£39
CHILD (4–11)	£29	£33

Children under 4 travel free.

Round-trip tickets are good for one year, but book your return journey four days before you plan to travel. Between the two countries the Hovercraft trip is noisy and fast, with a smooth-as-satin ride or a lot of bounce, as the weather dictates. People who order drinks are apt to get their comeuppance: what goes down, may come up.

Hovercraft and Seacat tickets are available from Hoverspeed, reservations, tel: 01304 240241 and British Rail centres and most travel agents. In Paris, Hoverspeed, tel: 0800 90 17 77.

Beware: some travel agents will try to apply a surcharge on any fare which includes continental rail travel. Others won't handle Senior Citizen rail tickets. If this happens to you, make your displeasure known on the spot and go to a more amenable travel agent.

STENA LINE
TRAIN/FERRY/TRAIN: Can be slower than the Hovercraft or Seacat, and conditions can vary. The boats sail in fog or dicey weather, when Hovercraft or planes may be grounded or delayed. You can jog around the decks. *Take your own picnic*, unless you *want* to eat in the restaurants or snack bars. For obvious reasons, you won't choose this mode of travel at football-match time. Up to four connections from Charing Cross to Gare du Nord a day, about eight hours.

	Single	Return	5-day return
ADULT	£44	£59	£49
YOUNG PERSONS (16–25)	£39	£55	£49
CHILDREN (4–11)	£23	£35	£28

Children under 4 travel free.

Reservations in Britain, tel: 01233 647022. In Paris, tel: 01 53 43 40 00.

EUROSTAR
Eurostar trains leave Waterloo about 10 times a day and take 3 hours to the Gare du Nord in Paris.

	One way	Return
ADULT	£77	£156
YOUNG PERSONS (under 26)	£40	£80
CHILDREN (4–11)	£31	£63

Children under 4 travel free.

Reservations in Britain, tel: 0171 922 6071; in Paris call SNCF for reservations: 01 45 82 50 50.

FOR UNDER-26S AND STUDENTS

Many travel agents specialize in inexpensive rail and coach and air fares for travellers in these special categories: they advertise in school and college magazines, and in *Time Out*, *City Limits* and free sheets such as *TNT*. STA Travel, 86 Old Brompton Road, London SW7 or 117 Euston Road, London NW1, tel: 0171 361 6161; and the Campus Travel Group, 52 Grosvenor Gardens, London SW1, tel: 0171 730 3402, are both long-established in this field.

CHEAP FLIGHTS

Magazines like *Time Out* and *City Limits*, *TNT* and *Girl about Town* are crammed with ads for cheap airfares. These days you don't have to depend on bucket shops for such good deals; most major travel agents will probably do you just as well and save you some footwork.

The Air Travel Advisory Bureau (in London, tel: 0171 636 5000 and Manchester, tel: 0161 832 2000) is a clearing-house for information about agents who offer cheap flights worldwide. We have found them quick, helpful and accurate, and one phone call to them could provide you with the names of five or six agents who might give you a good deal on the day of your enquiry, for flights – one-way or return – to Paris, saving you dozens of fruitless calls.

Major airlines insist that you book your return journey when you sign on for the outward leg, and you can't alter dates or flight times without a bitter penalty (be sure to take out adequate travel insurance to cover costs of cancellation for illness or whatever, approximately £16 – half-price for children under 16 – from the Air Travel Advisory Bureau). At peak holiday times all fares go up. But there are ways round these fixed price deals. Read on.

Among the best fares during the spring of 1997:

£59: For full time students and anyone under 26. Offered by, among others: STA Travel, 86 Old Brompton Road, London SW7 or 117 Euston Road, London NW1, tel: 0171 361 6161; and Campus Travel Group, 52 Grosvenor Gardens, London SW1, tel: 0171 730 3402

£75: British Midland, tel: 0345 554554
£83: British Airways, tel: 0345 222111
£83: Air France, tel: 0181 742 6600

Or try one of the following agents in London:

Flyair, tel: 0171 491 3330
Lupus Travel, tel: 0171 306 3000
Dawson & Sanderson, tel: 0171 839 2021
Major Travel: 0171 485 7017
Travel Power: 0171 571 8860
Vacation Club International: 0181 780 5551

ONE-WAY FARES: While the major airlines tie you up with all the restrictions they can devise, others are more flexible. Many airlines flying to the Middle and Far East pass on to you the benefit of something called the Sixth Freedom of the Skies, meaning that they can offer you a one-way-only seat to Paris at a moderate fare. Someone is waiting there to sit in that same seat on the longer leg of the flight. In Paris, check the travel agents mentioned above for one-way flights to London. For tickets from London, try these:

£28: For students under 29 and anyone under 26. Campus Travel Group, tel: 0171 730 3402 and STA Travel, tel: 0171 361 6161
£94: Off-peak. British Midland, tel: 0345 554554

IN PARIS: It's possible to book cheap charter flights, one-way or round-trip, to London/Dublin/Edinburgh, etc., through various agencies. In March 1996:

USIT
12 rue Vivienne, 2e (Métro Bourse); tel: 01 44 55 32 60
6 rue de Vaugirard, 6e (Métro Odéon); tel: 01 42 34 56 90
were offering one-way flights to London for 280F, round-trip 560F. Add to this approximately 20F in fees and 21F (single) or 61F (return) in airport taxes.

Cash and Go
54 rue Taitbout, 9e (Métro Chaussée d'Antin); tel: 01 44 53 49 49
has good prices for long-haul flights to Los Angeles or New York, for

instance, and often has charter flights to England, one-way, low cost; *and* they speak English.

Wasteels
a chain of travel agencies all over Paris, often has remarkable last-minute bargains on both major airlines and charter flights; at Métro St-Michel, tel: 01 43 26 25 25, or check the branch nearest where you are staying.

The agents we mention above are those whose information we have found accurate. Some others will advertise alluring prices which have mysteriously disappeared when you call. The practice is known as 'bait-and-switch', and originated in the used-car lots of Los Angeles, where it belongs.

PACKAGE TOURS
These come in all shapes and sizes and, naturally, all prices. They range from the antiseptic (everything through a coach window, with English commentary) to the spartan (transportation, bed and break-fast, no frills), to more luxurious but still affordable packages.

The advantage of the no-frills package is that it takes the guesswork out of the basic amenities, and leaves you free to explore the city on your own. The means of transportation (air, hover, coach and the rest) and the types of accommodation (1-star to 4-star) are varied, and you'll want to sort through the possibilities very carefully.

We have had good reports on UK package tour agencies which specialize in Paris (*French Leave* and *Time Off*) – there are a number of others which are undoubtedly equally good, but as we never give you information that hasn't come directly from someone who has been there, we can't comment on them.

Colour brochures featuring Paris have almost impenetrable charts – prices, number of nights, type of accommodation, supplements for holidays, and so forth. The chart we give you here is a simplified version from a major tour agency's brochure to give you an idea of the possibilities.

We've given the cost for *two nights only*, to make things easier; for longer stays, just add on the extra cost per night.

The tour operator whose brochure we've used offers much glossier stays in 3-star and 4-star hotels, even in luxury class Hôtel Louvre –

but if you travel in such circles, stop reading now and give this book to some deserving pauper.

The prices here are for good, centrally located, well-run 1- and 2-star hotels only. One-star places have basins and sometimes bidets in each room, 2-star will give you a private bath or shower and possibly a private WC. One-star hotels do *not* have lifts, 2-stars often do.

You can save £££ travelling by night by Euroline coach on the Dover–Calais service, at the lowest package tour prices, if you don't mind sitting up, drowsing in fairly comfortable surroundings. Most costly, of course, is travel by scheduled services from Heathrow to Charles de Gaulle, and coach direct from the airport to the city centre.

	City Sprint	Rail/Ship/Rail	Gatwick–Paris	Heathrow–Paris
Low Season (15 Nov.–19 Mar.)				
1-star	£95	£98	£130	£140
2-star	£99	£105	£135	£144
High Season (1 April–14 Nov.)				
1-star	£110	£115	£150	£160
2-star	£134	£140	£170	£182

Prices are based on *two people* sharing for *two nights*. Continental breakfast included. For single rooms, low season, add £15 per night for a 1-star hotel, £18 for a 2-star hotel; high season, add £17 for a 1-star, £25 for a 2-star. Extra nights, of course, are available at additional cost. Check the tour operator's brochure carefully for the small-print footnotes that add all sorts of supplements.

Many package tour operators offer special terms for Winter Bargain Breaks, Weekends and Long Weekends, and some good cheapies like a three- or five-night holiday by coach, ship and coach.

SEVERAL OF OUR WELL-TRAVELLED FRIENDS WARN: Think carefully before you sign up for package tour excursions – the Bateau Mouche cruises, trips to Chartres or Fontainebleau, the Moulin Rouge and Lido Cabaret shows – as they can be much more expensive than using this book and doing it on your own. Others are happy to have everything organized for them, and consider the extra money well spent.

Entrée/sortie (Arrival and departure)

PASSPORTS, VISAS, CUSTOMS

You ought to have a valid passport to enter France (although strictly speaking it isn't necessary for EC residents).

In Britain, standard passports are good for ten years, and cost £18 (for 32 pages) or £27 (for 48 pages). Get forms from your local post office. Two photographs needed. Return the application, with fee and photos, countersigned by someone impressive who knows you – vicar, solicitor, doctor, or JP – either to the passport office or to the nearest main post office in your city. Expect to wait about ten days for the passport in winter, or up to a month in busy periods. Don't leave it until the last minute.

LENGTH OF STAY

Up to three months, a resident of the EC countries needs no visa. For longer stays, apply at the Préfecture de Police nearest to where you are living. Take along your passport and a good reason why you want to remain in Paris. They will issue a *Permis de Séjour*. Keep this with your passport and produce it when necessary (in time of trouble or when leaving France). If you are going to study in France, take to the Préfecture some kind of proof of enrolment in a school or college.

On leaving Britain, you must for some reason show your passport to an immigration official. On entering France (airport, or at boat or Hoverlanding) a French official looks at it but probably won't bother to stamp it. Likewise on the return. As a foreigner entering either country, you *could* be asked the reason for your stay (business, tourism, family matters) and for how long. With the advent of the EC, this has become – in France, at least – the merest formality.

DOUANE/CUSTOMS

Again, these days, it's mostly a matter of waving you on. If they're looking for you for some good reason, they'll stop you. Or they may hold you up briefly, by pure chance, rifle your luggage, and leave you to repack. Contraband is illegal drugs, firearms (except hunting guns with permits), explosives, pornography. A respectful demeanour and a blank face will probably keep you from getting hung up in Customs at either end. Do not attempt to charm or chat up a customs officer anywhere. They are not susceptible to charm.

HEALTH

British travellers in France get a pretty good deal. Almost free medical care is available through the reciprocal scheme of the EC, and it applies to the self-employed and the unemployed as well as to full-time employees. If you're going abroad as a family, a single form covers all of you.

Before your departure get form E-111 from the post office and fill in both parts. There's a very useful leaflet with it that tells you everything you need to know about how to get medical treatment in Europe, and what to do to claim most of the cost back. It also warns you that it is NOT, repeat NOT, a substitute for adequate health insurance (see page 260). Then take the forms back to your post office and they'll process it.

If you're well organized, take your National Insurance number or your NHS number, and your passport to the post office, fill in the form, and the post office should be able to validate your E-111 on the spot. Guard it with your life, as it can't be replaced by post if lost, nor can it be reissued. Our advice is to take a couple of photocopies.

ARRIVING

First impressions can make or break your trip. If you step off the train or plane confused and disoriented, you can expect to stay that way for days. It helps to know what to expect: instead of floundering around in the chaos of the Gare du Nord you can begin immediately to develop a Paris expertise which will see you through your visit.

The airports are smoothly organized, well signposted and furnished with *bureaux de change*, information services and so forth. But like airports everywhere, Charles de Gaulle/Roissy and Orly are sterile, unamusing places, pervaded by a kind of travel *angst*, and you'll want to be on your way at once.

To reach central Paris from Charles de Gaulle or Orly, you have several choices:

CHARLES DE GAULLE/ROISSY

BUS: cheapest and reasonably fast: take the free bus from your arrival point to the SNCF station, buy a *carnet* of ten tickets for 44F, walk about 15 yards and find the service bus stop to Paris – No. 350 takes you to Gare du Nord, No. 351 to Nation. If you have bought a *Carte Paris Visite* in London, the ride costs you nothing – but don't put the little ticket into the ticket stamping machine as this will invalidate it. Otherwise, it's six tickets from your carnet.

ROISSYBUS: this bus leaves from the airport every 15 minutes, costs 40F, and arrives at rue Scribe, close to the Opéra.

The advantage of these buses is that you climb directly on and off, without having to cope with the railway turnstiles, escalators, stairs and platforms. The buses are blessedly uncrowded, and when you arrive in Paris you're at ground level ready to take another bus or the Métro. About 45 minutes' travelling time, depending on traffic.

ROISSY/RAIL: very fast direct train service to the Gare du Nord. Take that free bus to the SNCF station, where trains leave every 10 minutes from 4:30 a.m. to 11:30 p.m. Ticket to Gare du Nord is 43F50. Our only problem with this superb service has been manoeuvring luggage through turnstiles, and picking our way out at the Gare du Nord end. 35 minutes' travelling time.

AIR FRANCE BUS: swift and luxurious, to the Étoile and Porte Maillot in the 17e *arrondissement*. (For an explanation of the *arrondissement* system, see page 32 and the map on pages 270–71.) Buses run every 12 minutes, and your luggage is taken off your hands. 55F single or 95F return ticket. Children less than 4 years ride free. About 30–45 minutes.

ORLY

ORLY/RAIL: take the free shuttle to the SNCF station where (RER C) trains leave every 15 minutes from 5:34 a.m. to 11:15 p.m. for only 28F.

ORLYVAL: first take the Orlyval train from the airport, then the B4 RER train from the SNCF station and you will be in the heart of Paris in 30 minutes. Trains leave every 4 to 8 minutes, from 6:30 a.m. to 9:15 p.m. 52F.

ORLYBUS: high-speed, low-fare bus directly to Denfert-Rochereau Métro station, 14e *arrondissement*. A smartly designed coach with plenty of luggage space leaves every 15 minutes from 6:30 a.m. to 11:30 p.m. 30F per person (or 6 Métro tickets, *Formule 1* pass or *Carte Paris Visite* for four zones). About 25 minutes.

AIR FRANCE BUS: to the Gare des Invalides, Left Bank, 7e *arrondissement*. Runs about every 12 minutes, your luggage is dealt with for you, and it's around 20 minutes' travelling time. 40F or 65F return.

RAILWAY STATIONS

Boat and Hovercraft are linked to the Gare du Nord by fast train – about two and a half hours from Calais or Boulogne, and included in the cost of your ticket.

Railway stations are large, chaotic and always crowded, even early in the morning. It takes five minutes and three wrong answers to find anything, but there are centrally located information booths, usually with English-speaking personnel, who can provide authoritative answers.

If you're burdened with luggage, look for free energy-saving luggage carts. Avoid porters: the fixed charge per bag is 10F.

If you haven't provided yourself with some francs in cash before arrival, seek out the *bureau de change* and pick up some survival money. Not much: you'll probably get a better rate of exchange at one of the large commercial banks in Paris itself.

HELP

If you haven't already reserved a room and need help...
If you need a simple but comprehensible map of Paris, the Métro, buses...

If you need to know how to use the telephone, figure out the transportation system . . .
Or if you are merely tired and totally disoriented . . .

Look for the Hôtesses de Paris: These run a service provided by the Bureau de Tourisme de Paris, they speak all useful languages and they know almost everything. For the first-time traveller arriving in Paris without a place to lay the head, for someone arriving after dark, the Hôtesses can be invaluable. They have a list of hotels in each price range where they know there are vacancies at the moment. They will not call a specific hotel of your choice (they reckon that if you know that much, you can fend for yourself), but they will find you a room no matter how many phone calls it takes. The charge is 20F for a 1-star hotel, 25F for a 2-star, 40F for a 3-star, and when you're on your last legs, worth it. And they also make Youth Hostel reservations, 8F.

It has been our experience that they will not necessarily find the cheapest room in the best-value hotel. A sign displayed gives minimum prices for the kinds of hotels they use: 180F for a single, 350F for a double in a 1-star hotel, 350F for a single, 500F for a double in a 2-star, and so forth. This may be broadly true, but in practice you can do better for yourself (see 'Au lit', page 55). The Hôtesses can only book for you on the day you want a hotel, not in advance. They can be invaluable – if you don't speak much French, can't face the telephone system, and haven't the energy to start the search on the Métro with your luggage. Let the Hôtesses book you a room for your first night, and strike out on your own the next day.

Try to get them, either at the railway stations or at the main office, as early as possible, as from late morning until closing time, in summer, the queues build up to bursting point.

If the Hôtesses de Paris at the railway station where you arrive look slightly weary and sceptical, especially at the end of a long, hot day, don't be too surprised. Considering the number of idiot travellers who fall into their offices at all hours, often armed with nothing more than touching faith and a copy of an out-of-date or fanciful guidebook, expecting to find a double room in a good hotel, in a quiet neighbourhood, within walking distance of St-Germain-des-Prés, for 100F, their slightly disillusioned air may be justified. And they will indeed make umpteen phone calls, until they place you in a room.

Gare d'Austerlitz (arrival hall)
Mon-Sat 8:00 a.m.–3:00 p.m.

Gare de l'Est (departure hall)
Mon-Sat 8:00 a.m.–1:00 p.m., 5:00-8:00 p.m. (9:00 p.m. in summer*)

Gare de Lyon (arrival hall)
Mon-Sat 8:00 a.m.–1:00p.m., 5:00-8:00 p.m. (9:00 p.m. in summer*)

Gare du Nord (mainline hall)
Mon-Sat 8:00 a.m.–8:00 p.m. (9:00 p.m. in summer*)

Main Tourist Office (*Bureau de Tourisme, Paris*)
127, avenue des Champs-Élysées, 8e tel: 01 49 52 53 54

Métro George-V
Mon-Sat 9:00 a.m.–8:00 p.m. (9:00 p.m. in summer*)
Sundays and holidays 11:00 a.m.–6:00 p.m.

*Summer indicates Easter to 1 November

ALSO: tel: 01 49 52 53 56 for announcements in English of almost everything you need to know, 24 hours a day.

The tourist offices are a mine of information and a great source for free maps and other handouts. Most useful of these are several varieties of Métro and bus folders: individual pamphlets on certain sight-seeing bus routes; a comprehensive list of hotels and restaurants listed by *arrondissement* (see map, pages 270–71), alphabetically and classified by price and amenities. In addition, the main tourist office in the Champs-Élysées has posters displaying current cultural events; they give information about other parts of France; and there is an automatic SNCF ticket dispenser from which you can purchase tickets with your PIN number as well as an exchange office.

If you're just a little knocked out, but don't need the immediate assistance of the Hôtesses for hotel booking or map help, take time to get your breath. We strongly advise you to spend the next half hour getting acclimatized to Paris (what could be more pleasant?) before jumping on a bus or Métro.

First: find somewhere to leave your luggage. In all the railway stations there is a left-luggage place, the *consigne*. Cart your bags there in your trolley, and check them in. Cost 11F per bag. If you are travelling light, a storage locker (5F for a small one, up to 11F for a big one) will do nicely, if you can find one that's empty when you need it.

Then: get a bite to eat, a glass of wine or a cup of coffee. A *brasserie* is perfect, but don't head for one in the terminal (too hectic), or directly opposite (double the cost, as they know how to soak the tourist). Walk one street away, in any direction, find a *bar-tabac* or *brasserie*. Here you can sit down, catch your breath, relax for a bit before you go on. Try out your first five words of French. Begin to figure out how the money system really works. Don't be shy about laying the coins on the table, getting used to the colour and feel. Plan the route to your hotel, with the aid of *Plan de Paris* (see page 31).

For a little basic *brasserie* vocabulary, see under 'La nourriture', page 92. Smile. And finish with '*Merci, au revoir, monsieur* (or *mademoiselle*)', which will surprise them so much they'll smile back.

If you haven't already booked a hotel, and have (as you should have) absolute confidence in this book, consult the chapter 'Au lit', page 55, for information, and page 250 to find out how to use the phone.

GETTING TO YOUR HOTEL

If you are really weighed down, take a taxi. If necessary, write down the address and show it to the driver. There are taxi ranks outside all the stations and terminals. See the information on page 252 for tipping.

If you are ready to brave the Métro or the bus, see page 33 in 'Getting around'. At railway stations you can pick up a *Carte Paris Visite* or *Carte Orange* (see pages 36 and 38 for how to do it), and start using it to travel for almost nothing right away. The process for *Carte Orange*, including getting a picture taken in a photomatic booth, takes about five minutes; for *Carte Paris Visite*, a fast 30 seconds.

LEAVING PARIS

By the time you're ready to wrench yourself away from Paris, you should be able to do this part walking on your hands. But just in case:

IN RAILWAY STATIONS: Departure times, train numbers, destinations and track number (*voies*) are marked in huge letters, on an immense blue board in mid-station. Trains leave very strictly on time, and with almost no warning whistles or horns. Anyone coming to see you off will need a platform ticket, although as there are actually few officials at the gate this can sometimes be dispensed with.

AIRPORT BUSES: Air France takes you to Charles de Gaulle from Porte Maillot (16e arrondissement) and the Étoile (avenue Carnot, 16e *arrondissement*). They claim a 35-minute travelling time; knowing traffic, you should double that. Buses leave every twelve minutes between 5:40 a.m. and 11:00 p.m. Fare 55F. (Unless you are actually staying near Porte Maillot or the Étoile, the Roissy-Rail service from Gare du Nord is faster, easier and cheaper.)

The Air France bus to Orly leaves the Aérogare des Invalides (rue de Constantine, just north of the Invalides Métro, 7e *arrondissement*), and also from the Gare Montparnasse (15e *arrondissement*), every 12 minutes, and takes at least half an hour – allow plenty of leeway for traffic. Buses run between 5:50 a.m. and 11:00 p.m. Fare 40F.

TRAINS: Roissy-Rail: Gare du Nord to Charles de Gaulle. Tickets from automatic dispensers in the hall leading to the train, marked Roissy-Rail, or from a ticket window – but be wary of this last, as the booking clerk also issues the *Carte Orange* and *Coupon Jaune*, student passes, etc., and you can get blocked for ever while he does the paperwork. If you are well organized and don't lose things easily, get your return ticket to Charles de Gaulle when you arrive from the airport and are not pressed for time, and put it with your airline ticket. Trains run every fifteen minutes from 5:30 a.m. to 11:30 p.m., fare 43F50.

Orly-Rail runs between the Gare d'Austerlitz and Orly every 15 minutes, and takes about 35 minutes to reach Orly Sud and Ouest. Departures from 5:50 a.m. to 10:50 p.m., fare *28F*.

SERVICE BUSES TO AIRPORTS: DON'T, unless you're a masochist with plenty of time to waste, take the bus to Charles de Gaulle, even if you have the *Carte Paris Visite* and the ride is free – the nervous strain is just too much. However, the new fast direct service to Orly, from Denfert-Rochereau in the 14e *arrondissement*, is great – about 30 minutes' travelling time to Orly-Ouest, 35 minutes to Orly-Sud. Every 15 minutes, 6:05 a.m. to 11:00 p.m.

BUSES AND MÉTROS TO RAILWAY TERMINI: Consult your maps. If you're on a direct route, with no changes, there should be no problems. But if you must change anywhere on the Métro, forget it: negotiating stairs and intersections with luggage is out of the question. Take a taxi. In hot weather, and in rush hours, Paris buses are intolerably hot; the windows are made to keep out draughts, not to let in fresh air. Doors are closed when the bus is in motion – and sweaty human bodies can be really unpleasant.

Circulons (Getting around)

You'll probably spend much of your time in Paris getting from place to place, just wandering around with eyes open. Nowhere in the world will you have such beauty to absorb as you go! But getting muddled can take the shine off anything, even Paris. To make the most of your wandering, we suggest arming yourself with a really first-class 'atlas' of Paris.

The best we know is a thick little book called *Plan de Paris*, published by Éditions A. Leconte and available in bookshops and *papeteries*. The hardcover edition is dark red, and costs 99F, which seems like a lot, but it's packed cover to cover with everything you need to know. There are cheaper, paperback editions of the *Plan*, but with hard use they tend to lose the covers, the maps drop out, and you end up frustrated. Other atlas-type books exist, some with larger and more legible maps like the Michelin map, 22F, or *L'Indispensable*, 36F, but none we have found includes so much and such accurate information as the *Plan*.

The *Plan* of M. Leconte lists all streets, alleys, *quais* and squares alphabetically, with their beginning and ending points, *arrondissements*, nearest Métro stops, and a keyed map reference which takes you to the individual, coloured *arrondissement* map.

Each *arrondissement*, from 1er to 20e, has its own page. Métro lines and stops are printed in red. The maps themselves are laid out with alpha-numerical grids. Some plans (not, to be sure, the estimable M. Leconte's) are smallish and blurry, and therefore useless no matter how cheap. A good copy is child's play to use, and a treasure to keep long after your visit to Paris. Don't lend it to anyone.

The suburbs (*banlieues*) are also mapped in this book with the same format of street listings, map reference, etc., but probably won't be of much interest to you at this point.

A highly useful section lists addresses and map references for anything you want to know, and quite a lot you might never need: embassies, theatres, hospitals, schools, churches, monuments, police stations, city halls, race tracks, museums, post offices, state ministries, stadiums, tennis courts, swimming pools, shops, radio and TV stations, principal cinemas, cabarets, concert halls.

All the Paris bus routes are listed in numerical order, and what is even more important, shown in chart form, each with its starting and ending point and the principal stops in between. For that alone, the Paris Tourist Office should give M. Leconte a gold medal, as it is the only thing lacking in their otherwise excellent bus folder.

If you are in Paris for more than a day or two, and intend to move more than a quarter of a mile from your hotel in any direction, the *Plan* is indispensable. The good news is that you can get a copy before you leave London, from The French Bookshop, 28 Bute Street SW7. Cost £7.95 for the paperback edition. Tel: 0171 584 2840.

Less detailed but very useful maps of Paris, with pictured locations of principal tourist attractions – museums, monuments and so forth – are available free from the Bureau de Tourisme. And the big department stores (Printemps, Galeries Lafayette, among others) have prepared very much the same sort of thing, showing of course where *they* are located.

THE STREETS OF PARIS

THE *ARRONDISSEMENT* SYSTEM

In the mid-nineteenth century, Paris was thoroughly overhauled by Napoleon III's urban planner, Baron Haussmann. Slums were cleared (fortunately, he didn't get around to the Marais), sewers and aqueducts installed where the Romans had left off, and a web of wide thoroughfares, the Grands Boulevards, was laid. The city was thereupon divided into 20 *arrondissements* (there had previously been 12, based on the old traditional *quartiers*, some dating back 2000 years). Numbers 1–7 cover the three historic parts of Paris: the *cité* (official and religious, located on the central islands), the *ville* (the Right Bank, commercial and industrial), and the *université* (Left Bank, commercial and scholastic). To a great extent these medieval distinctions hold true today.

The *arrondissements* spiral clockwise from the centre of Paris (the 1er being part of the Ile de la Cité and the area around the Louvre). The numbers which you will see on street signs and in newspapers and magazines (and in this book) are expressed thus: 1er, which means *Premier*; 2e, which stands for *Deuxième*, and so forth. Each *arrondissement* has quite distinct identifying features or landmarks which can serve to give you your bearings. The Eleventh (you might as well get used to seeing it written as 11e) is roughly the area which stretches outwards from the Bastille; the 8e is Gare St-Lazare and the Madeleine; the 7e is the Invalides and the Tour Eiffel. Street signs in Paris are large, legible, and almost always include the *arrondissement* number (thus: avenue de l'Opéra, 1er).

With map, *arrondissement*, landmarks, street signs, and clearly written house or shop numbers, you shouldn't ever get *totally* lost, but it can happen, and for some reason even people with a good sense of direction find it hard to work out which way is north in Paris.

When you do feel really lost, the simplest thing to do is seek out the nearest Métro station: ask anyone, with the simple formula, '*Pardon monsieur (or madame) – le Métro, s'il vous plaît?*'

LE MÉTRO

It's impossible to lose your way in the Métro. You can't walk ten paces without a clear, explicit sign informing you of your destination. How to use all this information:

1   In the *Plan de Paris*, look up the name of the street you want to go to, and you will find the nearest Métro stop.

2   Find the station on the Métro map in front of the *Plan*, or in one of the small free maps dealt out by the municipal transport system at every chance. Or look on the big map outside the entrance to the nearest Métro station, or near the ticket office, or on the platform from which the trains run.

3   Trace your route. Each Métro line is known by its beginning and ending points. Between any two stations in the system, you will be coming from and going towards one of the terminals of the line. For example, line 12 runs from Mairie d'Issy to Porte

de la Chapelle. If you were at Gare St-Lazare and wanted to go to Pigalle, you would take a train in the direction of Porte de la Chapelle. From St-Lazare to Sèvres-Babylone, your direction is Mairie d'Issy. You then follow the appropriate signs to the platform where your train comes in. On Métro maps, each line is numbered and colour-coded. The terminals are marked in good, big, capital letters on the map, at the outskirts of the city.

4   If you need to change trains to get to the stop you want, it's equally easy. Paris Métro lines are linked together in a remarkable system of *correspondances* (intersections) of two, three, sometimes five or six lines. You may have to walk underground for what seems like miles before you find your train, and it's hard on the feet. But keep calm, and you will never be lost. The signs simply don't allow that to happen.

The Métro runs every day, but with reduced services on Sundays, holidays and after about 8:00 p.m., when intervals between trains become longer. Most trains begin running at 5:30 a.m., and stop at 1:15 a.m. But take care: if you have to change trains after 12:45 a.m you can easily find yourself stranded at the connecting station.

L'AUTOBUS

Trickier, and takes longer to get you from A to B, but infinitely more fun than the Métro. Like the train system, each bus is marked large and clear with its point of origin and destination. The buses are designated primarily by number. On the sides of the bus, the major stops are displayed so that even when it moves past you, you can read the route in a flash. An overall bus map, available at Métro stations, bus termini, and the Bureau de Tourisme at 27 avenue des Champs-Élysées, gives a fairly clear, colour-coded overview of the routes. But it's intricate and you could miss your bus while you're trying to work it out. Best of all is the chart-form bus information in the *Plan de Paris*.

If you read French and plan to use buses often and for a long period, try to find *Le Guide Paris-Bus*, now being reprinted after a lapse of several years by the publishers Prat/Europa in conjunction with the RATP (the municipal transport system). It shows you every bus route, the street address opposite each bus stop, and best of all, what other buses connect at every bus stop on every route. Using it, you quickly learn which combination of buses will serve you best, thus saving a lot of walking. In addition, the index tells you which bus, or buses, take you to every point of interest in the city.

Bus stops are clearly recognizable, often as a kerbside shelter, with a good visible display above of which buses stop there. Otherwise, look for the pole at the kerb with a numbered disc on top, and a panel that tells you everything you need to know about each bus.

Inside the shelters, you are shown a clear chart of the bus route, all its stops, a helpful marker that shows exactly where you are on the route and the nearest place to buy tickets. On the bus you will only be able to buy single tickets, not *carnets*, and this costs real money (page 37 for price). If you have a *Carte Orange* with a monthly or weekly pass, a *Formule 1* ticket, or a *Carte Paris Visite*, just hold it up for the driver to see. Single tickets are 'composted' (date stamped) in the machine near the bus door.

Inside, just in case you've missed the other information, there are two or three route maps, overhead. So you can know instantly where you are, what the next stop will be, and even, if the worst comes to the worst and you are really mixed up, which direction you are going in. The bus stops along the street display names clearly and legibly, so you know whether you need to hop off and change direction.

TIMES: In general, buses leave their starting points at 7:00 a.m., and run to about 8:30 or 9:00 p.m. Others have a night service (these all begin at the place du Châtelet, avenue Victoria, 3e); Sundays and holidays: buses Nos. 20, 21, 26, 27, 31, 38, 43, 44, 46, 52, 62, 80, 91, 92, 95, 96, and the Petite Ceinture bus which runs around the outskirts of Paris.

All Paris buses run on the request-stop system. If you are standing at a stop marked for only one bus, the driver will stop (if he sees you). But it may be safer to wave your arm or umbrella. If more than one bus serves your stop, you *must* signal the one you want.

The same system applies when you want to get off. No automatic stops. You must push a red, rectangular button on one of the upright stanchions near entrance and exit doors. This activates a sign in the front of the bus: *Arrêt demandé*. This system lets Paris buses move fairly fast, considering the narrow, often crowded streets in which they run.

NOCTAMBUS

There are ten night-service buses which run from 1:30 a.m. to 5:30 a.m., all beginning at Châtelet and fanning outward to the outskirts of Paris:

LINE

NA:	Châtelet to La Défense, via Étoile
NB:	Mairie de Levallois, via Opéra
NC:	Mairie de Clichy, via Pigalle
ND:	Mairie de St-Ouen, via Gare du Nord
NE:	Église de Pantin, via Gare de l'Est
NF:	Mairie de Lilas, via Belleville
NG:	Mairie de Montreuil, via Gambetta
NH:	Château de Vincennes, via Nation
NJ:	Porte d'Orléans, via Luxembourg
NR:	Rungis, via Place d'Italie

As the RATP says, '*Pas de voiture? Pas de Taxi? Pas de vélo? Pas de panique!*' – Just signal the bus. Night buses will stop anywhere you hail them, not just at bus stops. They run only one an hour. With *Formule 1*, or *Carte Orange*, or *Coupon Jaune*, or *Carte Paris Visite*, you travel free; otherwise it's three or four tickets, depending on distance.

MÉTRO AND BUS TRAVEL

Paris transport is heavily subsidized, a great break for the travelling poor as well as for hard-working Parisians. Tickets can be used on Métro and buses interchangeably, which saves a lot of time and trouble. Prices have risen somewhat since the last edition of this book, and although in 1997 they may go up slightly, the increases will in all probability be gentle. Beginning with the least expensive – and why we prefer these – here we go:

CARTE ORANGE: this is a catch-all heading for cards that give you all-inclusive travel by the week or by the month (you can even get a yearly ticket). The *Carte* itself is a small orange card in a shiny grey plastic folder with a little pocket for your weekly or monthly coupon. It's free. Take a passport-sized photo to any Métro station. You then buy a *Coupon Jaune* (valid from 1:00 a.m. Monday to 11:59 p.m. Sunday) or a *Coupon Orange*, good for one calendar month). The *Coupon Jaune* is on sale from the Sunday before it becomes valid until the following Wednesday. The *Coupon Orange* goes on sale the 20th of the previous month.

Now that the Paris region has been zoned, you will have to say at the pay window which zones you want to travel in – zones 1 and 2 cover the whole of the city, so that's the most useful one. Outer zones extend to the limits of the region. In our experience, these coupons are the greatest travel buy ever invented. If you're in Paris even for four or five days, the *Coupon Jaune* will give you your money's worth in hassle-free travel.

On the Métro, push your ticket through the turnstile and immediately slip it back into the plastic pocket of your *Carte*. On the bus, flash your *Carte* at the driver. On no account feed the ticket into the ticket punch machine. This will invalidate it. There are no refunds for idiocy.

If for some mysterious reason your ticket won't open the gate, go back to the ticket window and show it to them; they'll press a magic button and let you through. This is no great help if you've entered through one of those entrances without ticket booths (marked 'reservé aux passagers munis de billets'), because then you'll have to trudge along to a manned entrance.

What you get for your money: unlimited travel on Métros, buses, certain segments of the high-speed RER, the Montmartrobus, and the Montmartre funicular.

Coupon Jaune, zones 1 and 2, 1 week: 67F
Coupon Orange, zones 1 and 2, 1 calendar month: 230F

FORMULE 1: This one-day pass gives you unlimited travel as above. You get an identity card (no photograph needed) which you can keep forever. Buy a ticket (*coupon*) for each day you need it. 30F

TICKETS AND *CARNETS*: You can buy them singly (extravagantly) at a Métro station or on the bus, or in *carnets* of 10 from Métros or in many tobacconists' shops. On the Métro, push your ticket through the turnstile but don't discard it until you leave the train – there are occasional spot-checks of travellers, and the *contrôleurs* can be fierce, even taking you and your passport to the nearest police station to be fined. On the bus, tell the driver where you are going and he will tell you whether to punch one or two tickets. Suburban buses – those with numbers higher than 100 – will cost two to six tickets. Bus drivers do not sell carnets, only single tickets. And you can be controlled on the bus too, so keep your ticket handy.

Single tickets 7.50F
Carnet of 10 44F
Carnet for children under 10 years 22F
Children under 4 travel free

CARTE PARIS VISITE: It does open every desirable door in Paris, but strikes us as somewhat expensive. Decide for yourself. You can buy it in London from Continental Travel at the French Railways office. In Paris get it at the SNCF stations at Charles de Gaulle and Orly airports, at most Métro stations and from some banks and travel agencies. It allows you the same unlimited travel on buses and Métro as do all other forms of tickets. The 'Zones 1–3' pass gives you the city of Paris and its immediate suburbs. 'Zones 1–5' adds the surrounding region (e.g. Versailles) and Roissy and Orly airports.

Zones 1–3	2 consecutive days	70F
	3 consecutive days	105F
	5 consecutive days	165F
Zones 1–5	2 consecutive days	170F
	3 consecutive days	230F
	5 consecutive days	315F

As you see, a three-day *Visite* costs more than a weekly *Coupon Jaune*, and even more than three Formule 1 day passes. A five-day *Visite* is more than triple the cost of a *Coupon Jaune* ... but you *can* buy it any day of the week.

If you're really a dedicated money-saver, arrive in Paris on a Monday morning, pick up your *Coupon Jaune* and be on your way. Use it fifteen times and you're travelling free the rest of the week.

Now that you know how to get around – where to?

You might just want to set off at random – head in any direction on foot; hop on the first bus that comes along, take the Métro to the end of the line and try to find your way back as a pedestrian – no matter what, something will come of it.

Or perhaps you could use some pointers on the *quartiers* before you set out – a few landmarks – some guaranteed bus routes. Possibly some areas to avoid, as well.

Major monuments (the Tour Eiffel, the Arc de Triomphe, the Louvre and such) you should be able to find with one hand tied behind your back. If you're really in doubt, ask a tourist. What follows is a sampler: general reflections on a few *quartiers* (central and out of the way) and some routes you might like to try, on foot and otherwise. It's anything but exhaustive. You'll discover far more than we have space for here on your own.

PARIS BY BUS

Commercial sightseeing buses in Paris cost an arm and a leg, as the saying goes. Why pay from 125F for a trip when the glorious RATP offers you an incomparable set of bus trips for practically nothing?

If you are armed, as you should be, with the indispensable *Carte Orange* (see page 36), or your *Carte Paris Visite* (page 38), your sightseeing is on the house, so to speak. The RATP has even started a special Sunday service, called the Parisbus, which does the highlights in a 50-minute run. Full details below.

RATP have also laid out, in a well-designed folder called Billet de Tourisme, available at all major Métro stations, a list of seventeen sightseeing bus routes that can show you the most beautiful, historic, curious and provocative parts of Paris. These seventeen could take up your entire time in the city, of course, so we've narrowed down the choices to a magic seven – some of which will show you parts of Paris most tourists haven't even heard about.

If you have time for only one leisurely, luxurious bus ride, choose number 24. If Sunday afternoon is what you've set aside for an excursion, try the Parisbus.

PARISBUS

For a quick, enjoyable trip that will give you your bearings in Paris, take a ride on the Parisbus. It runs only on Sundays and holidays from noon to 9:00 p.m., and you get on anywhere along the route at the stops marked 'Parisbus'. It runs between La Défense and Gare de Lyon, passing Neuilly, Porte Maillot, Charles de Gaulle and Étoile, before running down the Champs-Élysées to Concorde, the Tuileries and the Louvre. On the outward journey, it crosses the Pont St-Michel and the Ile de la Cité to the '*Quartier Latin*' and on to the Gare d'Austerlitz and the Gare de Lyon. The return journey takes a slightly different route which passes Notre Dame, Pont Royal and the Musée d'Orsay before crossing back to Concorde.

BUS 24

From Gare St-Lazare, it takes you round the place de la Madeleine (luxury shops) into the place de la Concorde, then sweeps along the quai des Tuileries beside the Seine, past the Louvre. As you go, you have a most enticing view of the silvery buildings lining the opposite side of the river (the Left Bank – Rive Gauche). Glancing to your left, you can see the exquisite church St-Germain-l'Auxerrois, where all the kings of France worshipped privately. At the pont des Arts, look across the river at the Hôtel de la Monnaie (the Mint) and the Institut de France which houses the 'Immortals' of the Académie Française. Crossing the river on the pont Neuf to the Ile de la Cité, the bus passes the Palais de Justice, then crosses the Petit Pont to the Rive Gauche. From the Boulevard St-Germain, the route follows the quai St-Bernard, skirting the edge of the four-centuries-old Jardin des Plantes. If you stay on the bus all the way to its destination at Alfort, you will catch sight of the monumental new Palais Omnisport built on the site of the razed wine warehouses along the quai de Bercy – passing a real working-class area on the way. On the return journey, the bus goes along the left bank of the Seine, with a good look at Notre Dame; then past the Mint and along the quai Voltaire (where Ingres, Delacroix and Wagner lived at various times), before recrossing the river by the Pont Royal and returning to St-Lazare by way of the place de la Concorde and the magnificent rue Royale. Mondays through Saturdays, 7:00 a.m. to 8:30 p.m.

BUS 29

Also from Gare St-Lazare, the No. 29 takes you around the Opéra, down the rue 4 Septembre, passing the Bourse (the stock exchange), and the place des Victoires with its statue of Louis XIV on horseback. You suddenly come to the great ultra-modern dazzler, Beaubourg (Centre Georges Pompidou), towering over the small crooked streets of the Marais, almost the oldest part of Paris. The bus goes past the elegant place des Vosges, built for the king in 1612, then into the wide boulevard leading to the place de la Bastille. The Bastille prison itself is gone, but the new Bastille Opéra House now dominates the area, and the immense circle itself is very impressive. If you like, get off here and catch the No. 87 bus for another fabulous sightseeing trip to the Champ-de-Mars (for the Tour Eiffel and Napoleon's tomb), or stay with the No. 29 and go on, past the Cimetière de Picpus where many of the victims of *la guillotine* lie buried. Mondays through Saturdays, 7:00 a.m. to 8:30 p.m.

BUS 32

It begins at the Gare de l'Est, but you may want to catch it at one of its more interesting stopping places, such as place de la Trinité, going in the direction of Porte de Passy. The route takes you through the 'Quartier d'Europe', so called because almost every street is named after a capital city: Amsterdam, Budapest, London, Stockholm. Past the Gare St-Lazare, you are in the faded elegance of the boulevard Haussmann, named after the man who reshaped the city in the 1860s. Along the rue de la Boëtie, look for the wildly expensive and beautiful boutiques and galleries. Then up the Champs-Élysées, and to the Trocadéro, the palace built for the Paris World's Fair in 1937 and now the home of three museums. You may want to stop off here and see the Museum of Mankind – fascinating. The bus goes on to the smart, but not entrancing, Passy neighbourhood with its mansions and streets overhung with huge old trees. On the return trip, the route is slightly different, and you'll pass along the avenue Matignon and through Faubourg St-Honoré, wall-to-wall with the great couture houses. The bus will give you an overview, but this is really for people who like to walk. File it for future window-shopping. No. 32 runs Mondays through Saturdays, first bus from Gare de l'Est at 7:00 a.m., last one at 8:30 p.m.

BUS 52

Begins at the Opéra, takes you around the lovely shopping area of the boulevard des Capucines, past the Musée Cognacq-Jay (again, file for future reference), and through the place de la Madeleine with its entrancing food shops: Fauchon and Hédiard. Around the place de la Concorde (a circus of killer traffic has taken the place of the guillotine that stood there for years), and a wonderful view up the vista of the Champs-Élysées. The big avenue de Friedland takes you to the Étoile/

place Charles de Gaulle, where there is always a silent crowd at the Eternal Flame that burns over the tomb of France's Unknown Soldier. Beyond that, you are in the streets of the 16e *arrondissement*, a smart, conservative residential area. The avenue Mozart on the return journey is charming; the local café is called The Magic Flute. This is a pleasant place to step off the bus and have coffee, and walk around a neighbourhood that is real Paris, far off the tourist beat. The bus continues to the place de la Porte d'Auteuil and takes you to pont St-Cloud, a fairly sterile area, so you might want to end your trip at the place de la Porte d'Auteuil and either walk west into the Bois de Boulogne – NOT at night – or head back into central Paris on the Métro. No. 52 runs seven days a week, including holidays, first bus at 7:00 a.m. weekdays and 8:00 a.m. Sundays, last bus at 10:15 p.m.

BUS 63

Begins at the Gare de Lyon, takes you along the quai St-Bernard, and almost at once you are in the *Quartier Latin*, the home of Paris students from the time of the monks in the Middle Ages to the motorbikes and demonstrations of the 1960s. It traverses the rue des Ecoles, crosses the boulevard St-Michel, and passes the church of St-Sulpice before threading its way through the stately streets of the 7e. The 63 touches the fringes of the boulevard St-Germain, then takes you along the quai d'Orsay (political and diplomatic Paris). If you stay with it to the end of the route at Porte de la Muette, you see 'untourist' Paris – but it's more interesting to get off at the Trocadéro stop for an unparalleled view of the city from high on the hill. Take the bus back in the direction of the Gare de Lyon, and this time step off at St-Germain-des-Prés: yes, it's a cliché, but not to be missed because of its bookshops, its galleries, its cafés. There are still those who swear that a costly coffee at the Deux Magots is worth the price, just to see and be seen by *le Tout* Paris. And it costs nothing to browse in the side streets, to see Picasso drawings or primitive paintings. Bus No. 63 runs seven days a week, from 7:00 a.m. to midnight (leaving times from the Gare de Lyon).

BUS 72

Runs from the Porte de St-Cloud to the Hôtel de Ville, and back again, and on the way gives you sight of both modern and historic

Paris. In between, you will see some of the glitter and splendour, and some of the less savoury and picturesque parts too. To get the most from this 'tour', catch the bus at the Hôtel de Ville end: you travel first along the lower and less chic end of the rue de Rivoli, past the great sweep of the Louvre, along the Tuileries Gardens, and past the lovely Jeu de Paume gallery. Turning round the end of the place de la Concorde, it enters the cours de la Reine – high above you are the bright, shining, gilded Horses of Marly. It runs along to the wide streets named after the City of New York and after President Kennedy – if you want to get off here, you can climb a steep set of steps to visit the Museum of Modern Art of Paris (see page 170). From here, it takes you to the avenue de Versailles, most interesting for its buildings such as No. 142 by the architect Hector Guimard, in Art Nouveau style. Beyond this point, the ride isn't particularly exciting, except as all Paris's un-touristy neighbourhoods are; you may want to get off in the avenue de Versailles, wander a bit and absorb its feeling, then return by No. 22 to the Opéra. Mondays through Saturdays, first bus from Porte de St-Cloud at 7:00 a.m., last one at 8:50 p.m. On Sundays, there is a partial service, from Porte de St-Cloud to Concorde only.

BUS 83

Begins at Porte d'Ivry, in the 13e *arrondissement*, a seldom-visited but quite interesting part of Paris (some very good hotels and restaurants there, see page 131 for more about them). Running down the avenue des Gobelins, it traverses the boulevard de Port-Royal. On Saturdays, there's a street market worth stopping for in this street, near the rue St-Jacques. Here it skirts the 5e *arrondissement*, the Latin Quarter. The rue d'Assas on this route is absolutely littered with good little bistros and cafés. The bus passes the Jardin du Luxembourg, where you might want to stop to inhale some fresh air and watch the Paris kids at play; then it runs along the river by the quai d'Orsay, past Invalides. Along the way, you glimpse the Tour Eiffel, and the dome of the Invalides with Napoleon's tomb. The bus crosses on to the Right Bank into fashionable haute couture Paris, around the Rond-Point des Champs-Élysées and the Métro station of St-Philippe-du-Roule. You could go as far as Levallois, but you have really had the most interesting part of its route by now, unless you want to see working-class Paris as it really lives. If you prefer, finish your trip at the Rond-Point, and sit for a while on a bench in the pretty little park while all Paris goes by, or walk up the Champs-Élysées towards the Étoile. This is a wonderful bus ride to take late in the afternoon (but be prepared for crowds during rush hour), as you may be lucky enough to see the lights along the Seine and the Champs-Élysées coming on as dusk approaches. Mondays through Saturdays, first bus from Porte d'Ivry at 7:00 a.m., last one at 8:30 p.m.

MONTMARTROBUS

A minibus service for the inhabitants of the steep streets that snake around the Hill of the Martyrs. It's several years old, enchanting, hardly publicized and, as yet, sussed out by only a handful of tourists. For one ticket, or free with *Carte Orange*, *Carte Jaune*, or *Carte Paris Visite*, you get a breathless, bumpy roller-coaster ride from Pigalle to the end of the line at Métro Jules Joffrin. On the way you are treated to the Moulin de Galette, the place du Tertre, the lovely place des Abbesses, the pure-Utrillo rue Tholoze, the centuries-old Montmartre vineyards, and more views up and down each winding street than you can take in. If the scenery goes by too fast, you can hop off, take pictures or merely wander and gasp, and catch the next bus in ten minutes or so. The return trip takes a slightly different route, if anything even more *pittoresque et historique*. The drivers are nerveless and daunted by nothing: not even a beer *camion* stuck in a hairpin turn will blow their cool. The marvellous thing about Montmartre is that the moment you're out of the sleaze of Pigalle, the landscape reverts to quotidian serenity: an area in which real people live and work as they have for centuries. If you jump off the bus at the northern end (Mairie du XVIIIe) you can pick up a snack lunch in one of the unbelievable places in the rue du Poteau, and sit in the exquisite square de Clignancourt among flowers, trees and children. If you have any luck at all you'll get there when the band is playing in the toy-town bandstand. The Montmartrobus runs every ten minutes northbound from Pigalle from 7:30 a.m. to 8:00 p.m., returning from the Mairie du XVIIIe with the last southbound bus leaving at 7:50 p.m. promptly.

RATP TOURS

In addition to these free bus routes through Paris, the RATP has some extraordinary tours of its own from the place de la Madeleine

(8e) to – among other places – the châteaux of Chambord, Chenon-ceaux, Poitiers, to Bayeux for the Tapestry, to Colombey-les-Deux-Églises to see de Gaulle's house, to Beaune for the wine country, to Cabourg for Proustiana, to Mont-St-Michel, to Domrémy for the route of Jeanne d'Arc – and even a day's trip to Luxembourg if that's a thrill for you.

For information: Services Touristiques de la RATP, place de la Madeleine, near the flower market. Pick up the folder called 'Excur-sions (plus de 100 circuits)' from major Métro stations and all railway stations. Prices are low, compared to commercial bus tours, but you will need at least a minimal command of French to make sure you understand their instructions about leaving times and boarding places. They also have guided tour buses to Versailles, Malmaison, Paris by night, and so on, but only in French.

FOOTWORK

THE BATIGNOLLES

Just north of the Gare St-Lazare, 8e, in the web of streets named after European capitals, begins a pleasantly varied, fairly gentle cluster of neighbourhoods. Heading north up the rue de Rome, you begin to run into music stores: *luthiers*, guitar-makers, violin shops, sellers of sheet music. This was, until 1991, the *quartier* of the Paris Conservatoire, now moved to La Villette. But the *bar-tabacs*, cafés and restaurants that cater to music students are still here; the prices are accordingly low and the whole neighbourhood is a find for the pauper astray in Paris. And it leads you, very quickly, into an oasis of calm. Take a left on the boulevard des Batignolles, past the Théâtre Hebertot, and you are in the beginning of the rue de Levis – a street market, jammed on Saturday mornings, which most tourists miss because they've never heard of it. This leads to an airy little square, and you are in the rue Legendre, heading towards Montmartre. In three blocks, you've arrived at the Église Ste-Marie. Behind it is the square des Batignolles – placid, delightful, a good place to sit for a while. It's a small park, rather than a 'square', and contains a series of artificial duckponds, a carousel and raked gravel paths. If you're still energetic, continue eastward and gradually uphill into Montmartre. The Batignolles is a backwater of calm in

Paris – quiet, unimposing houses, a *petit-bourgeois* population. At one edge is the Place de Clichy, the epitome of sleaze; at the other, the tracks that lead back to the Gare St-Lazare. In between, absolute peace.

THE RUE MOUFFETARD AND THE FIFTH

Since medieval days, the precincts of the 5e *arrondissement* have been the student quarter of Paris. The rue Mouffetard itself has somewhat more diverse origins. It began as a Roman road from Lyon, developed into a rich residential area in the twelfth to fourteenth centuries, then fell into the hands of skinners, tanners and dyers (the Gobelins factory nearby is the only remnant of this period). The resulting stench gave the street its name: *mouffette* is French for skunk.

The Mouffetard today consists of a street market at its southern end, and a string of small shops and restaurants running north: *boulangeries, triperies, boucheries chevalines* (for horsemeat), *fromageries*. The restaurants run mostly to Greek, Arab and Vietnamese/Chinese food. Everything here is startlingly good value: it's impossible to pinpoint a restaurant that offers a better meal than its neighbour, for about 55–70F, usually with reasonably drinkable wine and service thrown in.

At its north end, the rue Mouffetard becomes rue Descartes. At No. 39, now a restaurant, the poet Verlaine lived and died – it has always been a *quartier* for the artist, the writer, the poet, the student, the poor scholar; and although it has been thoroughly discovered by generations of tourists, the Mouffetard and its neighbouring streets remain triumphantly what they are.

The surrounding streets include the rue Geoffroy-St-Hilaire with the only fully fledged mosque in Paris; the Arènes de Lutèce (remains of a Roman arena), the place Monge (outdoor market), the Panthéon and the Bibliothèque Ste-Geneviève, probably the first use of structural steel supports and lots of glass, worth having a look at. The 5e is loaded with schools, technical colleges, branches of the sprawling University of Paris, and at odd times of the day bands of students flood the streets. It's wonderful walking country. The most you'll spend, perhaps, will be the price of a good, cheap lunch or a sandwich eaten sitting on a college wall, or, extravagantly, a coffee, sitting at a café table resting your feet and watching the world of student Paris wander by.

RUE ST-DOMINIQUE AND THE SEVENTH

The 7e is rich but sterile. You'll see that the hotels and restaurants we have picked in this area are rather few and far between. Lots of trees, wide streets and most of the *arrondissement* seems to be made up of the Tour Eiffel and its gravelly park, and the Invalides – haunted grandeur, with Napoleon's tomb as the major *frisson*. In general, we find the neighbourhood parched and almost devoid of interest, certainly very low on anything that counts for strolling, listening, enjoying the free delights of Paris.

But turn the corner off the boring boulevard de la Tour Maubourg into the rue St-Dominique, and it's like opening the top of a magic trunk. Bustle, shops, sales, ebullient cross-bred dogs instead of blanketed Yorkshire terriers, girls in tight skirts and men in faded jeans, a most typical and joyous neighbourhood restaurant or two (see pages 118), even a few hotels that are worthy of note (page 72). The little side-streets that run off St-Dominique are equally beautiful, and it's almost impossible to believe that a hundred yards away are the flat-faced, dull apartment buildings and pompous antique shops. Spend half a day in this neighbourhood: you'll spend almost no money unless you decide to splurge on a down-filled ski jacket for a big 200F, or a slightly used Christian Dior scarf from a street barrow.

Another startling street that redeems the whole 7e from its sterility is the little rue Cler, a pedestrian precinct that is like a microcosm of a French provincial town set down whole in one of the richer areas of Paris. The shopping is entrancing, and there is a hotel (see page 72) which has a faithful year-after-year clientele, French, English, American, Japanese. Perhaps there are other rue Clers and rue St-Dominiques which we haven't found; if so, we apologize to the 7e and next year, perhaps, we will have the time to discover its 'villages'.

THE ASTONISHING EIGHTH

One of the least homogeneous *arrondissements* of Paris that we've encountered is the 8e, which ranges from the quiet music-student life beyond Gare St-Lazare, to the bustling commercial area around Printemps department store, the boulevard Haussmann and the rue Caumartin; and takes in the supreme elegance of the rue Royale and the place de la Madeleine. Imagine a neighbourhood that encompasses both a public bath-house where a hot shower costs next to nothing, and the super luxury atmosphere of Fauchon, the most expensive ood shop in the world! Hermès, with its silk scarves and perfectly made saddle-stitched handbags – 4000F is nothing here – is in the rue Boissy d'Anglas. So is Lanvin, which seems to exhale Arpège from its windows.

Look into the lovely Jeu de Paume on the edge of the place de la Concorde to see if there's an exhibition there. If you think of having a meal within 1,000 yards of its doors, be prepared to blow the week's budget – Maxim's is a few steps away. Yet in the same street that houses the creations of couturiers is a pleasant little café which offers the mannequins and the *vendeuses* (not the customers of course) a moderately priced lunch menu. The Hôtel Crillon is only a few feet away from the American Embassy, and it costs nothing to smell the expensive hyacinths in its window boxes, or to sit for a few minutes in the downy chairs in the lobby (looking as though you are waiting for a rich friend). Yet in the immediate neighbourhood, just off the place de la Madeleine, is a very good, moderately priced hotel (see page 75), such remarkable value that it is only sheer generosity that makes us put it in this book, instead of keeping the name for a few favoured friends.

The bit of the 8e that surrounds the Gare St-Lazare is too little known to those who merely take trains or buses from the station. Real people live here, work here, send their children to school, look for jobs, buy flowers and pastry, newspapers, electric toasters, shoes, get their hair done and their cars repaired. Walk along the rue du Rocher, or the rue de Vienne, have a very good meal at a price that would not even buy you a pub lunch in London; go into a sheet music shop in the rue de Rome, and you might find a flat, a cello, a baby-sitter, a ride to Marseilles, a tandem bicycle or a chance to play chamber music. Towards the river, it is mink jacket country; but even paupers can drop in for a free spray of the latest Hermès scent.

The 8e is not as beautiful or as historic as the Marais, not as bubbling as the student quarter in the 5e, not as snobbish as St-Germain-des-Prés, not as pretentious as Passy and the 16e – it's dead at night, except for the rich sweeping out of expensive restaurants – but for daytime walking its mix of characteristics makes it very special indeed.

THE UNKNOWN ELEVENTH

This *arrondissement* seems to go on for ever – a huge sprawling collection of neighbourhoods which have grown together without having much in common. At one end, it begins at the place de la Bastille – almost unrecognizable now that it is dominated by the monstrous new Opéra looming like a beached ocean liner at the eastern edge. Streets radiating out from the place, once shabby, characterful and crowded with family-run shops and humble restaurants, have been blasted out of existence, and rebuilt in new shapes since this 'artistic' complex has gone up.

The *Onzième*, however, is so big and so varied that it will survive everything, even the yuppification of the Bastille area. The rue St-Antoine is still the street of furniture-makers. The place d'Aligre (page 214) remains a real flea market, surrounding the fruit and vegetable stalls, tiny shops and the big covered market.

To get the flavour of the 11e, take the No. 46 bus from the Gare du Nord, which goes past the Bastille, to the rue de Charonne, the Faidherbe-Chaligny Métro stop – there are some wonderful restaurants around here – or all the way out to the Porte Dorée for the African Museum and the Château de Vincennes. If you get off the bus at Faidherbe-Chaligny, walk slowly down the rue de Reuilly. Have a look in the window of Christ et Rudel for the most extraordinary collection of knobs and knockers. Look into the *junqueries* along the rue de Chanzy. In the rue de Charonne there's the extraordinary Palais de la Femme, a women's hostel, with a really fine restaurant open to everyone (see page 128).

Among the most interesting streets in the 11e are the rue Godefroi Cavainac (at No. 16 catch the chef's shop flashing with copper pots) and the rue Jean-Pierre Timbaud, named for a hero of the Resistance of the Second World War. Rue Jean-Pierre Timbaud runs from the boulevard du Temple to the boulevard Belleville in the north. Here you will find little shops crammed with semi-antique and real, low-priced junk. At the other end, as you approach the Chinese, Vietnamese, Arab, Jewish *quartier* of Belleville, you could eat different food every day of the week.

Down near the Gare de Lyon is what is known to the Brigade des Stups (the drug squad) as the Golden Triangle. Up near the avenue de la République, around the Métro stops Parmentier, St-Maur, Père Lachaise, the quartier is staid bourgeois. At the place de la République, you can buy T-shirts at Tati for 15F, or spend £75 a night in a big posh hotel. Just off the boulevard Ménilmontant, you could visit the Edith Piaf museum; not far away, see where Maurice Chevalier once lived; and at Père Lachaise, see where Colette, Gertrude Stein and Jim Morrison now lie. All and much, much more, in the 11e – still unknown to most visitors to Paris.

THE OTHER PARIS

Jewish, Tunisian, Algerian. If you have a fancy for seeing what foreign parts of Paris are like, take the Métro to Pyrénées or Belleville, in the 19e/20e, on a Saturday night after sundown, or from about 9 o'clock on Sunday morning. Walk the length of rue Belleville, and here you will find that the old traditional Jewish working-class quarter is gradually meeting and mingling with the new wave of Arab, Chinese, Vietnamese Paris, without political thought or collision. Belleville dies at sundown on Friday, comes alive again on Saturdays and Sundays. Whatever the weather, all Belleville is out on the street, talking, eating, embracing, arguing, smoking, shopping. Here you gradually begin to realize that almost every face you see is male. Arab women, if they have been brought to Paris, keep steadfastly to their houses and families. The Arab man in Paris lives to work, and works very often in the low-end job no one else wants to do. On weekends, they are all out drinking coffee in crowded cafés and socializing on street corners. The women, if any, are buying fruit, vegetables, dripping-sweet pastries and fresh-killed chickens.

Here in the rue de Belleville and the rue Ramponneau, you have the feeling of being surrounded by a world infinitely more exotic than anywhere else in Paris. Half a dozen varieties of Arabic, plus Yiddish or a strange French heavily injected with words from both languages, are all around you.

It is true that the civilization of North Africa has affected Parisian life in all its aspects. Hardly a quarter of Paris (except perhaps the stuffy 7e and the formal 15e and 16e *arrondissements*) is without its restaurant serving couscous, *merguez, bric à l'œuf*, sugary Oriental pastries. But none is like Belleville.

In the last few years, the racial mix of Belleville has been further enriched by a new wave of South-east Asian residents, with their restaurants, shops and mini-supermarkets. The Belleville area, historically, is the preserve of not very well-to-do Jews, many who survived concentration camps, mainly strictly orthodox. Then came the influx of Arabs, many North African Jews and now the people from the Far East. It is intensely alive, with a cosmopolitan mixture of cinemas, posters, news-stands, food stalls. If you want to get your hair cut on a Sunday, make for Belleville.

If you are there on a Sunday morning, and of an adventurous turn of mind, go into one of the numerous places that sell take-away food. A *sandwich tunisien* is a North African/French sandwich: a crusty loaf split open and crammed with tuna, black olives, tomatoes, lettuce, hot green peppers, capers, bathed in an orange sauce that could start a fire. Drink only beer or mineral water, not wine (too sweet and too expensive). Finish with ruinously sweet Arab pastries, and you will have made a very adequate meal, about 24F all told.

Tourists are not exactly fawned upon in Belleville, any more than in Brixton, but nor is the casual stranger sent packing. We suggest you keep a low profile: flashy clothes and expensive cameras will do nothing for your image; at best you'll feel uncomfortable and out of place. But if you can manage not to look or behave like a gawker, there's no reason to avoid the area.

If you decide that you want to see this *quartier*, so rich in life and colour, don't wait, as many of the old, crumbling buildings are going or gone. Bulldozers have done for the worst slums, modern proletariat housing is going up. The boutiques are already moving in, but this richly varied multicultural part of Paris can never become banal, its many roots go too deep in the history of the city.

STREET SCENES

Much of the beauty of Paris, ranging from the small and exquisite to surprisingly grotesque, is alive and thrilling to the eye and the – possibly furtive – touch of the fingers. Not just the endless turning vistas of streets, trees, mansions and monuments, but the decoration in the form of carvings, capitals and statues which reveal themselves often in unnoticed places, and always free.

Paris churches are part of this 'living museum', and although there is never an admission charge, it's a civilized gesture to leave a few francs in the unobtrusive offering boxes near the doors.

In the oldest surviving church of Paris, St-Julien-le-Pauvre (in the street that bears his name), look for the marvellous group of flying harpies among its twelfth-century stone capitals. Otherwise it's a dull little place crowded with columns, which comes to life only when its occupants, an Eastern Catholic sect called the Melchites, sing on Sunday morning.

The oldest bell in Paris is in the tower of the Church of St-Merri, 78 rue St-Martin, 4e – it was cast in 1331. The bell-tower porch of the church of St-Germain-des-Prés was begun in 1040, and two of the windows in the church itself date from the middle of the eleventh century; while just outside in the little garden is an astonishing head of a woman by Picasso.

The last period of Gothic architecture, known as the Flamboyant, blazed out as though in reaction to the stark horror of the fifteenth century (plague, civil war and occupation by the English were all visited on Paris in a space of about thirty years). Perhaps the most fascinating survival is in the vaulted interior of the church of St-Séverin, at 1 rue des Prêtres-St-Séverin, 5e: an extraordinary spiralling central column seems to move and vibrate as it flings upwards and outwards a series of interlocked ribs.

This might be an appropriate place to mention that Paris churches *are* churches, and are primarily for worshippers. It would be wisest and nicest not to talk loudly, walk heavily, or jostle the chairs or benches: and as for the groups of tourists who chatter and flash their way around Notre-Dame, we would cheerfully see them suspended by their cameras from the mouths of gargoyles.

It is almost impossible to write dispassionately about the Sainte-Chapelle, the most queenly example of Gothic architecture in Paris, built to hold relics of the Passion and consecrated in 1248. It is no longer a church, but a historical monument, and in changing identities it has been very nearly vandalized. Its lower chapel now sells guidebooks and cassettes, its frescoed walls are scratched with graffiti. An unforgettable sight of recent years was a bare-footed tourist peacefully eating a sandwich under the great Rose Window.

For uncompromising medieval grimness, have a look at the tower of Jean the Fearless, built about 1374, and tacked on to the Hôtel Bourgogne, at 20 rue Étienne Marcel, 2e. At the other extreme is the Hôtel de Sens, aristocratic and elegant, standing at the corner of the rue de l'Hôtel de Ville and rue Figuier, 4e. Its conical tower and superb doorway are among the gems of the Marais. All through this district are scattered beautiful examples of noble buildings of the sixteenth and seventeenth centuries, which survived wars, plagues, riots and revolutions but nearly went down in the heedless twentieth century. Mercifully, they have been saved, restored, cleaned. See the Hôtel de Lamoignon at 24 rue des Francs-Bourgeois, 3e, dating from

1580, and another beauty, the doorway with pepperpot turrets of the Hôtel de Clisson, even earlier, and now tucked into the National Archives at 58 rue des Archives, 3e.

Centuries later, Paris produced a most tremendous variety of 'pompous' architecture – a riot of academic taste, from about 1850 to 1900, so bad as to be utterly endearing. A classic is the Hôtel de Ville, 4e. Don't miss the main staircase, whose decorations mix up cowboys, Indians and French merchants wearing solar topis in what seems to be Ceylon or Equatorial Africa.

The Universal Exposition of 1900 produced Art Nouveau and 'Le Style 1900', which has been loved, hated, collected and argued about ever since its birth. Many of Hector Guimard's sinuous, serpent-green Métro entrances still survive, and are now especially prized since the Museum of Modern Art in New York bought a discarded one and re-erected it in its garden.

At 10 rue Pavée, 4e, there's a synagogue designed by Guimard in 1913. A less famous architect, Jules Lavirotte, did a block of flats at 19 avenue Rapp, 7e, that has *everything*: peacocks, butterflies, enamel, entwined flowers and – peering out of the maze of design – a bust of Ophelia with streaming hair that turns into tendrils of vines. At 33 rue du Champs-de-Mars, not far away, Art Nouveau lilies crawl all over the front.

At the corner of the rue Victor Massé and rue Frochot, 9e, where whores patrol the street from about 4 o'clock in the afternoon, there's a most delightful piece of art deco stained glass set into the walls. And don't fail to see a perfect Paris townscape: the avenue Frochot, a locked private road with sedate houses, small front gardens, and an academy of painting, a prim little island in the midst of squalid Pigalle.

A series of Utrillo paintings unrolls when you walk into the rue Germain-Pilon, 18e, just off the place de Clichy. At no. 13 is a delightful courtyard and house, and nearby is the Grande Boulangerie Viennoise with beautiful painted glass art deco panels bordering its doors. Oddly enough, many Paris bakeries of the early 1900s have these little works of art.

At the top of the street you emerge into the rue des Abbesses – another Utrillo – and nearby is the tranquil place des Abbesses, with a famous, perfectly preserved Guimard Métro entrance.

Paris abounds in statues and carvings on its buildings, balustrades and pedestals – it's impossible to describe or even list the main ones, and anyway they've been photographed and written about almost to the point of boredom. Our personal picks: the brackets that support the flying buttresses of the church of St-Germain-l'Auxerrois in the place du Louvre, 1er – a delightful nightmare of hippopotamuses, monkeys, madmen and a rat busily destroying a globe of the world; the heart-stopping 'St-Francis in Ecstasy' of the sixteenth-century master Germain Pilon, in the church of St Jean-St François, at 6-bis, rue Charlot, 3e; the rearing Horses of Marly at the bottom of the Champs-Élysées; and the Seated Lion, by the nineteenth-century sculptor Barye, on the quay side of the Tuileries.

SCHEDULING

Prime time for Paris watching varies with various events.

Early morning (really early) from about 7:00 a.m., is the time to see what Parisians are really made of. For the most part, they actively enjoy work. Pavements are sluiced and swept, shopfronts washed down (with soap and polishing cloths) and market stalls are arranged like jewellery shops. The cafés are full of banter.

From noon on, life becomes more leisurely. Lunch may be drawn out over a couple of hours; by 4:00 p.m. the population strolls rather than bustles. At dusk, the fountains and monuments are illuminated: at least once, try to be standing in the place de la Concorde, ideally inhaling the scent of money from the Hôtel Crillon, at the magical moment when the lights go on in the square, along the river and all up the Champs-Élysées.

Au lit (Sleeping cheap)

The hotels that follow have been personally and recently vetted by our experienced Paris people. We emphasize *recently*, because it has been our experience that hotels can change, renovate, redecorate, re-price, go to rack and ruin, even disappear, with extraordinary speed in Paris. We have done our best, but be warned, and try not to be affronted if what we tell you today is different the day you arrive.

Many of our choices are those officially classed as 1-star in the *Guide des Hôtels* produced by the Paris Tourist Office. They collect their information from three professional bodies (the Syndicat Général de l'Industrie Hôtelière, the Chambre Syndicale des Hôteliers, Café-tiers, Restaurateurs de Paris and the Syndicat National des Chaines d'Hôtels et de Restaurants). With all that expertise, you aren't taking much of a chance. This professionalism means that hotels have been inspected for adherence to certain standards, their prices registered, their amenities and number of rooms verified. On the whole, the *Guide des Hôtels* is accurate, but between the time the data comes in and publication date, many things – including prices – can alter, especially if the hotel has upgraded its services or accommodation.

Every hotel we have included here is clean, well run and well above what we would consider a minimum standard of comfort. A certain number we have found are actually classed as 2-star, but with prices that bring them within our budget. Most of them are, as you would expect, walk-ups but a surprising number (including 1-star hotels) have lifts, making life easier for older people and those with luggage and/or small children. Many of the hotels now have a telephone in each room and a switchboard service night and day. In most cases, someone on the hotel staff speaks English, and where no English is spoken, we have noted the fact. You will then have to get by with smiles, goodwill and a little French remembered from school.

The price of every room in any hotel vetted by the Tourist Office must be displayed at the registration desk and again in the room. Most hotels display their range of prices and accommodation on an official printed form on the door or an outside window, so you can know even before entering what you are getting into. Others may put it up on an inside door. If you go in and don't see it, a polite request will bring it forth.

These days few hotels include *petit déjeuner* (the Continental breakfast of croissants, bread, jam, coffee, tea or chocolate) in their prices. If it *is* included, and you don't want to eat it or pay for it without eating it, say so politely but firmly *when you register*, and ask how much the room *alone* costs. Breakfast in an hotel can range from a fairly moderate 20F to a shocking 35F. Even at its cheapest it will be double the price of coffee and croissants taken standing at the *zinc*, the counter of the nearest *bar-tabac* or *brasserie* – and there you have the fun of tuning in on the conversation of Parisians going to work.

The 1-star classification of hotels is a rather loose mesh, taking in anything from a very clean, well-run hotel with a fax machine, and only ten minutes from Beaubourg – efficient but may not be the friendliest in the world – to a strange hostelry where the hot water runs out early, the towels are child-size, the proprietor never visible – but where you can have *charcuterie* lunches in your room, or hang dripping laundry from the radiators, without anyone taking the least bit of notice. A sweet, rather shabby, friendly place located near the rue St-Honoré is 1-star, and so are some of the others which we think will soon climb into the 2-star category.

One or two of the hotels we have found have no stars at all, although they are comfortable and spotless – many of them hope to be reclassified for the next *Guide des Hôtels*, but the inspectors haven't got round to them yet.

On the whole, we have found that you can get a single room with a *cabinet de toilette* (that is, basin, bidet and constant supply of really hot water) in a pleasant hotel for as little as 135F. A double room with a big bed is even more of a bargain, as it costs as little as 200F even in a very remarkable hotel in the Marais. If you want a shower expect to pay 155F for a single and up to 250F for a double room with a large bed. Twin beds and a bath can push prices up to around 300F, a few go as high as 450F – a considerable climb over prices a few years ago, but in every case, well worth the money.

In terms of other capital city prices, even the most expensive hotels on our list are not exorbitantly priced. Often the price of a room with a complete bathroom – shower or bath and WC and basin – will be the same whether it's occupied by one or two people. Less expensive rooms, those with a basin only, or with basin and bidet, may charge a lower price for one person, and put it up slightly for double occupancy. For a small supplemental charge, a third bed or cot can usually be put in a double room so that it sleeps three or even four, bringing the price per person down sharply.

Rooms that have no lavatory are always within ten feet of such a facility, and every hotel we have listed is careful to keep a shower or bath on almost every floor, for which you can expect to pay at least 15F and up to 22F for each use. You'd be surprised at how clean you can keep without a daily bath, in a room with that luxurious and versatile necessity, the bidet.

Expect to pay the highest rates for location: near the Opéra, around the Louvre, almost anywhere in the 1er, 6e, 7e, 8e, or 16e. St-Germain-des-Prés, which was for decades the refuge of the poor traveller, is now one of the costliest areas of Paris. A few old faithful hotels in the much-loved Latin Quarter, 5e, try to keep their prices down, but they seem to be closing for good or else renovating or upgrading. The Grand Hôtel des Balcons, near the universities, was a home away from home for generations of American, English and German students. It finally tottered under the weight of breadcrumbs, empty wine bottles and dripping laundry, and was renovated, now wearing well-deserved extra stars.

If you are willing to spend an extra ten minutes on the Métro, away from the tourist heart of Paris, you can save from 30F to 50F a day. Some of our hotels are in what may seem like unlikely neighbourhoods often brushed off by travel writers as 'uninteresting, working-class, too far from the action' – beyond the Bastille, around the place de la République. Up near the place d'Italie, in quiet Passy and so forth.

Actually every one of these *quartiers* has an indigenous life of its own, and many have changed or are changing with great rapidity.

We know all these areas ourselves, on foot, and consider every one well worth getting to know. They are often far more truly Parisian than the more obvious areas known as '*historiques et pittoresques*'. In these well-known neighbourhoods, they've seen tourists for generations, and you sometimes have the feeling that they couldn't care less if they never see *you* again. In more out-of-the-way places, you only need to take breakfast two days running at the counter of a café and the third day it will be '*Bonjour, Monsieur – comme d'habitude?*' – the usual? The news-stand person will probably hand you *Le Figaro* before you ask.

Some hotels which have been mentioned repeatedly in guide books begin to lean back and take it easy. In a well-known 1-star hotel in the Quartier d'Europe, our researcher found the shower head had fallen off, the windows didn't quite close and the blankets were like Kleenex. We dropped it. Now it's being renovated, and we're waiting until the new plumbing is in and the new prices set to go back and see it again.

Most hotels listed here have shaver points with 220-volt current, so you can use your electric razor, blow-dryer, mini-boiler for a cup of tea and so on. For Americans used to 110 volts, all appliances must be dual voltage or need a converter (see Electricity, page 225). Many hotels have reading lights above or near the bed, which is a necessity for a lot of us.

If you use the telephone from your hotel, expect it to cost more than a phone box would. It does give you the convenience of having someone deal with getting the number for you, in French. If the *concierge* has done anything extra for you – getting a taxi, theatre tickets, or whatnot – it's polite to leave about 20F in an envelope at the end of your stay. Service charges and TVA (VAT, in English) are included in your final bill, and the chambermaid needn't be tipped, unless of course she has done some washing or ironing chores for you. In this case leave some money in the ashtray in your room or in an envelope at the desk.

If you can dust off your school French and smile a lot, you will find that in almost every case the atmosphere in these hotels will be astonishingly warm, personal and friendly. A few phrases of hotel French follow (under Hotel French) and more general conversation about *la politesse*, which oils the wheels of Paris, can be found on page 246.

EATING AND LAUNDRY IN YOUR ROOM

Many Paris hotels have had their hospitality abused by travellers lured to the city by budget airfares and charters. So they now post polite notices in their lobbies or in their rooms: *Please, no eating and no washing*. We can well understand this, having seen some hotels almost vandalized by inconsiderate guests. We can only advise that if you *do* want to picnic – and it's a great temptation with all those succulent *pâtés* and jewel-like *pâtisseries* – do it with neatness and discretion. Tidy up after yourself. Don't carry an obvious, warmly smelling roast chicken in a plastic bag right past the desk. Put down newspapers on the floor, pick up your crumbs, don't stain the table with wine glasses, don't get grease stains and lipstick on the towels. We have eaten in hotel rooms for much of our adult life, from the elegant Montalembert long ago, to several of our favourite small hotels in the 1990s, without anyone ever saying boo.

When it comes to laundry, it's obvious that it isn't the washing, it's the *dripping* that drives Paris *hôteliers* up the wall. Hangers with wet shirts suspended from curtain rods or draped over radiators can make a soggy mess of a carpet. In the old Grand Hôtel des Balcons (now fully renovated and upgraded), students draped wet tights, bras, jeans and jerseys on curtain rails until even the walls ran with damp.

You'll be washing out your smalls in the basin or bidet, so have the courtesy to blot them reasonably dry in a towel, then hang them over a basin or a tiled floor. That way no drips will damage the carpets or curtains. If you feel self-conscious about this, wring them as dry as you can, and put them on hangers in the cupboard before the chambermaid comes to clean. While she's not a management spy, it is part of her job to let the front desk know what condition each room is in, each day.

We have found a few things indispensable for staying in modest-priced hotels: some light-weight plastic-coated wire hangers – buy them if you have to from a French supermarket – four or five clothes-peg clips to hang up socks and tights or to pull together curtains over an open window. An oversized metal clip from a stationer's shop comes in handy for all sorts of things.

HOTEL FRENCH

The notice-board dealing with prices of rooms is often couched in an esoteric shorthand, but once you've cracked the code it's quite easy.

Chambre avec e.c. (eau courante) – room with hot and cold running water, basin, no bidet

Chambre avec cabinet de toilette – room with basin and bidet in their own compartment

Chambre avec douche – room with basin, bidet and shower

Chambre avec bain – basin, bidet and bath (often with a hand shower)

Chambre avec douche/bain et WC – basin, bidet, shower or bath, and lavatory

Petit déjeuner – Continental breakfast (see page 94)

En sus means extra charge, e.g. *petit déjeuner* en sus, 20F.

BATHS, SHOWERS

As noted, if you are staying in a room without these amenities, you can command one by ringing down to the office. The charge will appear on your bill at the end of your stay. Really skinflint travelling couples can manage to work in two showers for the price of one if they are quick and wily, but don't say you read it here.

Part of a poor traveller's experience in Paris can be the public baths. Don't shudder and turn the page. They are clean, supervised by the city, offering showers with plenty of really hot water in private cubicles, and cater to the 700,000 or so Parisians who have no baths in their homes. Most baths are open every day, but close for a couple of hours around midday. A fairly fastidious friend agreed to try one for us, and was surprised to find out what an agreeable experience it was. Great value, clean as can be, well run and efficient. For the current price of 5F50, you get a shower stall and a dressing cubicle with mirror, tiled floor, hooks and shelf, and hot water for twenty minutes. This is plenty of time to get really clean, and to wash your hair. Everything is mopped up between clients. It's a good way to avoid spending 15–20F for a shower at your hotel. See page 218 for addresses and more information.

FINDING AN HOTEL ON YOUR OWN

If all the hotels listed here are full, wander round the neighbourhood you like best, after stashing your luggage at the station. Even have a look at hotels that have no stars at all. They are often clean, respectable, cheap and run by a couple that may not speak much English but want you to be satisfied. If you are staying more than three days, you could try asking if they have a weekly or monthly rate. They save on laundry, you save on hotel costs.

Note: the hotel day begins and ends at noon, sharp, and if you overstay you will be charged for an extra day. Most of the hotels in this book are very good about letting travellers leave a small amount of luggage, coats and so on (at their own risk, of course) in the lobby or office until time for the train or plane. Some, however, have been so thoroughly imposed upon by those who dump rucksacks, skis, carrier bags and raincoats for days on end, that they are no longer so willing. Others may have little space and really don't want their lobbies cluttered up with the increasingly hideous magenta and bright orange nylon luggage that travelling paupers lug around – don't be offended if they politely refuse to keep them for you. Take the stuff to the nearest *consigne* at a railway station, making careful note of their opening and closing times.

NEVER BOOK WITHOUT LOOKING

Go hotel shopping in the middle of the day, or not later than teatime, not at night or when you're dropping with fatigue. If they won't let you look at the room, say a polite 'merci' and be on your way.

FOR SOME CHEAP ALTERNATIVES TO HOTELS

See Other options, pages 87–91.

RECOMMENDED HOTELS

1ER ARRONDISSEMENT

Hôtel Lion d'Or 1-star
5 rue de la Sourdière, 1er
Tel: 01 42 60 79 04
Métro: Tuileries

Number of persons	1	2	3
Room with *cabinet de toilette*:	195F	270F	
with shower	260F	320F	380F
with bath		340F	
with shower and WC		380F	

Petit déjeuner 35   Shower 20

This small hotel on a quiet street is a long-established favourite of *Paupers' Paris* readers. Over the past few years it has added some rooms with shower and WC, and rates have risen somewhat, but not steeply. The location is superb, close to the Louvre, the Palais Royal, the Tuileries, the Seine and a fair number of good restaurants. It has many regular clients, situated as it is, so book early. VISA, American Express, Access/Mastercard and Eurocheques with Eurocard accepted. The *patron*, M. Ammour, speaks excellent English.

Hôtel du Palais 1-star
2 quai de la Mégisserie, 1er
Tel: 01 42 36 98 25   Fax: 01 42 21 41 67
Métro: Pont Neuf, Châtelet

Number of persons	1	2
Room with *cabinet de toilette*:	180F	230F
with shower	280F	320F
with bath and WC	350F	380F

Extra bed 70   *Petit déjeuner* 30   **Shower** *no charge*

Really basic accommodation but the welcome is warm and the rooms clean – and just at its feet is the delightful plant and flower market along the Seine. Rooms facing the *quai* have a view of the river, but will get the noise of the traffic continuously – ask for one at the back of the hotel. The *patrons*, M. and Mme Benoit, say theirs is the last inexpensive hotel on the *quai* and since the prices haven't changed since 1993, who can argue? You might ask if there are special rates for a week's stay, or off-season. A bit of English is spoken, but correspondence should be in French. VISA, Mastercard and Eurocheques with a Eurocard are accepted.

Hôtel Richelieu-Mazarin 1-star
51 rue de Richelieu, 1er
Tel: 01 42 97 46 20
Métro: Palais-Royal, Pyramides

Number of persons	1	1–2	2
Room with *eau courante*	190F		210–230F
with shower and WC		280–300F	
with bath and WC	310F		330F

Petit déjeuner 25F   Shower 10F

A minute hotel – only thirteen rooms and these are usually snapped up by regulars – to be booked well in advance. It's clean and tidy, recently redone, panelled in wood, decorated with posters (the earth seen from the moon) and very pleasantly staffed. Somewhat noisy on the street side, but location is all: you can hardly stay in a more central spot – a stone's throw from the gardens of the Palais Royal. No lift, but the rooms are fine and all credit cards are accepted. Write for reservations in French. The *patron* is M. Ben.

Résidence Vauvilliers 1-star
6 rue Vauvilliers, 1er
Tel: 01 42 36 89 08
Métro: Les Halles, Louvre

Number of persons	1	1–2	2
Room with shower and WC	180F		242F
with bath and WC		336F	

Petit déjeuner 28

Really small, really basic, but very, very central and to find a hotel so well located at these prices is quite unusual. The Vauvilliers is within walking distance of the Louvre, two Métro stops, the rue de Rivoli and some of our favourite restaurants. As you can imagine, it is heavily booked the year round, so telephone a couple of weeks in advance. English is spoken and things run efficiently. No credit cards, no Eurocheques, cash only. The *patronne* is Mme Religue.

3E ARRONDISSEMENT

Grand Hôtel des Arts-et-Métiers
4 rue Borda, 3e
Tel: 01 48 87 73 89   Fax: 01 48 87 66 58
Métro: Arts-et-Métiers

Number of persons	1	2
Room with *cabinet de toilette*	150F	200F
with shower	220F	250F
with shower and WC	250F	270F

Petit déjeuner 20F

This hotel has a welcoming and 'sympa' air, according to a Paris correspondent. There are telephones in each room and it is quite prettily decorated considering the low rates. What's more, in the Conservatoire National des Arts et Métiers, just around the corner in the rue St-Martin, you'll find Foucault's Pendulum! The rest of this great jackdaw's nest of a museum is being explored for our next edition. The *patron* is M. Jafar Naffer. American Express, VISA, Mastercard and Eurocheques with Eurocard accepted. Pets accepted, too.

Hôtel du Chancelier Boucherat 1-star
110 rue de Turenne, 3e
Tel: 01 42 72 86 83
Métro: Filles du Calvaire

Number of persons	1	1–2	2	3	4
Room with *eau courante*	150F		170F		
with *cabinet de toilette*.		190F		250F	
with shower			250F		
with shower and WC			280F		
with bath and WC				350F	400F

Petit déjeuner included in room price   **Shower** *no charge*

This pleasant and quiet hotel may not be at its best at the height of the tourist season, but it is trying to improve: tatty carpets replaced and a washer and dryer installed. The prices given are not necessarily those of the cheapest rooms – so you might be lucky and pay less. And if you arrive between November and May, ask for the winter prices as they are cheaper. The street is noiseless at night and the big room with two double beds for two couples or a family of three or four is a very good deal. English is spoken and major credit cards and Eurocheques accepted. The *patrons* are M. and Mme Martin.

4E ARRONDISSEMENT

Hôtel Andréa 2-star
3 rue Saint-Bon, 4e
Tel: 01 42 78 43 93
Métro: Hôtel de Ville

Number of persons	1	2
Room with *cabinet de toilette*	210F	220F
with shower	300F	350F
with bath and WC	330F	350F

Petit déjeuner 30F

We liked the good feeling in this hotel, where everything seems solid and the prices are reasonable. The air of *politesse* here is most agreeable and the people who run it seem to take pride in the comfort of the Hôtel Andréa. The rooms are well decorated, furnished with telephones and TV, and tidy – everything well kept and comfortable. The double room with bath was delightful, with a terrace from which you could see the dome of the Panthéon across the river. Altogether, a find, since it is very near Beaubourg, walking distance to the river and to Les Halles and with great transport. The big Samaritaine department store is just around the corner; and the Marais, with its great restaurants, museums, shops of every kind, is a short bus ride or one Métro stop away. English spoken. The *patron* is M. Valls.

Grand Hôtel Jeanne d'Arc 2-star
3 derue Jarente, 4e
Tel: 01 48 87 62 11   Fax: 01 48 87 37 31
Métro: St-Paul

Number of persons	1	2	3	4
Room with bath and WC	300F	390F	415F	470F

Petit déjeuner 35F

This charming little 2-star hotel is very clean, perfectly neat and decorated in white-lace bourgeois style. It has a lift, the rooms are large and well arranged. As the prices make obvious, it's a better buy for two, three or four people than for a solitary visitor. The street is peaceful and pretty, in the very heart of the Marais, close to the superb place des Vosges and to many of our best-liked restaurants. English is spoken and VISA, Mastercard and Eurocheques with Eurocard accepted. The *patron* is M. Memsenge.

Hôtel Castex 2-star
5 rue Castex, 4e
Tel: 01 42 72 31 52   Fax: 01 42 72 57 91
Métro: Bastille, Sully-Morland

Number of persons	1	2
Room with shower or bath		300F
with shower and WC	270F	320F
with bath and WC		340F

Petit déjeuner 25F

This little family hotel has been renovated and the prices have risen somewhat, yet they are still remarkably low for the location in the Marais and for the amenities offered. All the rooms have either a shower or a bath and a telephone. The rue Castex isn't one of the really picturesque streets of the Marais, but only two minutes away, across the rue St-Antoine, is the historic place des Vosges. To feel wealthy for a day, on a pauper's money, take a picnic lunch to the well-groomed gardens. The Castex accepts Visa, Mastercard and Eurocheques with Eurocard. The *patrons* are M. and Mme Bouchand.

Hôtel de Nice 2-star
42 bis, rue de Rivoli, 4e
Tel: 01 42 78 55 29   Fax: 01 42 78 36 07
Métro: Hôtel de Ville, St-Paul

Number of persons	1	2	3
Room with shower and WC	380F	420F	520F

Petit déjeuner 35F

We have always liked this hotel, which has a lift and is well painted
and wallpapered, clean and run by helpful English-speaking people.
However, traffic on the rue de Rivoli is continuous, night and early
morning, and you are advised to take ear-plugs. The site is superb,
only minutes from Beaubourg and on the edge of the Marais. Very
popular, so book at least a month in advance for peak periods;
reservations should be accompanied by a deposit for the first night's
lodging – traveller's cheques in francs only. VISA, Mastercard and
Eurocheques with a Eurocard are accepted. In the larger double
rooms an extra bed can be added for a supplement of 100F. The
patrons are M. and Mme Vaudoux.

Hôtel Pratic
9 rue d'Ormesson, 4e
Tel: 01 48 87 80 47
Métro: St-Paul

Number of persons	1	2
Room with *cabinet de toilette*.	150F	230F
with shower		275F
with shower or bath and WC		340F

Petit déjeuner 25F   **Shower** *no charge*

Clean and with evidence of extensive renovation: hall and staircase,
showers and bathrooms and almost all the rooms have been redone.
The Pratic closes at 1:00 a.m., which is not unreasonable. The staff
are a trifle cool, though always correct. But the prices are *rock-bottom*.
No credit cards, but traveller's cheques (in francs only) and Eurocheques (with a 40F surcharge) accepted. The *gerant* is M. Zaidi.

Hôtel Sévigné 2-star
2 rue Malher, 4e
Tel: 01 42 72 76 17
Métro: St-Paul

Number of persons	1	2
Room with shower and WC	325F	(double bed) 345F
		(2 beds) 363F

Petit déjeuner 16F

Long ago this good hotel was known as the Grand Hôtel du Sud et Pôle du Nord and we can't help feeling that the new, more aristocratic name doesn't have the same flavour. The old easy-going atmosphere is gone, but it's still well run and extremely clean and tidy. Unusually for a hotel so well renovated, they will accept three people to a room, which brings down the price per occupant; and if you and your companion share a double bed, that's cheaper too. Every room has a shower and there's a diminutive padded lift. To reach it, however, you must walk up half a flight from the lobby. Drawback: one side of the hotel is on the rue de Rivoli, with its – you guessed it – continuous traffic. On Friday nights when the motorbikes seem to rally at the Bastille down the street, it is NOISY. Ask for a room on the rue de Sévigné side and pack ear-plugs. Traveller's cheques and Eurocheques with Eurocards accepted, as well as VISA and Mastercard. The *patron* is M. Mercier.

5E ARRONDISSEMENT

Hôtel le Central
6 rue Descartes, 5e
Tel: 01 46 33 57 93
Métro: Maubert Mutualité

Number of persons	1	2	3
Room with shower	153F	216F	
with shower, basin and bidet		246F	

Petit déjeuner 28F

Basic is the word that springs to mind for this useful hotel, in the centre of the student quarter, next to the Polytechnic of Paris. You wouldn't want to spend long dreamy hours here, it's really a place to sleep and get ready for a busy day in this historic and endlessly interesting area. Nearby: the Cluny Museum, the Luxembourg gardens, boulevard St-Germain, bookshops everywhere, plenty of places to eat, sit, gaze. But we have to pass on the comment of an English college student, well versed in cheap Paris hotels, 'The communal toilet I saw is so small that the advantage of being a man is not applicable!' But as he says, it's simple, clean and the location is one of the best on the Left Bank. Book well in advance, this 16-room hotel is very well known on the student grapevine. Eurocheques are accepted as a deposit for a booking, but not in payment for the actual stay. As you would expect, no credit cards. No English is spoken, but somehow the residents get along. The *patron* is M. Julio Neiva.

Hôtel des Grandes Écoles 2-star
75 rue du Cardinal Lemoine, 5e
Tel: 01 43 26 79 23   Fax: 01 43 25 28 15
Métro: Cardinal Lemoine

Number of persons	1–2
Room with shower or bath	490F
Room with shower or bath and WC	620F

Extra bed 100F   *Petit déjeuner* 40F

'Unquestionably my favourite hotel, quite expensive but not as high as other places on the Left Bank which are much less beautiful and friendly,' says our Paris friend. To reach this unbelievably pretty hotel, you walk through a rustic-looking courtyard off the rue Cardinal Lemoine. Turn the corner and you see a miniature country mansion in its own gardens. The rooms are delightful, each decorated differently – and the elegance and charm of the furniture and decorations are worthy of at least two more stars. There's a lift, but the hotel's not very accessible for anyone with a wheelchair, as there are steps up to the entrance door. English is spoken; telephone reservations are taken between 2:00 p.m. and 6:00 p.m. VISA,

Mastercard and Eurocheques with Eurocard are accepted. The very agreeable *patronne* is Mme Le Floch. It is wise to book at least two weeks ahead in high season and a week before during quieter months.

6E ARRONDISSEMENT

Delhy's Hôtel 2-star
22 rue de l'Hirondelle (6 place St-Michel), 6e
Tel: 01 43 26 58 25
Métro: St-Michel

Number of persons	1	2
with *cabinet de toilette*	233F	356F
with shower	356F	436F

Petit déjeuner 30F   Bath or shower 25F

Delhy's is in a pretty, little narrow street leading off the busy boulevard St-Michel and if you like the Left Bank, you couldn't want a better place to stay. It's basic, clean and very quiet – that alone makes it a find in this fairly noisy neighbourhood. Obviously, the rooms with *cabinets de toilette* (basin and bidet) are more comfortable than the very slightly less expensive ones with basin only. Credit cards are accepted and Eurocheques with Eurocard. Everyone here is pleasant and English is spoken. Mme Françoise Kenniche is the helpful *patronne*. Book a month in advance in high season, ten days ahead in spring or autumn.

Hôtel de Nesle
7 rue de Nesle, 6e
Tel: 01 43 54 62 41
Métro: Odeon

Number of persons	1	2
Room with shower	225F	275F

Petit déjeuner included

The Hôtel de Nesle is a riot. Full of students and backpackers, it has the atmosphere of the laid-back, what-the-hell 1960s. It may seem chaotic, but the *patron*, David, runs the place with benign autocracy and a nice sense of fantasy. Each room is decorated in a different style – one is 'Grandma's room', with lace, old furniture, sepia photographs; another has medieval murals. There's a Turkish bath, the *hammam*, with deep blue tiling and lion's head basin, and a washer and dryer for the use of clients. Breakfast is served on brass trays to the sound of Arab music – and staff and guests join forces to keep everything going. One day when we were there, an American motorcyclist was helping plant shrubs in the terrace level garden behind the hotel. Drawbacks? Some of the rooms are small and the partitions thin, so it might be noisy. Booking weeks in advance is imperative, especially if there's a big jazz or rock event scheduled, when fans congregate at the Nesle. Cash only, paid in advance when you arrive.

Regent's Hôtel 2-star
44 rue Madame, 6e
Tel: 01 45 48 02 81   Fax: 01 45 44 85 73
Métro: St-Sulpice

Number of persons	1	2
Room with shower or bath and WC	350F	450F

Petit déjeuner 40F

Almost too expensive, we said a few years ago – but prices have gone up little since then. If you want to spend your money on a relaxing, comfort-filled stay rather than on opera, music or films, this is the place. The little garden is beautiful, full of flowers and breakfast is served there in good weather. The hotel itself is quiet, clean, neat, respectable and gives you space, ease and a feeling of being lapped in comfort without the cost of a 3- or 4-star luxury hotel. It has a lift. We advise booking well ahead in high season, as the Regent's is known to French travellers who like easy charm at affordable prices. VISA, Mastercard and Eurocheques with Eurocard accepted. English is spoken, but it is best to write for reservations in French, if possible, using the Tourist Office form letter as guide (see page 13). The *patron* is M. Cretey.

7E ARRONDISSEMENT

Hôtel du Champ de Mars 2-star
7 rue de Champ-de-Mars, 7e
Tel: 01 45 51 52 30
Métro: École-Militaire

Number of persons	1	2
Room with shower and WC	355F	390F

Petit déjeuner 35F

Although it has recently been renovated by the new *patrons* M. and
Mme Gourdal, the rates here have hardly gone up in the 4 years since
we last wrote about the Hôtel du Champ de Mars. It's not the
cheapest hotel in Paris, but given the superb location and the fact that
it's a two star, it's a good buy for two people visiting Paris. Our
French researcher remarked that it was 'clean, nice, cosy – some
rooms not as bright as others, but as it has a lift and is on a delightful
street, I'd recommend it'. The street is 'neighbourhood' Paris and
endlessly fascinating. At night it's very quiet. Have your morning
coffee in a neighbouring café. All the rooms are equipped with
televisions and English is spoken. VISA and Mastercard are accepted
and Eurocheques on all banks except those of the UK.

Grand Hôtel Leveque 1-star NN
29 rue Cler, 7e
Tel: 01 47 05 49 15   Fax: 01 45 50 49 36
Métro: École-Militaire

Number of persons	1	1–2	2	3
Room with *eau courante*	195F		225F	425F
with shower		290F		
with bath and WC		345–360F		425F

Petit déjeuner 25F   Extra child's bed 80F

Most of the 7e *arrondissement* is so correct, so sterile, that it's a happy
shock when you turn a corner and stumble into anything as full of
life as the rue Cler. It's a pedestrian street, busy in the daytime with a

street market and many shops. At night it quietens down to a pleasant hush. The Hôtel Leveque is a walk-up and we like the rooms on the two top floors best – so this is a hotel meant for the fit. The rooms are well furnished and the upper ones are light and airy. Some of the rooms are big enough for three people to share, so a room with a complete bath and three beds must be one of the best value-for-money offers in this neighbourhood. English is spoken and despite the lack of a lift, those who stay here seem to settle in and stay for ever. Reserve well ahead, especially in high season. VISA, Access and traveller's cheques in francs accepted. The *patronne* is Mme Fouchet.

Hôtel Malar

29 rue Malar, 7e
Tel: 01 45 51 38 46   Fax: 01 45 51 38 46
Métro: Latour-Maubourg

Number of persons	1	2
Room with shower	280F	320F
with shower and WC	340F	380F
with bath and WC		400F

Petit déjeuner 28F

The Malar is well known to savvy travellers – we can't claim it as our discovery. All the rooms have showers or baths and many have WCs. Several of the double rooms can accommodate a third bed at a supplement of only 60F, useful for a travelling family or three really good friends. Perhaps the atmosphere is somewhat more formal and 'correct' than it was when we first saw it years ago – due, no doubt, to the pressure of those tourists who have discovered the 7e *arrondissement*. The Malar is still a pleasant place to stay and you will love the *quartier*. English is spoken. The Hôtel Malar accepts VISA and Mastercard as well as Eurocheques with Eurocard. The *patron* is Mme Caill.

Prince 2-star
Avenue Bosquet, 7e
Tel: 01 47 05 40 90   Fax: 01 47 53 06 62
Métro: Invalides

Number of persons	1	2
Room with WC and bath	300F	350–490F

Petit déjeuner 30F

This hotel is a favourite of ours and has been for nearly ten years. All rooms have bathrooms with either baths or showers and TVs. There is a room for handicapped travellers, a lift and a garden. Located in one of the more interesting parts of the 7e, the avenue Bosquet is the epitome of *haut-bourgeois* Paris. Although it has a lot of traffic, rooms facing on the street are double-glazed for quiet. Reserve several weeks in advance, as it is very popular with French families and business people from all over the country. English and German are spoken and the *patron*, M. Roussel (and his son) are very helpful. American Express, VISA, Mastercard, Eurocheques with Eurocard accepted.

Le Royal Phare 2-star
40 avenue de la Motte-Picquet, 7e
Tel: 01 47 05 57 30   Fax: 01 45 51 64 41
Métro: École-Militaire

Number of persons	1	2
Room with shower and WC	315–410F	350–410F

Petit déjeuner 30

M. le Rousic, the *patron*, speaks little English but understands it well and is always busy but helpful. The hotel has been redone over the years and his personal involvement really shows. The Royal Phare has a lift, TVs in the rooms and there are reading lights at the beds, something many Paris hotels don't have. A happy atmosphere and very good value and close to excellent shopping (Prisunic, Monoprix), and to the charm of the rue Cler for more shopping, strolling and gazing. In the avenue de la Motte-Picquet traffic begins early, about

7:00 a.m., if that matters to you, but it's quiet at night. AMEX, VISA and Eurocheques with Eurocards, possibly a surcharge for the latter.

8E ARRONDISSEMENT

Hôtel de Marigny 2-star
11 rue de l'Arcade, 8e
Tel: 01 42 66 42 71   Fax: 01 47 42 06 76
Métro: St-Lazare

Number of persons	1	2
Room with *cabinet de toilette*	235F	400F
with shower or bath and WC		490F

Petit déjeuner 35F

A truly remarkable bargain, if you can manage to get one of the six 235F rooms in this charming 2-star establishment. It's about a hundred yards from the Madeleine and a five-minute walk to Gare St-Lazare and the place de la Concorde. The Marigny actually provides pillows in addition to the usual Paris hotel bolster and it is one of the few that provides an individual piece of soap for the weary, dusty traveller. Sparkling clean and prettily furnished, too. But watch out for the self-service lift as the doors can give you a rap on the elbow if not firmly controlled. Reading lights. Visa, Access cards, traveller's cheques and Mastercard accepted. M. Maugars is the *patron*.

9E ARRONDISSEMENT

Hôtel de Lille
2 rue de Montholon, 9e
Tel: 01 47 70 38 76   Fax: 01 48 00 04 55
Métro: Poissonnière

Number of persons	1–2
Room with *cabinet de toilette*	150F
with shower	200F
with shower and WC	230F

Petit déjeuner 25F   Bath or shower 15F

Although the entrance looks a bit dark, persevere. The rooms are clean and tidy, though they don't provide twin beds, only doubles. And don't be put off by the aroma of garlic which may greet you as you come in – if this bothers you go elsewhere. Or even leave Paris itself. Rates at the Hôtel de Lille have hardly gone up in the past few years, it is inexpensive and the transport is good. The neighbourhood, which at first glance looks drab and commercial, will yield some unexpected and interesting places if you don't pass through it unseeing. No English spoken, but if you make an attempt at even hit-or-miss French you will be all right. No credit cards. The *patron* is M. Amir.

10E ARRONDISSEMENT

Hôtel Bonne Nouvelle
125 boulevard Magenta, 10e
Tel: 01 48 74 99 90
Métro: Gare du Nord

Number of persons	1
Room with shower	191F
Room with TV and shower	211F

Petit déjeuner included

The *patron* is M. Selam. A very Parisian hotel, this, somewhat old-fashioned but remarkably well located, just down the street from the Gare du Nord where the train from the airport brings you. There are buses and Métro stations galore within a few minutes' walk. The prices are low, so the Bonne Nouvelle is true to its name ('good news'). The boulevard Magenta is noisy, eighteen hours a day, so take earplugs. The rooms are smallish but clean, without any attempt at good taste in decoration. Some English is spoken – but a little French does help. Because of the location and the low rates, it is heavily booked during the tourist season, so write for reservations. It's best to do so in French, basing your letter on the Tourist Office form letter, page 13.

Hôtel Jarry 1-star
4 rue Jarry, 10e
Tel: 01 47 70 70 38   Fax: 01 42 46 34 45
Métro: Gare de l'Est or Chateau d'Eau

Number of persons	1	2
Room with WC	140F	170F

Bath or shower free

In the not very interesting 10e *arrondissement,* this hotel is a pleasant surprise: very clean, sober, nicely redone in considerable taste and the *concierge* speaks good English. Conveniently located for the Gare de l'Est and there are some goodish restaurants and brasseries in the neighbourhood. No lift but there are telephones in the rooms, a bar in the hotel and VISA and Mastercard are accepted. The *patron* is M. Mahfouf.

ôtel du Jura

6 rue Jarry, 10e
Tel: 01 47 70 06 66
Métro: Château d'Eau

Number of persons	1	2
Room with WC	140F	185F
with shower		210F

Bath or shower 20F

A more modest place, but comfortable, neat and respectable; a remarkable bargain with well-arranged rooms and continental breakfast included. It can be a bit noisy and is beginning to need redecoration and repairs, but they're on the way, we're told. And while the 10e isn't one of the historic areas of Paris, it has its own neighbourhood character and some very good shopping. Those who run the hotel are kind, helpful and willing to speak English of a sort and to help you with your French. No credit cards or traveller's cheques.

Little Hôtel 2-star

3 rue Pierre Chausson, 10e
Tel: 01 42 08 21 57   Fax: 01 42 08 33 80
Métro: Jacques Bonsergent

Number of persons	1	2
with shower or bath and *cabinet de toilette*	275F	350F

Petit déjeuner 30F

A clean and pleasant place, completely renovated with lift. All the rooms have showers or baths, telephones and TVs. The hotel has a homelike feeling and the *patron*, M. El Baz, is a sociable man who likes to take care of his customers. VISA, American Express, Mastercard, Eurocheques with Eurocard and traveller's cheques accepted.

11E ARRONDISSEMENT

Cosmos Hôtel 1-star
35 rue J.P. Timbaud, 11e
Tel and fax: 01 43 57 25 88
Métro: Parmentier

Number of persons	1	1–2
Room with *eau courante*	180F	
with shower and WC		210F

Petit déjeuner 25F

This 41-room hotel has a lift, is very clean and fresh and has TVs and telephones in every room. The largest of its double rooms with bath can sleep four people, in two big beds. Add to that the pleasure of this Paris-village street – restaurants, several Chinese/Vietnamese places, cafés, brasseries, *junqueries*, small supermarkets and art shops. There are great street markets Tuesdays and Fridays, one on the boulevard Richard Lenoir and the other in Belleville at the north end of the street. Transport is excellent; the No. 96 bus stops almost at the doorstep and takes you straight to the Marais, the Left Bank, the Gare Montparnasse – and runs seven days a week. Prices at the Cosmos are still low, as it's known only to the French. No English is spoken, so write or telephone in French. The *patronne* is Mme Vedrines. VISA, Mastercard and Eurocheques with Eurocard (with a surcharge of 90F). Pets accepted.

Hôtel Notre Dame 2-star
51 rue de Malte, 11e
Tel: 01 47 00 78 76   Fax: 01 43 55 32 31
Métro: République

Number of persons	1	1–2	2
Room with *cabinet de toilette*	190F		
with shower		230F	
with shower and TV			280F
with bath, WC and TV			330F

Petit déjeuner 32F   Bath or shower 20F

We are very fond of this hotel, which is getting well known to
English, American and German visitors to Paris. Close to the great
square at République, with its shops, restaurants and several Métro
lines, it couldn't be more conveniently located. The hotel itself is so
pleasant; the reception area is charming and the breakfast room is
furnished with fresh flowers. The atmosphere is peaceful (though the
rue de Malte is far from quiet in daylight). You're advised to book
well in advance from late spring through early autumn. VISA
accepted. Pets allowed. The *patrons* are M. and Mme Ades.

Hôtel Plessis 2-star
25 rue de Grand Prieuré, 11e
Tel: 01 47 00 13 38   Fax: 01 43 57 97 87
Métro: République, Oberkampf

Number of persons	1	2
with *cabinet de toilette*	195F	215F
with shower	270F	295–315F

Petit déjeuner 32F

This hotel is very well run by an enterprising couple, M. and Mme
Montrazat, the latter of whom speaks English and knows a great deal
about this interesting neighbourhood. Staying here you are within a
brisk walk of the Musée Picasso and the charming small streets of the
11e, yet the very busy place de la République is just down the street.
The hotel has double windows and new doors – quite efficient against

the noise. There is a lift and a bar, and the rooms have hairdryers, telephones and cable television. All credit cards are accepted.

Hôtel Rhetia 1-star
3 rue de Général-Blaise, 11e
Tel: 01 47 00 47 18   Fax: 01 42 61 23 17
Métro: Voltaire

Number of persons	1	2
Room with *cabinet de toilette*	170F	190F
with shower	210F	230F

Petit déjeuner 10F   Bath or shower 10F

The Rhetia is a hotel we discovered more than ten years ago and a very good choice for those who like to explore parts of Paris that never make the guidebooks. Prices are moderate and the atmosphere is quiet and friendly; once you get to know the neighbourhood it's easy to put down roots. The pretty square opposite is bubbling with children after school. The Rhetia is well run, unpretentious and known to French rather than foreign tourists. The hotel has TVs and telephones in the rooms and allows pets. Cash only.

Hôtel Sans-Souci 1-star
113 boulevard Ménilmontant, 11e
Tel: 01 43 57 00 58
Métro: Ménilmontant

Number of person(s)	1	1–2
Room with *eau courante*	120F	
with shower		180F

Shower 20F

Basic, but clean and respectable. Most of the rooms are off the boulevard, hence quiet, and the hotel is just five minutes' walk from the green peace of beautiful Père Lachaise. We know this neighbourhood well and like the mixture of people, shops and restaurants of all kinds almost within an arm's length. Book well in advance, in French, following the form on page 13. These low rates mean that there are many long-stay tenants, students and young people. Edith Piaf was born near here, in the rue Crespin-du-Gast. The very French street market on the boulevard Ménilmontant is open Tuesday and Friday mornings from about 8:00 a.m., while the Belleville market, more raucous and rambling, runs west from the Ménilmontant Métro stop. No credit cards accepted. The *patron* is M. El Djama.

13E ARRONDISSEMENT

Pacific Hôtel Gobelins
8 rue Philippe-de-Champagne, 13e
Tel: 01 43 31 17 06
Métro: Place d'Italie

Number of persons	1	1–2	2–3
Room with *eau courante*	138F		
with WC		153F	
with shower			223F
with bath and WC		253F	

Petit déjeuner 25F

A hotel with an old-fashioned air and with a lift – not all that common in 1-star establishments. We have always liked the neighbourhood, a well-to-do bourgeois one, only a few minutes from the good shopping of the place d'Italie. The reception is polite and efficient without noticeable warmth, but the comfort of the rooms and the good tiling and plumbing in the bathrooms makes up for this slight drawback. There's a *gendarmerie* almost at the door, so the crime in this quiet area is probably low! Pets and credit cards (except American Express) accepted. The *patronne* is Mme de Roode.

Hôtel Rubens
35 rue de Banquier, 13e
Tel: 01 43 31 73 30
Métro: Gobelins

Number of persons	1	2
Rooms with *cabinet de toilette*	128F	150F
with shower or bath	205–235F	

Petit déjeuner 15F

This hotel never seems to change – it is remarkably good and the rates are still low. The rooms are delightful and every bathroom we have seen here has been comfortable. The street is quiet with no through traffic, but the hotel is within close reach of good restaurants (Lebanese, Vietnamese, South-east Asian). The neighbourhood has an interesting life of its own which one can happily settle into – if you yearn for the bright lights and the bustling streets, there's very quick transport by bus and Métro into the centre of Paris. The Rubens provides reading lights. Credit cards accepted. The *patronne* is Mme Grillère.

14E ARRONDISSEMENT

Hôtel du Parc 2-star
6 rue Jolivet, 14e
Tel: 01 43 20 95 54   Fax: 01 42 79 82 62
Métro: Montparnasse Bienvenue, Edgar-Quinet

Number of persons	1–2
Room with *cabinet de toilette*	250F
with shower and WC	360F

Petit déjeuner 30F

While the building is old, it has been well maintained and improved by the owners. We like the view across the little triangular park which adjoins the busy boulevard Edgar-Quinet, or the very Parisian roof-scape seen from the rear windows. Double-glazing means the rooms are quiet and they're clean, cheerful and pleasant to stay in.

The street is a nice backwater of Montparnasse, with small shops and restaurants ranging from Japanese sushi bars to inexpensive family-run Italian bistros. There is a lift in the hotel and hairdryers, telephones and TVs in the rooms. VISA, American Express and Eurocheques with Eurocard accepted. The *patrons* are M. and Mme Jacob.

Hôtel de la Loire 2-star

39 bis, rue de Moulin Vert, 14e
Tel: 01 45 40 66 88   Fax: 01 43 20 38 18
Métro: Alésia, Plaisance

Number of persons	1	1–2
Room with *cabinet de toilette*	235F	
with shower		260F
with shower or bath and WC		340–360F

Petit déjeuner 25F

The atmosphere here is almost like a country town rather than a street on the edge of an international metropolis. The Hôtel de la Loire has a range of small but efficient rooms set along the edge of a pretty little garden. Upstairs, larger rooms provide accommodation for a family of three or four. All rooms have TVs and telephones and there is a lift. The Alésia neighbourhood is a good shopping area and exploring it will give you a view of how Paris really runs. Mme Noël, the *patronne*, has a welcoming manner and really seems to enjoy running her 'country inn'. VISA, Mastercard and Eurocheques with Eurocard. Pets are allowed.

17E ARRONDISSEMENT

Hôtel Flaubert 2-star
19 rue Rennequin, 17e
Tel: 01 46 22 44 35   Fax: 01 43 80 32 34
Métro: Ternes

Number of persons	1	2
Room with *cabinet de toilette* and shower or bath	370F	500F

Petit déjeuner 30F

This new addition to our list is a real find. Known primarily to French visitors and business people, the Flaubert is a well-kept secret from tourists. The windows of the reception and dining area are lined with tropical plants and parakeets, and many of the 37 rooms overlook the courtyard garden that grows wilder than a jungle. All rooms are furnished with little soaps and shampoos, telephones and TVs. A clean, tidy and friendly hotel, there are facilities (including a lift) for the disabled and special rates for weekend or longer stays. The prices are not rock-bottom but the charm and comforts make it worthwhile. A famous outdoor food market, Marché Poncelet, is only five minutes away and rue Rennequin is lined with restaurants from all reaches of the globe. VISA, Mastercard and Eurocheques with Eurocard accepted. Pets allowed.

18E ARRONDISSEMENT

Hôtel André Gill 2-star
4 rue André Gill, 18e
Tel: 01 42 62 48 48   Fax: 01 42 62 77 92
Métro: Pigalle

Number of persons	1	1–2	3
Room with *eau courante*	160F		
with *cabinet de toilette*		240F	
with shower or bath and WC		360F	530F

Petit déjeuner included

Although the André Gill is just up the hill from the racket of Pigalle, it is tucked away into a sort of courtyard backing onto the rue des Martyrs. It's an oasis of peace and calm, yet very easily reached by Montmartrobus from the Métro. The neighbourhood is a complete delight, with attractive restaurants and food shops, and although the hotel is just five minutes' walk from Sacré Cœur, it's a world away from the *hurluburlu* of Montmartre. It has a lift, a reception room and many of the thirty-two rooms have private baths or showers. Some rooms have delightful coloured glass windows dating back many years. All credit cards accepted. The *patron* is M. Brahim Lounis. Pets allowed.

Hôtel de Bouquet de Montmartre 2-star

1 rue Durantin, 18e
Tel: 01 46 06 87 54   Fax: 01 46 06 09 09
Métro: Abbesses

Number of persons	1–2	3
Room with shower or bath and WC	350F	440F

Petit déjeuner 30F

This is a hotel located in the centre of Montmartre and here you are paying for the location. The bathrooms are small, the wallpaper clashes gaily with the bedspreads and the furniture is bargain warehouse. But the neighbourhood has vistas that remind you of Utrillo paintings wherever you look and a lot of good, small, inexpensive restaurants within walking distance. To cut costs, try the *Bains/Douches*, the public baths of Paris (see page 218) rather than pay the fairly high price for a shower here. And take your morning *café au lait* and *croissants* at the nearest café for considerably less. English is spoken, no credit cards. The *patronne* is Mme Gibergues.

Hôtel Central Montmartre
37 rue Hermel, 18e
Tel: 01 46 06 09 13
Métro: Jules Joffrin, Simplon

Number of persons	2
Room with WC, bath or shower	210–370F

The Central Montmartre is in an area we're very fond of. The Montmartrobus stops at the door, the rue Ordener at the corner is wonderful for food shopping, restaurants, flowers, or just wandering. There's a pretty park nearby, and if you're lucky, on a summer's night you may hear a band playing. The hotel itself is modern and charming, with a telephone in each room, and prices which are really reasonable. The furniture is good and the décor tasteful. There are no tourists in this slightly out-of-the-way neighbourhood, yet a bus will take you down the boulevard Ornano to the Champs-Élysées in a surprisingly short time. All credit cards accepted. The *patronne* is Mme Lamyre.

Other options:

BED AND BREAKFAST: B & B on the English plan is slowly catching on. **Café Couette** is an organization which operates all over France and has recently started up in Paris. Write to or visit them at 8 rue de l'Isly, 75008 Paris. Their office is at the back of a courtyard and hard to find, but persevere, an English-speaking representative is usually there.

ROOMS TO LET: check the notice-boards at the American Church, 65 quai d'Orsay, 7e (Métro: Alma-Marceau, Invalides). They are plastered with notices by English-speaking residents who want to let rooms and flats. Most holiday lets are for two, three or four weeks; rooms to rent may be offered for longer periods. You will see ads for studios or for bedrooms with use of bath or kitchen in a flat. Take a notebook, a lot of franc pieces or a Télécarte (see page 250). St Michael's Church of England, 5 rue d'Aguesseau, 8e (Métro:

Madeleine), has a similar service and very helpful people who can tell you everything about living in Paris.

STUDENT HOUSING: students are well catered for in Paris. Take your International Student Identity Card, or if you don't have one a current photograph and proof of your full-time student status, with 38F to CIEE, 49 rue Pierre-Charron, 8e (Métro: Alma-Marceau).

The Cité Universitaire, in the quiet southern part of Paris, often has rooms to let during university holidays. Contact them at 18 boulevard Jourdan, 14e (Métro: Cité-Universitaire), where you may find someone who speaks English.

A very useful organization for the young is UCRIF (Union des Centres de Rencontres Internationales de France), which has 11,000 beds on offer all over the country. Find them at:

Office de Tourisme
127 avenue des Champs-Élysées, 8e
Tel: 01 47 23 6172

Gare du Nord
Tel: 01 48 74 68 69

Siège Social UCRIF
21 rue Béranger, 3e

Also first class at finding accommodation for young people:

Accueil des Jeunes en France
139 boulevard St-Michel, 5e
Métro (RER): Port Royal
Tel: 01 43 54 95 86
Open from March to October, Mondays through Fridays, 9:30 a.m. to 6:30 p.m.

Near the Bastille at:
151 avenue Ledru-Rollin, 11e
Tel: 01 43 79 53 86

Gare du Nord, near the Halle des Arrivés:
Tel: 01 42 85 86 19
8:00 a.m. to 10:00 p.m.

Near the Pompidou Centre at:
119 rue St-Martin, 4e
Métro: Hôtel de Ville
Tel: 01 42 77 87 88
9:30 a.m. to 6:30 p.m.

In the Marais at:
16 rue du Pont Louis-Philippe, 4e
Métro: Pont-Marie, St-Paul, Hôtel de Ville
Open June to September, Mondays through Fridays, 9:30 a.m. to 6:30 p.m.

There are four beautiful and historic converted houses in the Marais, 4e, given over to housing students. Check at the Maubuisson Hôtel des Jeunes, 12 rue des Barres, 4e (*Métro*: Hôtel de Ville, Pont-Marie).

YOUTH HOSTELS: the *Ligue Française des Auberges de Jeunesse (LFAJ)*, 38 boulevard Raspail, 7e (*Métro*: Sèvres-Babylone), is *the* address to use if you have a YHA card, no matter what your age. Paris hostels are not comfortable, not very well located and certainly offer little privacy, but at their prices who can complain? A three-day stay is generally the limit, but that's probably all you would want.

If you want to stay longer than a week or two, check the noticeboards near the restaurants, cafeterias and in the entrance halls of the universities. One young friend, on a year's foreign study from Cambridge, found free lodgings. He had a room in a Left Bank flat in exchange for tutoring the flat's owner in English, all the while polishing up on his own French. For such good deals, check these sources:

CROUS
39 avenue George Bernanos, 5e (*Métro*: Port-Royal)

Assas
92 rue d'Assas, 6e (*Métro*: St-Placide)

Cité Universitaire
19 boulevard Jourdan, 14e (*Métro* (RER): Cité Universitaire)

CIDJ

101 quai Branly, 7e (*Métro*: Bir-Hakeim)

Your own college or university may be able to add to this very brief listing of student-type places to stay.

RENTING A FLAT in Paris, for a family or group planning to stay a long time, can work out cheaply: the best source we know is the *Offres Meublés* column in *Le Figaro*. But take a French-speaking friend when you negotiate any agreements! Several agencies which advertise in the *International Herald Tribune* are said to be efficient: they charge a finder's fee, of course.

EXCHANGING: perfect for paupers. A French person or family occupies whatever you have to offer, from a bed-sit to a house, and you go to their room/studio/flat. An experienced 'exchanger' has these tips to offer:

1   Make your arrangements through an exchange agency which lays down certain well-established rules. Or check the Announcements column in *The Times*, London.

2   Be specific about what you are offering: number of bedrooms, baths, equipment, use of telephone, daily help, linen, washing machine, car, motorbike, exact dates when you plan to leave and return.

3   Be sure you understand what you are getting into: same as above, but with such important extras as how many flights of stairs, lift, concierge, etc.

4   Pets and plants can be catered for in exchanges, but specify *that* early on; some exchangers may be allergic or unwilling to tie themselves down.

Everyone we know who has done exchanges has been satisfied and plans to do it again. Most have had happy surprises: one family thought it was getting a four-room house and found that they had four *bedrooms*: another was invited to spend the weekend in a Normandy cottage during their Paris stay; a third has established a long family friendship which includes the free use of a Paris flat over Christmas week. *Not* so great: the exchanger who arrived late at night and found the cupboard bare, not so much as a teaspoon of instant coffee or a slice of bread for breakfast, in an intimidatingly clean kitchen!

Agency exchanges cost about £35 a year, but work well because they are managed by experienced people who have a good set of guidelines for you and your prospective exchangees. The one we have used, which has many Paris members longing to do swaps in the UK and North America, is INTERVAC, 6 Siddals Lane, Allestree, Derby, DE 2DY. Our family has done exchanges through them for about nine years, with 99 per cent great success and the occasional comic episode. One such episode was a Paris Christmas, which included a temperamental front door lock and only one key for three people, a very high-strung electrical system which blew fuses constantly, a bath/shower room with no door, bizarre linens, an invisible concierge. The plus points were: a perfect location one minute from a good Métro stop, a library of paperback thrillers in French, a fridge full of exotic foods, a bottle of wine, a dishwasher and washing machine, a lift and a Christmas tree.

There are other exchange agencies: look in the telephone book or read about them in newspaper and magazine articles. INTERVAC is the one we know personally and use often.

La nourriture (Eating well)

WHAT TO EXPECT

For anyone coming from a country where only Indian, Chinese or Greek food is inexpensive, Paris makes a welcome change. True at today's exchange rate of 7F60 to the pound, it's no longer the bargain paradise that it was, when you could divide prices by ten. But you can still eat well as the Parisians do, in interesting surroundings, for between a third and a half of what a comparable meal would cost you in London, Manchester or Edinburgh.

The great Paris restaurants, admittedly, can cost you a month's salary at one sitting, but that's not what this book is about. Almost everywhere in Paris there's an immense range of affordable and very good food.

Our basic requirements in setting out this list is what is called *le menu*. It is price-fixed, posted in the window (even some of the 3-star restaurants will publicly display their menu, but these will be from 300F up). Some offer a three-course menu, with a quarter-litre of wine, beer or mineral water and service included. Others will include service, or will say *prix net* which means the same thing, but will not include drink. In most cases wine will be modestly priced at from 10F to 20F for a quarter-litre, two good glasses.

Some restaurants we have chosen do not offer three courses, but have opted for a two-course *formule* – starter and main course. A few have no set menu, but their à la carte choices seem so good, and the total is not staggering, that they are included here.

Now for the good news: almost every one of the restaurants here will feed you well, with a glass or two, for not more than 100F – as this is written, you'll get 7F60 for your pound, so a meal to enjoy will be about £13.50. A few go as high as 160F, all inclusive, but they have been chosen as special occasion meals.

Best news of all: quite a number of new restaurants, and old favourites, have menus at from 50 to 85F including service, and often drink as well. As this book was being re-edited, and reports were flooding in from our diligent eaters in Paris, we were pleasantly amazed to see how many said 'the menu is 65F', or 'a very good meal for 50F'.

In no case has any restaurant been included just because it is cheap. Our reporters like to eat well, and in many places we've had to edit out some of their enthusiasms simply for the sake of space. In order to keep on offering really good food at affordable prices, many restaurants will offer their special menu only at lunch. Others have dropped *boisson incluse,* so you pay for what you drink, or skip it if that suits you better. A few offer food that is conventional, not particularly distinguished – but always of good quality, well cooked, and probably making up for a somewhat banal menu in having a fun atmosphere and the Parisian flair for making a meal an event. In these cases, we've set down exactly what you can expect in the most forthright terms: no one who contributes to *Paupers' Paris* owes any obligations to any establishment, so what you read is what you get. Unless of course a restaurant has changed hands, changed character, upped its prices between press time and reading time.

Now about drink: follow the lead of many Parisians. If wine, beer or mineral water is not included in the menu price, feel free to skip it. Contrary to what you have heard, not *all* Parisians drink wine with every meal. Ask for *'une carafe de l'eau, s'il vous plaît'* and you'll get a jug of clean, safe, very cold drinking water, which you'll probably like as much as pricey mineral waters.

We have grouped these restaurants by *arrondissement* (see page 32 to find out how these work), so that if you find your first choice is packed, another won't be far away. Many of these places hardly ever see a tourist, because they are good bourgeois eating-places patronized by serious eaters, and no one eats more seriously than the French. Each year, more and more accept credit cards. In the main they are clean, simple, usually with a spotless paper tablecloth put down over a longer-lasting cotton one; paper napkins – but sometimes linen ones – endless baskets of fresh, good French bread, and undistinguished but palatable wine, beer or mineral water.

Sanitation (*le lavabo*) varies from spotless to mildly squalid, and a few places still have *toilettes à la turque* reminiscent of the Dark Ages. Not once in our experience has the bill been padded in any way, and rarely has a restaurant made any sort of mistake on the bill. However, we advise you always to run an eye down the bill before you pay. Although service is included in all prices, it's good manners to leave any small change on the little tray. Coffee is almost never included in the set menu prices, and ordering it in a restaurant can bump up the price by about 10F. You'll sleep better without it anyway.

Many Paris restaurants close on Sundays, and some are open only for lunch or only for dinner. Most close on public holidays, some close Christmas Eve and New Year's Eve. Many which open on Sunday are closed one other day during the week, and a surprising number are open in August. They take their holiday in off-season months, so that visitors in the summer have many more choices than in years past.

We found as we re-edited the book that Paris restaurants are changing their hours of opening, weekly and annual closing times at the speed of light, and are far more flexible to the demands of their customers than ever before. What we set down here is as accurate as possible as of summer 1996, but please don't send us thunderbolts by post if a good little French restaurant has become an expensive chilli parlour or South-east Asian café!

Have the occasional snack lunch or dinner in your room (or outdoors), which can save you on a restaurant meal (see page 59, about hotel eating). Or go to one of the very good value '*Selfs*' (page 141), where three courses with your choice of drink can be as little as 35–55F.

Café eating – those alluring little corner spots with outdoor tables and awnings – can tear a carefully calculated budget wide open. But if you're exhausted in mid-morning or late afternoon, sit down and spend 8F for a cup of (black) coffee, or 12–15F for a *citron pressé* (real lemonade). The chance to rest your weary feet, write your postcards, read the newspaper, and sit as long as you like, is worth the money.

For breakfast, if you choose not to eat at your hotel (often overpriced and not nearly as enjoyable as mingling with the French on their way to work), take your coffee and croissants at *le zinc* (the counter), not sitting down at *la terrasse* (a table) which ups the bill by about 30 per cent. And never order tea in Paris! You get a cup, a teabag, and a jug of water that's hottish but never boiling, and you'll pay about 12F. Brandy might be cheaper.

All Paris tap water – in hotels, flats and restaurants – is safe to drink. But if you worry about what a change of water can do to your digestive system, it's good to know that you can buy small bottles of good mineral waters to put in your carry-around bag. And huge (1½-litre) plastic bottles of Vittel, Evian and private-label still mineral water, at supermarkets for about 3F. *Eau gazeuse* – Perrier and the like – are usually available only in glass bottles, but they are still cheap.

RESTAURANT MANNERS

Restaurants – except for *'Les Selfs'* (page 141) – are run by a *patron* or *patronne*, with waiters and waitresses. All very human, all very connected to their clients. We're not talking here about McDonald's or their like. Contrary to myth, those who work in restaurants are not to be addressed as *'Garçon!'* If you want fast, friendly service, and advice if you need it, it pays to be polite. As you enter the restaurant it doesn't hurt to say *'Bonjour'* or *'Bonsoir, monsieur'*; and as you leave, *'Au revoir'*.

French restaurants – especially the ones you'll find listed here – don't give you a lot of elbow room, and curiously enough you find that you don't need it. You may be just barely able to squeeze into your seat; or seated opposite a stranger instead of with a table to yourself, and seated very snugly at that. Yet, the general air of *politesse* and enjoyment, is such that tight spacing doesn't seem like encroachment on your personal living space.

You'll find it easy to adapt to. Your neighbours are absorbed in their food, or each other, and there is no lack of privacy. A *'Bonsoir'* or *'Bon apétit, madame'* will not be taken amiss if you happen to catch someone's eye. If no one wants to get into conversation, it will be obvious; if everybody does, this soon becomes known. In any event, there is no stuffiness or awkwardness about your proximity. Best of all, women who eat alone in restaurants need not worry about being put at the worst table, near a draughty door, or in a forgotten corner. They are never ignored, and are always treated with respect, and even a little encouragement.

RECOMMENDED RESTAURANTS

1ER ARRONDISSEMENT

Auberge du Palais Royal
10 rue Jean-Jacques-Rousseau, 1er
Tel: 01 40 26 51 53
Métro: Louvre, Palais-Royal

The Auberge is nicely hidden away in a narrow, crooked street, and further hidden behind brown curtains, which give it privacy and atmosphere. Most of its patrons, at lunch, are government or business people who talk quietly, there's a subdued hum of conversation rather than a noisy chatter. The decor too is subdued in tone but cheerful in feeling, the room is decorated with theatre posters, fresh flowers, and candle-lit at night. The *patron* is friendly and welcoming. The menu is 70F, *boisson comprise* at lunch and 70F at night (not including drink or 120F if it's included), and the menus are identical at both meals. The *andouillette* was delicious and the *faux-filet* was well cooked and flavoured with bundles of herbs, the crisp potatoes roasted with rosemary. Other choices of starters would have been *fromage blanc* with garlic and herbs, garlic sausage or lentil salad. In the winter, you can have soup as a first course. Main courses are few, each is good: *escalope panée*, grilled chicken, *brochette* of tender lamb pieces. For dessert, there are *tartes maison* (*rhubarbe, noix de coco, pomme, poire*) Their chocolate mousse has a light texture and is made with care, not the usual dense commercial mousse. Good cheeses and fruit tarts are on the menu too. Service and a quarter-litre of wine are included. Open noon to 3:00 p.m., 7:00 to 10:00 p.m. Closed Saturdays and Sundays and Christmas.

Au Petit Ramoneur
74 rue St-Denis, 1er
Tel: 01 42 36 39 24
Métro: Châtelet, Les Halles

Having known this restaurant, so conveniently located near the Forum des Halles and quite close to Beaubourg, for almost ten years, we always wonder if this is going to be the year that the proprietors retire? Or that the overhead awnings finally give way in a cloudburst? Will one of the tightly packed clients knock over the communal bottle of *rouge*? But all is still well. One of our eaters, a Paris-based Englishman, ate there for the first time, and said that it's a real treasure – a *Paupers' Paris* special, the kind of place most tourists would pass without noticing anything but the sleazy street. Inside there's a noisy little room lost in a happy time-warp. Photographs of Les Halles-as-it-used-to-be are everywhere, and the *patrons* can remember the time of the great market, its little restaurants, and the market-porters, butchers and early-morning revellers who were their clients.

The menu is ridiculously good value, 68F including a half-litre of red wine or a half-bottle of mineral water and service. First courses might be *terrine de campagne*, fillets of marinated herring, *pâté de foie* with green peppercorns; then a choice of *petit salé* with lentils – a very Les Halles dish – and so forth. Desserts are conventional and the pastry is fine. The menu is offered at both lunch and dinner. Open 11:30 a.m. to 2:15 p.m., 6:30 to 9:30 p.m. Closed Saturdays, Sundays, major holidays, and 15 August to 1 September.

Le Galtouse

15 rue Pierre Lescot, 1er
Tel: 01 45 08 04 61
Métro: Les Halles, Etienne-Marcel, Châtelet

Somehow this one has slipped past the guidebooks. The two-course *formule* at 69F, service included, is amazing value. It's one of the best meals you can find in an area which can be rather hit-or-miss when it comes to eating. This confident little restaurant has a touch of old-fashioned French class to it. The à la carte menu is impressive and rather high-priced, usually a good sign that the *prix-fixe* dishes will be cooked by people who know what they are doing.

Le Galtouse offers a first course choice of *salade de fruits de mer*, a rabbit terrine, onion soup, a big salad with cheese and walnuts, then a main course of *faux-filet*, grilled trout, or for a supplement, lamb chops, all with baked potato with chives, and two other vegetables. Desserts are à la carte and range from 23F for *crème caramel* to 35F for profiteroles. The cheeses are 25F. A meal of such quality for 69F, or the minor extravagance of the three course *menu* for 110F, is really rare. The dining-room is very attractive, with fresh flowers, big mirrors, candles, a luxurious air. A woman friend who has eaten there says they are kind and thoughtful to the lone female client. Service is included in prices, drink extra and not cheap at 25F for a quarter-litre of good red. Open noon to 2:30 p.m., 6:30 to 11:00 p.m., every day except Christmas.

L'Incroyable
26 rue de Richelieu, 1er
Tel: 01 42 96 24 64
Métro: Palais-Royal

This famous little place is still literally incredible. People working and living nearby come here week after week, year after year, as do members of our 'extended family' in Paris. The three-course menus range from 70F to 100F including service (70F at lunch)! The restaurant is perched on either side of stairs that join the rue de Richelieu and the rue de Montpensier – entrances in both streets. The menu gives you a choice of six starters, six or seven main dishes which could include squid *provençale*, and duck breast with freshly made pasta and gruyère cheese, finishing with a choice from four or five desserts and cheese. Their fruit tarts are made in their kitchen, and cost extra. A quarter-litre *pichet* of wine is 11F, as is Vittel water. This is an early-hour place, opening at 12:00 to 2:15 p.m., when it is usually empty. Dinner is 6:30 to 9:00 p.m. – eat early, go home early. Closed Saturday nights, Sundays, Monday nights.

Le Palet
8 rue de Beaujolais, 1er
Tel: 01 42 60 99 59
Métro: Palais-Royal

This restaurant is hidden in a pretty little street very close to the Louvre, and so far it has escaped the notice of tourists, who stick to the more obvious places. We liked the rustic atmosphere, the stone walls and the changing art exhibitions which customers enjoy wandering around to gaze at between courses. On the ground floor there's a bar and some tables, and downstairs a room converted from a vaulted wine-cellar, with tables tucked in between the arches. The *formule* is 65F–95F, with a main course and either a starter or a dessert, all chosen from the slightly more expensive 95F three-course menu. First courses included a *tartine*, a big salad with walnuts, *crudités du marché*, mushrooms *à la grecque*, *cervelas*, etc. Main courses: *faux-filet* with a choice of shallot or black-pepper sauce, poached turkey liver, lamb fillets, and what they call '*l'idée du jour, selon l'humeur du Chef!!!*' All are served with crisp fries or a selection of vegetables. The dessert list is copious, including a flan with coconut, sorbet and lemon tart. Try *Coupe Damnation* which includes chestnut purée, crème fraîche, and hot chocolate sauce!

Wine such as a Touraine rosé, the house red or Bergerac Blanc is served in *pichets*, around 16F for a quarter-litre and 30F for a half-litre. Service is included, so you could eat well there for 90F or 120F. Open noon to 2:30 p.m., 7:00 to 12:00 p.m. Closed Saturday lunch, Sundays, and one week over Christmas. On other holidays, Le Palet closes for lunch, and opens for dinner. No annual closing.

Le Relais du Sud-Ouest
154 rue St-Honoré, 1er
Tel: 01 42 60 62 01
Métro: Louvre, Palais-Royal

Year after year, the Relais goes on being a delight – nearly ten years ago, we discovered it on a rainy day when we were foot-weary from a morning at the Louvre just around the corner. Most tourists never get as far as the rue St-Honoré for lunch, and are probably intimidated by the grandeur of such an address. What they are missing! It's unaffected and traditional, packed at lunch and dinner by the locals, almost entirely French. The service is brisk, friendly, and the stone walls, old photos and wall panels – painted to look like wood – never change. At lunchtime, the menu for 65F includes service and drink, and has a choice of six starters, such as artichoke hearts, good *crudités*, tuna salad, fillet of herring, etc. Main dishes change every day, always include good steaks and usually a fish dish. Desserts could include *gâteau basque*, pastry – or cheese. This menu is available only at lunchtime. A more expensive one, still only 85F service included, is served at lunch and dinner – with such goodies as a *coeur d'artichaut*, *cassoulet*, fresh salmon steak, saddle of lamb, duck with plum sauce, and a selection of desserts. Drink is extra – a quarter-litre of the house red is about 15F. Open 12:15 to 2:30 p.m., 7:00 to 11:00 p.m. Go early at lunchtime – if you arrive after 12:30 you may have to wait for a table, or be courteously told the house is full. Closed Sundays, for three days over Easter, and for Christmas; open New Year's Day and 14 July. Closed August.

Le Stado
150 rue St-Honoré, 1er
Tel: 01 42 60 29 75
Métro: Louvre, Palais-Royal

The *patron* of Le Stado is a former rugby player, and the stone walls are hung with mementos of his career and of the team of Tarbes or 'le Stadoceste Tarbais' in the south-west region. The cooking is extremely good, hearty Pyrénées food, and the service is warm and welcoming. Starters are the usual *crudités*, *charcuterie* and *pâté*, with a fine garlicky *rillette du pays* or a salad with nuts or gizzards; typical main courses are beef brochette, rumpsteak, *terrine des landes, maigret de canard, lapin chasseur*, veal kidneys, and chicken livers. We are fond of the sporting, rather noisy ambiance and the back-slapping, chatting owner. The cheese is brought to you on a plate for your choice; and one member of our family always goes for the coffee dessert, *Moka St-Michel*. The general lunch menu costs 65F. Dinner is a bit pricier with meals at 85F, 100F, 160F, 180F. Wine is not included with lunch or dinner. Open seven days a week, noon to 2:30 p.m., 7:30 to 11:00 p.m. Open August, Christmas.

2E ARRONDISSEMENT

Anadolu
rue de Turbigo, corner rue Volta, 2e
Tel: 01 42 05 42 01
Métro: Sentier

One of the very unpretentious little cafés which stand on every street corner in the business section of Paris. On the edge of the wholesale jewellery/leather goods/luggage area, the Anadolu is a godsend: it serves huge sandwiches of spit-roasted lamb (*shawarma*) shaved into slivers and put into a giant 'pocket bread', like a monster pita. Then in go onions, lettuce, tomato slices, seasonings, and a dollop of very hot sauce. Sandwiches at the table are 22F, at the bar or 'to go' are 20F. The set menu is 55F, with the usual Middle Eastern starters of tarama, vine leaves, feta cheese and salad, then lamb brochette, steak, lamb chops and a choice of ultra-sweet desserts. All prices include service, and wine and beer are inexpensive. The one or two waiters are genial and handle a constant stream of customers. Open early morning for coffee, pastries, croissants; sandwiches are served all day. The 52F menu is available for lunch and for dinner from 6:30 p.m. until about midnight. Open seven days a week, closed some holidays – no annual closing, as far as we could make out.

Note: the loos are unisex and should be used only in real necessity.

Le Drouot
103 rue de Richelieu, 2e
Tel: 01 42 96 68 23
Métro: Richelieu-Drouot

The same management as Chartier (page 122), it's large and too well-known. Normally we wouldn't include it here, but if we don't, we'll get a postbag full of letters telling us about how good it is, what excellent value. All true. It's near the Opéra, hence useful for pre- and post-Printemps and Galeries Lafayette excursions. Specialties include the *oeuf mayonnaise* and beef stew. A three-course meal with wine runs between 70F and 91F, according to the daily offerings – leek salad, *boeuf bourguignon* with steamed potatoes, and *tarte Tatin* (caramelized apple tart), with a quarter-litre of slightly better than ordinary wine, plus a 12 per cent service charge. A la carte menu runs from 38F to 90F. Open 11:30 a.m. to 2:30 p.m., 3:00 to 10:00 p.m., seven days a week. No annual closing, but closed major holidays.

Restaurant Kurde Dîlan
13 rue Mandar, 2e
Tel: 01 42 21 46 38
Métro: Sentier

If you're near Les Halles, walk away from crowded and costly places, into the streets around rue Montmartre, where we found this gem, one of the few Kurdish restaurants in the Western world. The character of the food is unmistakably from the old Ottoman empire: *bostanà balcara*, aubergine purée with red and green peppers, garlic, olive oil; tarator, spinach with garlic and yogurt; grilled lamb marinated in lemon, yogurt, diced red pepper and parsley. An exotic soup called *sorba* is made with rice, lemon, yogurt and mint. There are nineteen cold starters, and a dozen grilled dishes, served with salad, rice and superb Kurdish unleavened bread. Desserts are lush: try *firini*, fine semolina baked with a sugar syrup, pistachio nuts and butter. No set menu, but prices are not high: soups 18–20F, starters 22–28F, main dishes from 40 to 50F, desserts 20–25F. Beer is around 15F. The Dîlan is open noon to 3:00 p.m., 8:00 to 11:30 p.m. Closed for lunch on Sundays and holidays but open in the evening. Closed Christmas. No annual closing. VISA, Access and Diners' Club cards accepted.

4E ARRONDISSEMENT

La Canaille
4 rue Crillon, 4e
Tel: 01 42 78 09 71
Métro: Sully-Morland

One of our student scouts of years past wrote 'Very cool – *assez sympa, décontractée*,' another called it 'sort of campy'. It's a good night out in a thronging place with a really optimistic atmosphere – big, imaginatively decorated with trendy lights, and a youngish, very talkative crowd. Go early, or brace yourself for a wait. Everything runs on greased wheels here – you write out your order, it is whisked away, and eventually your meal will come, although service can't be very fast in a place so popular, so packed with appreciative eaters. Try the express lunch (entrée, plat, desssert) at 70F for quick service. The menu is short; attention is paid to quality rather than variety with lunch at 73F and dinner at 85F. Unusual starters: pumpkin mousse with a green sauce, a *terrine* of fresh and smoked salmon with a creamy lobster sauce – almost unbearably good, and certainly the dish of the week. Main course choices were sautéed rabbit with mustard sauce, chilli, or a lamb brochette with couscous and a 'desperately hot' sauce. Desserts are quite ordinary, sorbets (commercial, not home-made), several pastries, a small selection of cheeses. For a larger selection of foods, the *grand menu* is available at lunch and dinner for 139F. Service is included, drink extra – a quarter-litre of wine 15F, mineral water 17F. Open 11:45 a.m. to 2:15 p.m., then 7:30 p.m. to midnight. Closed for lunch Saturdays and Sundays.

Le Cristal
13 rue Beautrellis, 4e
Tel: 01 42 72 38 34
Métro: St-Paul, Bastille, Sully-Morland

Le Cristal is in one of the prettiest streets of the Marais, and it's small, with space for only about twenty-four people. We and our friends have been going there since 1982, through several changes of management and menu. Two menus: one at *midi* for 65F, includes a salad with anchovies marinated *à la provençale*, hard-boiled eggs with a *forestière* sauce, then a filet of herring for the main course. The 98F menu offered at lunch and dinner is longer, and certainly not expensive for what it gives you – *oeufs de caille*, duck *pâté*, or salad, then good main courses like duck breast with green peppercorn sauce, goulash, salmon with tartar sauce, and fried kidneys. Desserts were fairly conventional but excellent – lemon tart, *tarte Tatin* and *crème caramel*. An *apéritif* is included with lunch and dinner as well as dessert. Our one reservation? The main courses were accompanied, on a spring night, not with superb fresh vegetables or with a salad, but with vegetables straight from the tin, a real shame. Service included in prices, wine is available only in half-bottles at 50–55F, mineral water 25F, so anyone eating alone must either spend real money for wine, or ask for the usual carafe of fresh cold water, free. Open noon to 2:30 p.m., 7:00 to 11:00 p.m. Closed Saturday lunch, Sundays, Monday nights, and 'some time in August'. Open holidays including Christmas (unless it falls on a Saturday or Sunday), Good Friday and Easter Monday.

Le Loir dans la Théière
3, rue des Rosiers, 4e
Tel: 01 42 72 90 61
Métro: Saint-Paul

Bring your mother here. For a light lunch and a superb dessert, a good cup of tea (one of the few places in Paris . . .), stop over at Le Loir while strolling through the Marais. A restaurant and *salon de thé*, it is 'baba cool'. Grab one of the old leather armchairs if you can, then sit back and browse the painted walls until your eye rests on the dessert table. Great tarts, lemon pies, red fruit crumbles and rich confections like *fondant au chocolat* or *fondant au citron* will make your mouth water – don't forget to order lunch. Everything is à la carte, teas are 20F a pot (enough for two to share); lunch runs from 40F for a *tarte Pascualina* with salad to 48F for the *tartes salées (chèvre, roquefort)*: desserts are 38F, but large enough to share. Offers weekend brunch from 80F to 115F. Open from 11:00 a.m. to 7:00 p.m. everyday. Never closed.

Galerie 88
88 quai Hôtel de Ville, 4e
Tel: 01 42 72 17 58
Metro: Hôtel-de-Ville

For a fun, inexpensive sampling of world food and a lovely evening view of the spectacularly lit trees along the Seine, don't miss this jewellery-shop-turned-restaurant. Candlelight illuminates the middle Eastern *tchachkas* that hang from the wood beams and good music – usually blues – is always playing. Turkish doors, Tibetan jewellery, dried flowers, and unmatched chairs and tables create the relaxed ambiance in which to enjoy a range of 35F–40F east-meets-west dishes: big Greek, Mexican, Moroccan, Italian or French salads; pasta with *crème fraiche*, gorgonzola, basil, tomato sauce or *crottin de chèvre* ... Or try the substantial *Assiette 88*, a selection of dips like *taboulé*, tapenade and guacamole for 60F. Desserts include scrumptious pecan pie, chocolate brownies and lemon tart, all for around 25F. Open every day for lunch, snacks and dinner from 12:00 p.m. to 1:00 a.m.

Le P'tit Comic
6 rue Castex, 4e
Tel: 01 42 71 32 62
Métro: Bastille

This little place has a new manager, Marie-Thérèse, who has kept the *Bandes Dessinées* (comic book) decor. She cooks, serves and keeps an eye on everything. In addition to *crêpes*, there are salads, such as the delicious 'Gourmande', tuna, baby corn, tomato and so forth, a big bowl for 45F. Among the *crêpes* are 'Tyrolienne', which is a savoury affair with ratatouille and minced steak, 45F; and 'Bigoudine', a substantially filled Breton *crêpe*, also 45F. The most inexpensive main-course *crêpe*, 'La Pleureuse', rolled around sautéed onions, is 27F, for vegetarians try the 'Vegetarian' with ratatouille and mushrooms for 30F. For dessert try the 'Bonne Maman' at 20F a basic, jam-filled *crêpe*. Ideal, as *Le Monde* commented, after you've been to some theatre event around the Bastille Opéra. Cider, usually drunk with Breton food, is available only in bottles, which three or four could share, 35F. Wine and mineral water are over-priced, we think. All in all you can eat here à la carte for around 80F, or try the 90F menu which includes *cidre* for two. Service is included in all prices. Open 11:30 a.m. to 3:00 p.m., 7:00 to 10:00 p.m. Closed Sundays and Christmas Day. Open Good Friday and Easter Monday, New Year's Day, and 14 July.

Le Petit Gavroche
15 rue Ste-Croix de la Bretonnerie, 4e
Tel: 01 48 87 74 26
Métro: Rambuteau, Hôtel de Ville

'An odd, scuzzy little restaurant, with zinc bars upstairs and down, peeling paint, toilets to avoid, a revolting stuffed deer in one corner, radio music – and one redeeming quality: good food,' reported an American in Paris a few years back. Add to that the location, in the depths of the now-fashionable Marais. Somehow it has managed to remain unchanged in the nine or ten years we and our friends have been going there. Le Gavroche rambles over several floors, with tables fitted in wherever. A reasonable red wine is just 12F a quarter-litre. The menu changes all the time. At dinner, the *formule* is 48F and might include the *faux-filet* with roquefort sauce or veal escalope Normandy-style in cream and cider sauce. The lunch menu is an equally good value at 45F, coffee not included. A la carte entrées cost about 26F, main course 48F and dessert 20F, so the *menu à prix-fixe* is excellent value. Service is not very fast, but extremely amiable. Although this restaurant has been in a number of (French) restaurant guides, tourists don't seek it out, perhaps put off by the faded street entrance, or the look of the bar as they glance in. Appreciate it for what it is, an old-style Marais restaurant before yuppification set in. Open noon to 2:30 p.m., 8:00 p.m. to 2:00 a.m. Closed Saturday lunch, and Sundays. In August, open for dinner only, from 4:00 p.m. to 2:00 a.m.

Relais de L'Ile
37 rue St-Lois-en-l'Ile, 4e
Tel: 01 46 34 72 34
Métro: Sully-Morland

This lovely restaurant was described as shoebox-small (but with a gallery) by the Bramhalls, who discovered it for us. It's remarkable value, astonishing in this very up-market street. There are two good short menus at lunch, at 57F and 89F. One has a choice of two huge main-course salads followed by a selection of five or six sweets. The price included a big basket of very good bread and a quarter-litre of red or *rosé* wine. The second menu offers a starter, main course and dessert with wine. For dinner the menus are 89F and 119F.

Friends living in Paris were enthusiastic about the food and the setting – paintings everywhere, soft music. They liked the *salade fraîche*, a platter of varied greens with tomato, egg, *salade russe*, and the thick slice of coarse country *pâté* with a generous serving of salad greens. The main courses that day were grilled chicken marinated in lemon and honey, and a big plate of lamb steaks sprinkled with fresh herbs. Desserts are à la carte at 25F, and extraordinary – home-made cream in shallow saucers, strawberry melba made with real vanilla ice-cream. But their pleasure in the meal was marred by the cool treatment – the waitress brought mineral water when asked for a *carafe d'eau*, and charged them extra for it on the bill, which is illegal. The special menus are served only at lunch, and Le Relais is closed Sundays and holidays. Credit cards accepted.

Le Temps de Cerises
31 rue de Cerisaie, 4e
Tel: 01 42 72 08 63
Métro: Bastille, Sully-Morland

There's a poster of Jacques Brel on the wall of this friendly little corner restaurant in the Marais, and it's likely that he would have been at home here. You'll be caught up in the flow of talk from the workers in overalls and the young Parisians of the *quartier*, and the *patron* really does keep the lively spirit of the place going. The food, as a Breton friend, Patrick, remarked, is honest and correct. But the quality is variable, and the best bet is to stick to simple dishes such as cold beef salad with ratatouille, or roast pork with *haricots verts*. The first courses are usually very good, smoked fish (according to season) with potato salad, or *charcuterie*, or *crudités*, and excellent desserts: fruit compote, *gâteau fourré*, ice-cream. If *Far breton*, a pudding made with *pruneaux* and raisins, is on the menu, the day you're there, choose that. All this, and walls papered with photographs of the Marais as it once was, comes to just 68F, service included. A quarter-litre of house wine is 10F, but a better bet for two might be the Côtes du Rhône at around 30F the half-litre. Open as a café from 7:30 a.m. to 8:00 p.m., but serving lunch only from 11:30 a.m. to 2:30 p.m. – go before 12:30 or after 1:30 to be sure of a table. Closed Saturdays, Sundays, holidays and August.

Vancouver
64 rue de la Verrerie, 4e
Tel: 01 42 72 67 63
Métro: Hôtel de Ville

Once again, we're glad to report that prices in this much-liked restaurant have crept up only a few francs in two years. The two-course *formule* is only 59F at lunch, with ten choices of starters – rabbit *pâté* with hazelnuts, quiche made in their own kitchen, avocado with a sprightly sauce; five choices for the main course including steak with our favourite roquefort sauce, escalope of veal Normandy-style, or *andouillette* with sharp mustard sauce. Desserts – an irresistible chocolate charlotte 30F, tartes 25F – will up your bill a bit, but as wine and service are included, a fine lunch could be as little as 88F. Dinner prices are higher, but if you can content yourself with an *escalope of saumon* for 65F and a huge bowl of three sorbets for 30F, with a carafe of water instead of drink, you'd have a lush meal for under 100F. Wine or beer at night is 16F. All prices include service. Open noon to 2:30 p.m., and 7:00 to 11:00 p.m. Closed Sundays, Christmas Day, August, and national holidays. The outside tables get taken up early; the service is outstandingly pleasant and fast, and the rooms inside are serene and lights are low. Don't go if you're allergic to dogs, as a large friendly fellow wanders around to greet guests.

5E ARRONDISSEMENT

Aux Savoyards
14 rue des Boulangers, 5e
Tel: 01 43 26 20 30
Métro: Jussieu, Cardinal Lemoine

Aux Savoyards, like many other restaurants around this 'street of restaurants' is, and always has been, a place for students. They eat here, or wait outside for a table to clear, or often work part-time on the staff

– it all adds up to a somewhat hectic and very 'in' feeling. Don't expect to linger, or have a quiet meal. The service is fast – otherwise they could never cope with the crowds that want to come in. A meal, with service and perfectly passable wine, costs just 65–70F à la carte. Ask for the menu as you enter, at lunch the fixed price menu is 75F for three courses, at dinner choose between the 90F and 130F menus. *Entrecôte*, hamburgers, chicken, sausages, salmon – all cooked well, rural fashion, with no fancy sauces or names. Open noon to 2:30 p.m., 7:00 to 11:30 p.m. Closed August.

Le Baptiste
11 rue de Boulangers, 5e
Tel: 01 43 25 57 24
Métro: Jussieu

A beautiful little room with provincial decoration on stone walls; copper jugs, plants and so forth. Lovely food. Menus are written on wooden paddles, and include, at 71F, *chèvre* on salad greens, fresh *cervelas* sausage vinaigrette, herring fillets served with potato salad. Main dishes are few but well cooked, such as sirloin *steak au poivre*, fish, and a *plat du jour*. Cheese or fruit salad or the usual *crème caramel* follow. Service is included, wine extra at 18F the quarter-litre. A la carte, a three-course meal could cost as little as 71F, or as much as 185F, service included, drink extra. Recently, one of our 'Paris family' liked the eggs baked in tomato sauce, and chicken-liver *pâté* in a cream and cognac sauce. Main courses include duck breast cooked in honey sauce (overdone, said the French girl), and cod fillet in cream sauce. Other choices were veal fillet in mushroom sauce, kidneys cooked with cassis. For dessert, apple tart, fresh fruit salad, *tarte Tatin*, or the Damnation (a sinful creation which lives up to its name) made of *crème de marron, crème fraîche,* and chocolate. A quarter-litre of drinkable Côtes du Rhône was 18F. Go before 8:00 p.m., as it's popular. Service is brisk, not chatty, but friendly, the manager keeping things moving during the busiest times. Open noon to 2:00 p.m., 7:00 to 10:30 p.m., and 11:00 p.m. Fridays and Saturdays. Closed Saturday lunch, Sundays; closed on public holidays. No annual closing.

Le Blé d'Or or Freddy Gosse (*boulangerie- pâtisserie*)
243 rue St-Jacques, 5e
Tel: 01 43 54 62 31
Métro: RER Port Royal (B-line)

This delightful shop is not a restaurant – it is one of the best of those *boulangeries–pâtisseries* that make Paris a paradise for the greedy. The classic Paris-Brest pastry is almost beyond words – go and try it for yourself. 'Airy pastry, the filling made with pure Normandy butter, creamy, praliney and almost overflowing,' as one of our resident reporters describes it. At Freddy Gosse's, a short walk from the Sorbonne, in the Latin Quarter, all their cakes and crusty bread are made in purest French tradition. The staff is warm and even the smallest fruit tart is wrapped and presented with a flourish. We'd suggest that if you have had a two-course *formule* without dessert in a Left Bank restaurant, walk up to Freddy Goose's for a pastry that is almost literally out of this world. Their croissants, too, are superb – rich, but not too buttery. From here, it's a short stroll with your sweet course to the tree-shaded, fountain-playing gardens of the Luxembourg where you can eat as Parisians do, from the 'designer paper' wrappings. Freddy Gosse is closed Saturdays, Sundays, two weeks in August, open most holidays.

Le Bouche Trou
20 rue des Boulangers, 5e
Tel: 01 40 51 73 25
Métro: Jussieu

This restaurant is new to us, drawn to our attention by the fact that Verlaine, the Symbolist poet, once lived in a room upstairs (where was Rimbaud?). It's typical of the good little unfussy traditional restaurants in this popular street. The menus on offer are between 69F and 120F, including service but not drink. On any given day you might browse a menu with pickings like *museau vinaigrette* (this translates as pig's nose in oil-and-vinegar dressing – much better than it sounds), sardines, *oeuf mayonnaise*, fish fillet *à la Normande* with cream and cider sauce, steak *au poivre* (or some highly spiced sausage), then the usual *crème caramel*, ice-cream, pastry, as dessert choices. According to one of our reliable Paris eaters for a little more you can enjoy the slightly more expensive dishes such as snails, mussels, fish soup, quail *pâté* among the starters; frogs' legs *à la provençale*, grilled steak, escalope Viennoise, or lamb cutlets as main dishes, with *profiteroles*, sorbets, and chocolate mousse to follow. Wine is expensive at 20F the quarter-litre, and beer is 19F. The *carafe d'eau* is fresh, cold, and free. Open 11:30 a.m. to 2:30 p.m., 7:00 to 10:30 p.m., Mondays through Thursdays. Friday and Saturday nights, open until 11:30 p.m. Open most holidays, but check by phone for Easter and New Year's Day.

La Trattoria
5 rue d'Arras, 5e
Tel: 01 43 29 51 28
Métro: Cardinal Lemoine

This is a pleasant find in one of the small streets that surround the University of Paris. Already colonised by enterprising students, it seats barely two dozen people, but makes up in personal attention for what it lacks in size. The 'Trat' is run by a lively Italian couple, and the menu, at 60F, is much like that you'd find in southern Italy – nothing very startling, but everything good, and lots of it. Also, this inexpensive menu is served until 8:30 p.m. They'll feed you on tomato and lettuce salad, or Italian charcuterie such as mortadella and salami, with good crisp-crusted bread, then tagliatelle, spaghetti Napoli, lasagne, or scallopine of veal. Cheese, chocolate mousse, apple tart or ice-cream round off the meal. Service is included, wine is extra – 16F for a quarter-litre. So for 66F you will have dined well alla casalinga – Italian home-style. After 8:30, everything's à la carte, and main dishes such as lasagne or tagliatelle will cost you about 42F. So an early supper here is one of the bargains of the neighbourhood. Open noon to 3:00 p.m., 7:00 p.m. to 1:00 a.m. Closed Saturdays and Sundays at lunchtime. Open most holidays, and in August when many other restaurants in the university area are closed for the month. VISA, Access and Eurocheques are accepted, and it's possible AMEX cards will be too, by the time you go there.

6E ARRONDISSEMENT

Restaurant B.E.P. of the École Ferrandi
11 rue Jean Ferrandi, 6e
Tel: 01 49 54 29 33 or 01 49 54 28 00
Métro: St-Placide

This just has to be the best-kept culinary secret of Paris, according to our friend Gloria Girton. It's actually the training school run by the Paris Chamber of Commerce. Thus, the menu is always changing. The tables are most attractively set, and we wish that all Paris waiters and waitresses were as nice as the ones training here. The menu is a *prix-fixe* at 90F for lunch (the 200F dinner might just be too steep), service included, and it's a feast. For instance, fish in a sauce of cream, shrimps and mussels; or the best roast beef in France, sliced very thin and served with a *marchand de vin* sauce and very delicate roasted potatoes. Other main courses looked equally inviting. After that, you are offered a choice of seasonal salad or an exquisite cheese tray, and then dessert – four courses in all. *Crèpes Suzette* were prepared at the table with great élan, but there were also fresh strawberries, pastries, fresh fruit in *eau de vie*. Half a bottle of very good Beaujolais was only 19F, and the rest of the wine list is excellent ranging from 15F to 130F. Open from 12:30 to 2:30 p.m., the B.E.P. seats 40–50 and is open weekends and during student vacations. Not to be missed.

Bistro de la Grille
14 rue Mabillon, 6e
Tel: 01 43 54 16 87
Métro: Mabillon

Be prepared to spend real money here, as the menu is 95F for lunch and 150F for dinner, service included, drink extra, even so it's less than you'd pay in many an English restaurant recommended as good value for money. Le Bistro is one of the most recommended *branché* restaurants: plugged-in to the BCBG circuit of Paris restaurants. (BCBG's are the French equivalents of London's Sloanes, fun to watch and listen to.) The walls are adorned with photos of film stars you'll probably half recognise. The welcome is warm, the service friendly, and, even if you have to wait for a table, you never get parked and forgotten in a corner. The dining-room is pure nineteenth century, the cooking true French traditional. Starters can include marrow-bones with toasted French bread, salad with hot *chèvre, Bleu de Bresse*; *tarte Tatin*, chocolate cake, or a plate of pastries. A quarter-litre of wine is about 20F, and beer a very reasonable 18F – a good choice with something like the *daube*. Open all day, for coffee and croissants at 7:00 a.m., until about midnight, every day of the year. For holiday dinners, however, phone first. Reservations are really necessary. At lunch, try to arrive before 12:30, or wait at the bar for a table.

La Bolée

25 rue Servandoni, 6e
Tel: 01 46 34 17 68
Métro: Odéon, Luxembourg

Une Bolée is the word for a bowl of real Breton cider, the correct accompaniment for the many kinds of *crèpes* and pancakes and *galettes* offered here. For times when you want a light but satisfying meal, perhaps when you've had a lavish lunch or are planning a splurge dinner, make for La Bolée. You can tuck into the traditional cheese-, ham-, tomato-filled *crèpe*, or go for the mildly outrageous – 'Le Hot Dog' with sausage, mustard, gruyère, only 26F; 'L'Americaine', hamburger, ketchup, *gruyère* and fried egg, 38F; or 'Le Maritime' with fish, spinach and cream. There are several kinds of salads available too, only 28F–36F. For dessert, there's a really wild choice: 'La Normande', home-made apple compote with caramel and cream, or flambéed with Calvados, for 35F, or 'Le Bleuet', filled with vanilla ice-cream, blueberry jam and whipped cream, for 35F. More conventional sweet *crèpes* are priced form 18F to 28F. Coffee, beer, and Breton cider, are comfortingly cheap. Open Mondays through Saturday lunch from 11:30 a.m. to 2:30 p.m., 6:00 to 10:00 p.m. Closed Saturday nights, Sundays, open most holidays, closed 15 August, closed Christmas Day.

La Cabane d'Auvergne
44 rue Grégoire de Tours, 6e
Tel: 01 43 25 14 75
Métro: Odéon

La Cabane is described as 'warm, cosy, welcoming, really French and rustic, not touristic at all.' Here is a restaurant where you never feel rushed, even though it's one of the better-known streets of the Quartier Latin. The atmosphere is that of an *auberge* deep in the country, far from the crowds of the Left Bank. Auvergnat food is 'serious' food, and here it's authentic, not pastiche. No *prix-fixe* menu is offered here, but servings are huge – a main-course dish of *confit de canard* with *cèpes* (wild mushrooms) would do for two. Lunch will cost between 50F and 70F and dinner will set you back 200–250F à la carte. Main courses include *coq au vin* (house specialty at 200F–250F), *cassoulet*, *petit salé* with lentils – all these dishes will serve two people. First courses may be home-made game *pâté* – venison, quail, wild boar, duck, or a salad of *frisée* lettuce with strips of sautéed bacon. There's an old-fashioned bar in the corner, for a glass of wine while you wait. The crowd is friendly, talkative, and enjoys both the food and the country-inn atmosphere. You must reserve for dinner. Open noon to 2:00 p.m., 7:30 to 11:00 p.m. Closed Sundays, one week at Christmas, one week in May, and all of August. Open some holidays, but check by phone before going.

Marco Polo
8 rue de Condé, 6e
Tel: 01 43 26 79 63
Métro: Odéon

Full of Italians, which means good food, Marco Polo will give you an excellent two-course lunch for 90F ... but it's worth it. You must go there for lunch as in the evening everything's *à la carte* and you'd pay between 85F and 125F for main dishes, 60F–70F for pasta. However, in this popular neighbourhood, food of this quality and at this price is rare. And it's perfect for vegetarians as both starters and main courses can be meatless. Begin with tomato and mozzarella salad, or carpaccio (raw beef sliced transparently thin), progress to big plates of pasta served with various sauces – walnut, mushrooms-ham-and-cream, gorgonzola, carbonara, bolognese. Service is included, and a quarter-litre of nice red wine is 20F. Open noon to 2:30 p.m., 7:00 to 11:00 p.m. Closed Saturdays and Sunday for lunch, major holidays, but usually open 14 July, closed 15 August.

Orestias
4 rue Grégoire-de-Tours, 6e
Tel: 01 43 54 62 01
Métro: Odéon

A wonderful little restaurant established in 1927 and run by a troupe of manic Greeks who operate on the 'always room for one more' principle. The tables are long and open, offering minimum privacy and maximum chance to get to know people. They are very obliging: one steamy summer day we arrived at nearly 2:30 for lunch, and were fed with speed and amiability. Unbelievably, the menu ranges from only 37F to 46F à la carte and a *plat du jour* from 30F to 60F, service included: vine leaves, salad or *tsatsiki* (yogurt beaten with finely chopped cucumber, garlic, salt and lemon juice), then lamb on a skewer, roast chicken, lamb chops, etc., and fruit, yoghurt, pastry to finish. *A la carte*, you could have a big plate of assorted Greek hors d'oeuvres which include taramasalata, vine leaves, feta cheese, *tsatsiki*, lettuce and tomatoes, for 32F, and as a main dish *moussaka*, stuffed peppers with rice, various grills and *brochettes*, all immense portions, and ranging from 28F to about 55F. Wine – try the Retsina (Greek resin wine) – is inexpensive, about 10F for a quarter-litre. It's an entertaining, noisy, crowded, hospitable place and once you've discovered it you will probably want to return again and again. Open noon to 2:30 p.m., 5:30 to 11:30 p.m. No groups after 7:30 p.m. Closed Sundays, but open holidays and August.

Osteria del Passe Partout
20 rue de l'Hirondelle, 6e
Tel: 01 46 34 14 54
Métro: St-Michel

This beautiful little restaurant is tucked away in a lane under an arch, just off the raucous boulevard St-Michel. It's a real find, in this vastly overpriced and overcrowded district. Work your way through the spidery handwriting of the menu, and you find a very well-chosen selection of Italian and French dishes. There are two menus at lunch: 65F and 70F, each including service. On the less expensive one, first courses may include a salad of fennel, oranges and black olives, a *terrine* of courgettes with tomato coulis, ricotta with tomatoes, etc. Then pasta with most unusual sauces, such as macaroni with guinea-hen, orange rind and cream, or spaghetti with tomatoes, *petits pois*, spring onions and slivers of bacon. Desserts are very Italian, very traditional – have the *tiramisu* – a very special Italian cake made with coffee, rum and *marscapone* cheese. The 66F menu is even more special – a remarkable mousse of herring with lemon, and then *carpaccio* (paper-thin slices of raw fillet of beef) with salad, and the tiramisu of course. At dinner, the menu prices go up to 86F, 94F and 130F, with such delicacies as *tagliatelle alla panna e funghi* (thin noodles with cream, wild mushrooms), and fricassée of guinea-hen in a red sauce. Drink is extra, a small pichet of wine is 15F, rosé is 16F, beer or mineral water is 18F. L'Osteria is open noon to 2:30 p.m., 7:30 to 10:45 p.m. Closed for Saturday lunch and Sundays. Usually open on holidays, but telephone first to make sure. No annual closing, at the time of writing.

Le Polidor
41 rue M.-le-Prince, 6e
Tel: 01 43 26 95 34
Métro: Odéon

Polidor is really *Vieux Paris*, extremely popular and usually packed, so best to go early when daily specials are still available. A two-course menu – starter and main course, or main course and dessert – at 55F is offered at lunchtime Mondays through Fridays, 100F for dinner. The starters are fairly conventional, but there's a different main course each day. Thursday, it might be kidneys with a Madeira sauce, Wednesday, chicken with a creamy sauce suprème, Monday, *boudin noir* (a black pudding-like sausage) with puréed potatoes. Desserts are quite remarkable, *baba au rhum*, ice-cream, good sorbets, *gâteau de riz*, *tartes*, chocolate mousse. Le Polidor has been around since 1845, but with its elegant decor of mirrors, lamps, chairs, the feeling is that of a 1930s film set. Wine is not expensive, available by the glass, carafe or bottle. The establishment has many delightful quirks, such as the huge bottle of champagne displayed all year long, then opened with a bang on New Year's Eve. The dining-room has beautiful old floor tiles, and little drawers where the rolled napkins of long-gone patrons were kept for them. The courtyard *toilettes* are *à la turque* and ancient, be warned. Open every day, noon to 2:30 p.m., then 7:00 p.m. to 12:30 a.m., except Sundays when it closes at 11:00 p.m. This is our choice for Christmas lunch in a true Parisian family setting.

Restaurant de Beaux Arts
11 rue Bonaparte, 6e
Tel: 01 43 26 92 64
Métro: St-Germain-des-Prés

Everyone knows this restaurant, and it has been in guidebooks for years, but nothing has changed its busy bustling character or the quality of the food. There's an amazing variety of choices – twelve different starters and as many main courses to pick from – all for around 75F, which includes service and wine! Year after year, the *boeuf bourguignon* gets praise. You can usually find a non-meat dish on the menu, fish is well cooked and served. Desserts are conventional; try the house specialty, apple tart and caramel semolina, but the quality is never less than exceptional. The high-speed shuttle service of the waitresses is something to see, and a wave of noise hits you as you open the door. In winter, there's usually a great *pot-au-feu* with marrow-bones. There are perpetual queues, and you aren't encouraged to dally for long periods over choosing, so consult the menu posted outside and be ready to give your order quickly. Open noon to about 2:15 p.m., 7:00 to 11:00 p.m. Don't be disappointed if you go late in the evening and many of the best choices are gone. Open every day of the year, including holidays.

Le Sybarite
6 rue du Sabot, 6e
Tel: 01 42 22 21 56
Métro: St-Germain des Prés, St-Sulpice

The rue du *Sabot* is a beautiful, narrow, short street on the Left Bank, near St-Germain-des-Prés and St-Sulpice, with several boutiques and *dépots de vente* – elegant resale shops where rich women leave their gently-worn clothes to be sold at lowish prices. Le Sybarite, an offspring of Sud-Ouest (page 99) is garlanded with mentions in the Gault-Millau guide and magazine, the Guide Deuzère, the Touring Club de France, etc. It's an experience in what the French can do to produce really super food for a meal at a price that would barely buy you one course in London wine bar or restaurant – 80F, service included at lunch. Their secret is to keep the choices few, and offer only a short selection of what is best in the market each day. First courses could be *mesclun aux noix* – tender little leaves of several kinds of salad greens, with walnuts – or an *entrée du jour*, possibly *foie gras confis*, or an egg dish. Steaks are a speciality, such as *pavé grillé au thym*, or a *plat du jour*. End with cheese, pastry, ice-cream or sorbet. A half-litre *pichet* of red wine from the Gard area at lunch is only 15F, so for 80F one person can get the *plat du jour* including entrée, plat, dessert and *pichet*. To select from the larger menu, pay 125F at lunch and at dinner. Ordering à la carte from the fifteen entrées and fifteen dishes available will cost you around 175F. They accept Visa cards. Open noon to 2:00 p.m., 7:30 to 10:30 p.m. Closed Saturday lunch, Sundays.

7E ARRONDISSEMENT

Au Pied de Fouet
45 rue de Babylone, 7e
Tel: 01 47 05 12 27
Métro: St-François-Xavier

Straight out of the late 1940s ambiance, this tiny, friendly restaurant is not for the claustrophobic. Don't come in a crowd, the five or six tables cannot take a large group. And come early, or be patient and wait. Coffee after the meal is served at the bar, so you don't have to hang about in the doorway while people sit over their cups. Everything is *à la carte,* but inexpensive – entrées 15F, main courses between 40F and 55F, desserts 16F. The choices are interesting; *rillettes* and *tabbouleh* as well as soup or salad, with main courses including ravioli in cream sauce, sautéed chicken livers, beef *terrine*. The fruit tarts are famous, plum, gooseberry, cassis, lemon; cheeses include very good brie and *cantal*. If you are there on a rare quiet evening, André or Martial may show you the napkin rings kept for their regulars but don't ask if you blush easily. Adam Steinhouse and a young French friend, Benoit, warn that the toilets are 'indescribable'. Open noon to 2:00 p.m., 7:00 to 10:00 p.m. – last serving at 9:45 p.m. Closed Saturday nights, Sunday, and August.

Chez Germaine
30 rue Pierre Leroux, 7e
Tel: 01 42 73 28 74
Métro: Vaneau

You must go early, otherwise prepare to queue for ten minutes to half an hour – it's that good, and that popular. The gregarious atmosphere will draw you into conversation that could last all evening if you weren't aware of hopeful eaters peering through the windows. Everyone at Chez Germaine knows exactly what you've chosen for your meal, as it is bellowed across the room to the kitchen. M. Babkine says *interdit de fumer* and he means it, so this is a great place for non-smokers. The menu is an astonishing 65F for hors d'oeuvres, main dish, dessert and quarter litre of wine including service. Even the à la carte list is inexpensive, so you'd find it hard to spend more than about 70–90F. The *prix-fixe* menu is short, but the food is really traditional, well cooked, satisfying. In late years the clientele has become somewhat more BCBG (Paris Sloanes), but the restaurant still has its own atmosphere of innocent enjoyment. Open noon to 2:30 p.m. – go early or you'll have to wait; and at night from 7:00 to 9:30 p.m. Closed Saturday nights, Sundays, and August.

Le Roupeyrac
62 rue de Bellechasse, 7e
Tel: 01 45 51 33 42
Métro: Solférino-Bellechasse

One of the few affordable places within walking distance of the Musée d'Orsay, Le Roupeyrac changes little over the years. At lunch, it's crowded with people from nearby ministries, so go early. Saturday lunchtime is a wiser choice. This is a simple restaurant in an elegant neighbourhood, and does not attempt to give you a long menu. For 77F, it offers starters such as *pâté*, mushrooms *à la grecque*, *crudités*; then brains in black butter, which we always enjoy, or steak, or grilled pork chop, all with good fries. End with cheese, or extremely good chocolate mousse, ice-cream, *crème caramel*. The *à la carte* menu is really good, with several choices which usually include a very distinguished fish dish such as marinated and grilled fish, at 45F, and a great choice of desserts. A three-course meal could be about 130F. Wine here is served in a small *pichet*, 22 cl, and depending on the quality costs from 10F to about 15F. All prices include service. Open noon to 2:45 p.m., 7:00 to 9:30 p.m. Closed weekends and public holidays.

8E ARRONDISSEMENT

L'Assiette Lyonnaise
21 rue Marbeuf, 8e
Tel: 01 47 20 96 80
Métro: Franklin-D.-Roosevelt

L'Assiette is a real, authentic Lyonnais *bouchon*, a place that serves not only lunch and dinner, but also welcomes you to drop in for a substantial snack anytime between 9:00 a.m. and 11:30 p.m. – snack such as the traditional *machon* (a platter of *charcuteries* and salads with cold roast meat), and a glass of Beaujolais. L'Assiette is the real thing, friendly and bustling, just what you'd find in the narrow streets of Lyon itself. There are no *prix-fixe* menus, but the *à la carte* choices are interesting and inexpensive: *tripes Lyonnaises* with a gratin of macaroni for 56F, or *andouillette* in a mustard sauce with *gratin dauphinois* (potato baked in a casserole with cream and cheese) for 60F are typical. That very Lyonnais delicacy called *tablier de sapeur* (the fireman's apron), tripe breaded and sautéed, is served with steamed potatoes and tartare sauce and for starters, you could have a salad of tomatoes and real mozzarella, 32F, or *oeuf en gelée*, 28F. Their cheeses include the famous *cervelle de canut*, a soft cheese with herbs, garlic and a dash of vinegar, 20F. Desserts such as *tarte Tatin* or *crème brulée* are all 24F. Service is included in the prices, drink is extra. Lunch is from noon to 3:00 p.m., dinner 7:00 to 12:00 p.m. Reservations are advisable, even for lunch.

Hyotan
3 rue d'Artois, 8e
Tel: 01 42 25 26 78
Métro: Franklin-D.-Roosevelt

The entrance to this remarkable Japanese restaurant is so under-played that you could easily miss it – look for an unassuming white sign with the name in black Japanese lettering. At the top of the stairs, you see an old Japanese drinking-gourd, the *hyotan*. Inside, it's as if a corner of Tokyo had landed in a street just off the Champs-Elysées. Nine out of ten of the patrons here are Japanese, and it's run by a husband and wife who do all the cooking. Bottles of Japanese 'Scotch' whisky and *sake* line the walls, labelled with the names of the regular customers for whom they are reserved. Shoji screens at the windows, and totally authentic Japanese food – extremely fresh ingredients, labour-intensive preparation, everything done by hand – and not so cheap. But it is superb; try the *tonkatsu* (deep-fried pork pieces in batter with a 'fantastic' sauce), or *taki sakama* (baked fish), noodle dishes like *udon*, *soba* and *ramen* which come in a bowl of soup with vegetables, seaweed and shreds of pork. The miso soup is very good. Everything's *à la carte*, nothing more than 55F. You could eat well here for between 90F and 110F. Including service. Keep the cost down by not ordering wine, which doesn't go well with Japanese food; try Kirin beer, which is a steep 42F but enough for two. (A bottle of *sake* – a Japanese drink made from rice – is 48F.) Tourists haven't found the Hyotan yet, perhaps because the entrance is so unobtrusive. Open evenings only, 7:00 p.m. to midnight. Closed Sundays, one week between Christmas and New Year's Day, and two weeks in late July or the first two weeks in August.

9E ARRONDISSEMENT

Chartier
7 Faubourg Montmartre, 9e
Tel: 01 47 70 86 29
Métro: Montmartre

A cliché restaurant, listed in all guidebooks, but the value is so good it must be included. It's possible to eat a really superb meal for 80F–100F, everything included: *terrine de lapin*, *cassoulet parisienne* or *escalope de veau forestière*, and *gâteau St-Sylvestre* or *mousse au chocolat*, and a quarter-litre of wine – just to give you the gist. Service is quick, not too much Gallic charm, but the customers are always an interesting mixture of students, tourists and impecunious Parisians. Look for the *menu conseillé*, which is always good value, but note that 12 per cent service is added to its basic cost. The 1920s decor alone makes Chartier worth a visit. Open 11:00 a.m. to 3:00 p.m., 6:00 to 9:30 p.m., seven days a week, no annual closing.

Duhau
32 boulevard Haussmann, 9e
Tel: 01 47 70 80 01
Métro: Chaussée d'Antin

Open for lunch only, with a menu at 70F, this is an offshoot of one of Paris's best-known *traiteurs*, famous for their luxurious prepared take-away dishes. The menu one day offered quiche, *charcuteries* and *crudités*, then steak, grilled ham, one *plat du jour* – it changes every day – such as Basque chicken with cheese or dessert – fresh fruit salad, and a glorious chocolate mousse. The menu changes each week, and you might have prosciutto ham with Charentais melon, served with a glass of white wine, and chicken baked with spices, or grilled fish. For dessert, a rich and wonderful *îles flottantes* or cheese. It's a cool retreat from the great boulevard outside, very welcome after strenuous shopping at the Galeries Lafayette. The service is leisurely. After lunch, look into Duhau's main shop, and see what Parisian chefs make of food when they are really trying. Service included, wine only 10F a quarter-litre, and half a bottle of mineral water 8F. Open 11:30 a.m. to

2:30 p.m. Closed Saturdays and Sundays in July and August. No annual closing.

Le Relais Savoyard
13 rue Rodier, 9e
Tel: 01 45 26 17 48
Métro: Cadet, Notre-Dame-de-Lorette

The same family has run the Relais Savoyard for the past quarter of a century, and it has its quota of regulars from the neighbourhood – visitors from the outer world, so to speak, are looked upon as rather an oddity. Service is efficient and polite. The chef, if he has time to talk, is very friendly and chatty. In this simple pine-panelled restaurant, the food is good bourgeois cooking, very, very French. The à la carte menu has a wide selection: sausage in white wine for 75F, *rochette* (a mixture of potatoes, buttered toast and cheese (excellent for sharing with a friend) for 85F, the house specialty *fondue savoyard* for 78F, and *fondue bourguignonne* for 110F per person. The menu is 80F, including red wine and service. Among the hors d'oeuvres, *cervelas* salad, *crudités*, tomato and mixed salads, herring with potatoes in oil, grapefruit, and black radish – a huge radish is brought to your table and you cut off the slices you want. Main courses recently included *poule au pot*, chicken in cream sauce, boudin sausage with sautéed apples, a plate of cold country ham with salad. Along with the quart of wine, choose dessert or cheese: the home-made apple tart was exceptionally good; other choices are *crème caramel*, cake or cheese. Open noon to 3:00 p.m., 7:30 to 10:00 p.m. or possibly a little earlier or later, depending on how busy they are. Closed Sundays, certain public holidays, and August.

Xavier Gourmet
19 rue Notre-Dame de Lorette, 9e
Tel: 01 45 26 38 46
Métro: St-Georges

Another notable find, Xavier is a rather sophisticated blend of tea-room and restaurant, always busy, always good. Examples: trout in aspic with smoked salmon sauce and a green salad, 45F. A *crêpe* stuffed with raw mountain ham, raclette cheese from the Savoie, with green salad and tomatoes, 40F. A sandwich, on wonderful chewy *Poilâne* bread, or tomatoes, mozzarella, fresh basil and olive oil, served with a green salad, 40F. Best of all are the pastries. A glass of good wine is 10F–15F, service is included and it's easily possible to walk out satiated for 55F. Open 11:45 a.m. to 2:30 p.m. and 6:45 p.m. to 1:00 a.m., seven days a week, including holidays. No annual closing.

10E ARRONDISSEMENT

Au Gigot Fin
56 rue de Lancry
Tel: 01 42 08 38 81
Métro: Jacques Bonsergent

A bistro in 1920s style, popular with the local working population – you must go early in the evening to get the best choices, as everything is freshly cooked each day and represents what the chef liked in the market that morning. There's a menu at 60F for lunch only, and three others, at 85F, 110F and 170F, served at lunch and dinner. Our eaters opted for the 85F menu and were offered some good choices as starters – *mousseline* of duck liver (very tasty and a good portion), hot *chèvre* with salad (over-seasoned and rather oily), or herring with potato salad or a cold meat salad. Main courses were roast turkey, tender and very good, sliced and served with sautéed potatoes, leg of lamb redolent of garlic, and always a *plat du jour*. It was an opulent meal, and they chose fruit sorbet, raspberry and lemon, for dessert. Service is included in all prices, and drink is fairly reasonable – wine from 12F to 20F a quarter-litre, mineral water 12F, beer 15F. Open 12:00 to 3:00 p.m., (the 60F menu is such a bargain that it gets crowded by 12:30), 7:00 to 11:00 p.m. Closed Saturdays and Sundays.

11E ARRONDISSEMENT

La Cheminée
7 rue Jean-Pierre Timbaud, 11e
Tel: 01 49 23 06 76
Métro: Oberkampf

This new addition to our list offers very traditional French cuisine at delightfully unParisian prices. The lunch menu is 52F and includes two courses: an appetizer and main dish or a main dish and dessert. Dinner is *à la carte* and will cost, all included, from 50F to 100F. Copious helpings of everything (à la carte minimum 50F), a cosy decor and a fireplace create the pleasant ambiance to which the patrons keep returning. Try the *terrine paysanne maison* for an entrée and remember it's all-you-can-eat so save room for the *entrecôte grillée sauce aux cèpes* and the *tarte maison*. With prices like this you might just be able to share a bottle of the Château Guichard 1992 bordeaux, 68F. Reservations required at the end of the week, so call in advance. Open weekdays, Saturdays from 12:45 to 2:15 p.m. and 7:30 p.m. to 11:00 p.m. Closed Sundays.

Cannibale Café & Restaurant
93 rue Jean-Pierre Timbaud, 11e
Tel: 01 49 29 95 59
Métro: Couronnes, Ménilmontant

A great place to enjoy a relaxed meal if a) you've had a long day, b) have children, c) a dog, d) yearn to combine your thirst for a beer with a laid-back meal – or e) all of the above. The Cannibale is a café (all day, beginning at 7:00 a.m.), restaurant (until 12:00 a.m.) and bar (until 2:00 a.m.) combined in an airy, mirrored space, often adorned with good photograph exhibitions. The patrons range in age, but the ambiance is youthful, *décontractée* and alternative. The music is one of its highlights – you'll hear Russian folk songs, Algerian pop and Indian *ragas* all in one evening. Children are welcome, in fact they're *invited* (the café provides a tiny table and benches with crayons and paper). Friendly dogs tend to roam freely, licking the odd hand or lying under the tables. The menu (which changes daily) is imaginative and always a tasty *mélange* of French and anything exotic, large portions of quiche and salad, to curried chicken embellished with mango and bananas, or grilled lamb cutlets with mint, 50F. Desserts include sorbets and basic French sweets for 15–20F. Beer and wines run 13–18F. Open everyday from 7:00 a.m. until 2:00 a.m. No annual closing.

Bois et Charbons
8 rue de la Main d'Or, 11e
Tel: 01 48 05 77 10
Métro: Ledru-Rollin

It takes persistence to find this small gem, as it's on a short street off a narrow alley of furniture-makers' shops that runs beside no. 133, faubourg St-Antoine. At first glance, the place looks unpromising, with half a dozen workmen drinking at the bar. Go though into the little dining-room, still very unpretentious, with the occasional unpainted patch on the wall, and the smell of good cooking will lift your spirits. The menu at lunch, for 60F, has few choices, written on a blackboard. Every dish is a winner. At night, everything's *à la carte*, but not expensive. Starters were all in the range of 15F–25F: and included home-made *terrine de volaille* and *terrine de lapin*. The Lyonnais speciality *cervelle de canut* is soft white cheese sparked up with fresh herbs. Calves' liver as a main dish was thinly sliced, with vegetables and sautéed potatoes liberally sprinkled with parsley. The *plat du jour* ranged from 50F to 75F. Desserts are all 20F, the chestnut cake served with *crème fraîche* and a thin icing of bitter chocolate is exceptional. Expect excellent quality and good presentation. Service is included in all prices, wine quite expensive at 20F for a quarter-litre pichet. The hours are 10:00 a.m. to 3:00 p.m. for lunch on weekdays; dinner from 8:00 to 11:30 p.m.; Fridays and Saturdays from 8:00 p.m. to midnight. Closed for lunch Saturday and Sunday. Sunday drinks and music from 7:00 p.m. to 9:00 p.m. Closed 15 August and Christmas. If you plan to dine here, phone early in the day and make your reservation, so the friendly cook/waitress will know how many to expect.

Les Cinq Points Cardinaux

14 rue Jean Macé, 11e
Tel: 01 43 71 47 22
Métro: Charonne

We have known this little place for more than ten years, when our friend Rory Cellan Jones found it in a dilapidated alleyway off the rue St-Antoine. Now that the street has been bulldozed, the restaurant has reappeared at this pretty and peaceful spot. It still serves simple, well-cooked food, and most of its patrons are still the working people of the neighborhood. The owner has decorated the plain walls with the original tools used by the artisans of this craftsmen's area, brought from the old site. Don't be misled by the ordinariness of the bar as you come in, you are here to eat, like everyone else. At 55F a *formule* for lunch, the prices are exceptionally low with five entrées to choose from. We liked the juicy roast pork with cauliflower *au gratin*, and for dessert – wonderful red currant tart. A quarter-litre of wine is 8F50, and a half-litre of a light, pleasant Beaujolais-style wine is 18F. Les Cinq Points is now open for dinner, with menus at 60F and 98F. Sample delicacies like frog legs and *chèvre chaud*, duck mousse, and move on to a thick tournedos steak with bordelaise sauce for only 98F. Open noon to 2:30 p.m., 7:30 to 10:00 p.m. Closed Sundays, holidays and August.

Pizza Tavola

10 rue de la Rouquette, 11e
Tel: 01 47 00 20 85
Métro: Bastille

In a magical street just a few steps away from the place de la Bastille, there's one of the best Italian restaurants we know. Although it calls itself a pizza place, it's more than that. They do make real Sicilian pizzas, thin-crusted, irregular, spread with home-made pizzaiola sauce, and toppings put on with a generous hand. But they also do pasta freshly made, with sauces tasting as though mammina is standing over the cooker in the kitchen. And their non-pasta main dishes are said to be as good as their *canneloni* and *fettucine alla crema*. Pizzas cost 39F–80F, main dishes are 50–80F. We like their big servings of cassis, lemon or mango sorbets from one of the best Parisian ice-cream makers. An à la carte meal here, lunch or dinner, could be as little as 65F including drink and service. The delightful owner has been decorated by several gastronomic groups. He loves to chat, and speaks good English. Open noon to 3:00 p.m., 6:30 p.m. to 2:00 p.m., seven days a week. Major credit cards accepted.

Palais de la Femme
94 rue de Charonne, 11e
Tel: 01 47 97 26 04
Métro: Charonne

One of the many surprises in the long list of good restaurants in the 11e is in this fine building, a residence for young women alone in Paris. The hotel is open to women only, but the superb self-service restaurant in its magnificent high-ceilinged room is open to everyone. In addition to the main room, there's a new pizzeria in the basement, and a tea-room in the lobby. Everybody eats here – writers from a smart magazine down the street, fashion models from a shoot in the place d'Aligre, elderly locals who love it for the fine food and the low prices. You can heap a plate with *crudités* for 11F; *steack haché* with leeks, peas and *frites*, 28F40; pastry from 11F; mineral water 4F a small bottle, beer and soft drinks, 7F. Service at the counter is very friendly, and you're asked only to take your tray to the service hatch after your meal. What a place! Open for lunch 11:30 a.m. to 2:00 p.m. every day of the year including all holidays.

La Ravigotte
41 rue de Montreuil, 11e
Tel: 01 43 72 96 22
Métro: Faidherbe-Chaligny

This restaurant is a real find, tucked away in a part of Paris which saw a lot of goings-on in the French Revolution – there are plaques commemorating this or that event in all the surrounding streets. This is one of our top-priced restaurants, but very much recommended for serious eaters – plan to go there one evening when you've had only a snack for lunch and are feeling adventurous, and mildly rich. It's in an area with real character, and owned by the original proprietor's charming grand-daughter. She will suggest the evening's best choices. The menu is 93F, service included: among the dishes, smoked duck breast, or a *fricassée* of snails, then a choice of *tête de veau*, home-made *cassoulet* (excellent), duck with tarragon, steak with shallots, and a delicious fish called *eglefin*. For dessert, try the bitter chocolate mousse, or profiteroles with chocolate sauce, or have cheese. Service is included, drink is extra – a quarter-litre of wine is really pricey at 28F, so have mineral water or 'une carafe d'eau'. Open for lunch Mondays though Saturdays, noon to 2:30 p.m. Dinner is served only Thursdays, Fridays and Saturdays, 7:00 to 10:30 p.m. Lunch menu, 75F. Closed Sundays, and August.

Relais du Massif Central
16 rue Daval, 11e
Tel: 01 47 00 46 55
Métro: Bastille

We have known this simple family restaurant for years. Now, since the Bastille area is changing and upgrading so fast, we asked a friend living in Paris to visit it for us. As we hoped, the warm welcome and 'really splendid food' is unchanged. Even on a Monday night, the place was full. There are three menus: one at 64F which changes every day, but the day we went they had such starters as red cabbage vinaigrette, *pâté de campagne*, egg mayonnaise, followed by veal escalope *milanaise*, grilled steak or half a chicken with dessert or cheese. For 98F, start with a warm salmon tart or a ham and onion one, or melon *à l'italienne*, then move on to thinly sliced duck, or almond-crusted trout. The most expensive at 115F was praised; first courses included a seafood pie packed with goodies, and frogs' legs with rice in a *provençale* sauce, with lemon-scented wipes to clean up sticky fingers, or snails or fresh asparagus vinaigrette. For a main course, our friend had scallops *provençale* with rice, so good that she wiped the plate clean with crusts of bread. Another choice was a dish of big, juicy, grilled prawns served with crisp potatoes. Even if you're full (the portions are large), you'll find the five or six dessert choices tempting: cake with lashings of whipped cream; banana, apple, or pear tart, and chocolate mousse. Service is included, wine extra but inexpensive, 10–15F for a quarter-litre. Open noon to 3:00 p.m., 7:30 p.m. to midnight. Closed Sundays, holidays, and August.

12E ARRONDISSEMENT

Le Limonaire
88 rue de Charenton, 12e
Tel: 01 45 23 33 33
Métro: Ledru-Rollin, Gare de Lyon

This good little neighbourhood place hasn't changed in years. A tiny restaurant on a tree-studded corner, in turn-of-the-century style, decorated with musical instruments on the walls, plants, old photos, a piano in the corner and an old *orgue de barbarie*. The ceiling is pressed tin, the bar is beautiful, traditional zinc. There is no *prix-fixe* menu, but 95F will see you beautifully fed, and another 10–16F will get you excellent wine, Côtes du Rhone or fruity red Visan. Starters include a variety of terrines: tuna, or chicken livers with blueberries, or a Basque terrine, 22F, or friton de canard de Lot, also 22F. The plat du jour comes with a glass of wine, and could be an unusual veal dish cooked with lemon and herbs, or chicken done in any number of imaginative ways, with potatoes and salad, about 52F. If you are lucky, their famous chocolate/hazelnut cake, with crème anglaise will be on the menu for 25F. Wine is available by the big glass for about 9F. Open noon to 2:30 p.m., 6:00 to 10:00 p.m., call for reservations if you plan to eat after 8:00 p.m., Tuesday through Sunday. Closed August and major holidays.

13E ARRONDISSEMENT

Bangkok-Thailand
35 boulevard Auguste-Blanqui, 13e
Tel: 01 45 80 76 59
Métro: Corvisart

Pure Thai restaurants, unalloyed with Vietnamese or Chinese influence, are rare in Paris, which is why we like this one – although the
decor has to be seen to be believed, with plastic bric-à-brac, amazing
paintings, a plethora of Buddhas (there must be a collective noun to
describe these, perhaps a Smile of Buddhas?), insistent music. Never
mind: enjoy the food, the smiling welcome, the good service. The
food is subtly spiced and has a tantalizing flavour that owes much to
coriander leaves. At lunch the menu is 60F, including service, and
offers a variety of Thai soups, nems (spring rolls with an irresistible
thin sauce), or Thai salad. Then beef with basil, pork with spices, beef
with sautéed onions, all served with rice. Fruit, or a deep-fried beignet
of fruit, are the desserts, served with tea or coffee. At night the menu
price soars to 100F. Open noon to 2:30 p.m., 7:00 to 10:30 p.m. Closed
Sundays and holidays, and for two weeks in August.

L'Espérance
9 rue de l'Espérance, 13e
Tel: 01 45 80 22 55
Métro: Corvisart

Don't turn and walk away when you see the rather dingy exterior of
L'Espérance, or the run-down look of the neighbourhood. As soon as
you go up the few steps to the restaurant itself, the atmosphere alters
at once. The waiter and the other diners give a smiling welcome, and
you can join in the conversation if you're so minded. The price is
hard to believe: 55F50, including service and drink! There are three
or four choices of starters. The leeks vinaigrette are home-made and
very good, or you might have anchovies, sardines or herring. For your
main course, steak with shallots is very good, with thin crisp *frites*
freshly made and hot. Roast chicken sausages, and roast pork are
usually on the menu. Desserts sound banal, but are really fine: mocha

cake and fruit tart especially. As well as the standard brie and camembert, the cheeses include *gruyère* and *chèvre*. How do they do it? If you're looking for elegance, you won't find it here, but it's simple and satisfying. Open seven days a week, noon to 2:30 p.m., 7:00 to 11:30 p.m., and Christmas, Easter, New Year's Day.

Hawaï
87 avenue d'Ivry, 13e
Tel: 01 45 86 91 90
Métro: Tolbiac, Porte D'Ivry

In the heart of the Quartier Chinois of Paris, this restaurant combines Vietnamese, Chinese and Cambodian food, and was highly praised by a Chinese student living in Paris and by one of our most experienced eaters. They tried a variety of dishes, and report that you can eat well for 35F–46F for a *plat* at lunch, ar dinner 65F–80F, or have a real splurge for 125F; and they suggest that you have a soup and two other dishes, perhaps steamed spring rolls and a hot rice dish, or the spring rolls and a cold noodle dish. For those not familiar with Southeast Asian delicacies, a 'soup dish' like the Tonkinese *xelua*, *nho* or *taubay*, 31F, gives you a big bowl with 'everything' in it. Try the steamed spring rolls – a Vietnamese speciality quite unlike the Chinese ones with their irresistible dipping sauce. For 70F, two can split the *Riz au porc grillé*. The menu is heavy on meat, so the Hawaï is no place for vegetarians. Drink is extra. Hawaï is clean but the service is brutal and nearly non-existent. Servers and hungry customers hover, waiting for you to finish your meal and leave an empty seat. Open 10:30 a.m. to 3:00 p.m., 6:00 to 11 p.m., 365 days a year . . . great idea for an offbeat Christmas lunch.

14E ARRONDISSEMENT

Au Vin des Rues
21 rue Boulard, 14e
Tel: 01 43 22 19 78
Métro: Denfert-Rochereau

This adorable little restaurant changes its menu daily, but a typical selection might be a plate of Lyonnaise salads which includes marinated anchovies, pigs' ears vinaigrette, pickled lambs' feet, crayfish with home-made mayonnaise, or marinated salmon with a salad of potatoes in olive oil all between 45F and 55F. If you are still able to eat another mouthful after that, cherry *clafoutis* (thick pancake from Limosin) and lemon tarts, among other choices, are 35F. They always have a nice selection of Beaujolais red at about 15F a quarter-litre. Without dessert, you'll be spending about 90F–100F, service included, for a superb meal, in a very pretty room embellished with pictures, posters, maps and drawings. It's near the lively and attractive rue Daguerre where a street market bubbles and sparkles. Open 1:00 to 3:30 p.m., dinner Wednesdays and Fridays only, 9:00 to 11:00 p.m. On other evenings it's a wine bar presided over by the owner. Closed Sundays, Mondays, and August.

Crèperie de St-Malo
53 rue de Montparnasse, 14e
Tel: 01 43 20 87 19
Métro: Montparnasse

The rue de Montparnasse has always been rich in Breton restaurants, and this is one of the choicest, very 'sympa'. It's much more than a *crèperie*, offering several menus. Even the least expensive, the Menu Forestière at 88F50, gives you such choices as a *frisée* salad with chicken livers and bacon, then a Breton *galette* (a big flat pancake) wrapped round ham, cheese, an egg or mushrooms, finishing with a *crèpes* as above. For a little more, luxuriate in *moules marinière* for a first course, or home-made fish soup, thick, delicious and partnered by a very good *rouille* – then grilled salmon with Béarnaise sauce, luscious grilled sardines in season or *dorade* – finishing with a sweet *crèpe* or *crème caramel*. Service is included in all prices, and Breton cider is a must. The St-Malo is open 365 days of the year, 11:30 a.m. to 3:00 p.m., 6:00 p.m. to 2:00 a.m.

Le Jéroboam
72 rue Didot, 14e
Tel: 01 45 39 39 13
Métro: Plaisance

A lovely little bistro which offers three *formules* at lunch. One, 64F including service, a second *formule*, at 75F, added a hot vegetable plate to the cold buffet. For 75F, you could have a lavish dish, the buffet and a lush chocolate cake. A quarter-litre of wine is 16F. At night, there's a two-course menu at 129F including service. The last time one of our most food-loving friends was there, the first courses were smoked salmon salad, consommé with sherry under a puff-pastry dome, fried camembert with a salad; then *pot-au-feu* with marrowbones, among other hearty dishes, all very well cooked. Servings of dessert are huge: the chocolate cake was big enough to divide in two, 30F, and a real OTT dessert, *armagnac soufflé* with prune-caramel sauce, the same price. Open noon to 2:30 p.m., 7:30 to 10:00 p.m. Closed Sundays and Monday evenings. The annual closing is usually from the last Sunday in July to the end of August. Open some holidays, but ring first to check.

Midi-Trente
56 rue Daguerre, 14e
Tel: 01 43 20 49 82
Métro: Denfert-Rochereau

We got a superlative report on this *salon de thé*/restaurant, found by a Paris friend when strolling around Montparnasse. Its odd opening hours make it possible to have a late breakfast with coffee and remarkably good pastries, or a very special lunch, or to drop in after lunch elsewhere for coffee and dessert, or real tea. The *à la carte* prices seem rather high, at first, but you can lunch there for about 72F, with a wonderful starter such as *pâté* with *confiture d'oignon*, a delicious onion marmalade, 22F, and a main course like the salad of broccoli, walnuts, cantal cheese, prosciutto and salad greens, 48F. Or have a main course and a fabulous dessert like cherry cobbler or rhubarb compote, for only a little more. If you let yourself go, you could have three superb courses and wine for about 130F, but that's real extravagance. It's a good place for vegetarians; try *quiche aux courgettes* with *chèvre* and salad, or a platter of anchovies, ripe tomatoes, basil, real mozzarella and curly lettuce, each 50F or sample one of the many *tartes salées* and *sucres*. Prices include service – the house wines are well selected but expensive. You are recommended to sit on the terrace under an awning in summer, or if indoors, get a table near the bar. In the afternoon, Midi-Trente stays open as a tea-room with a selection from a famous Paris tea-merchant. Open 11:00 a.m. to 6:00 p.m. only. Closed Sundays and evenings.

Le Plomb de Cantal

3 rue de la Gaité, 14e
Tel: 01 43 35 16 92
Métro: Gaité

It would be easy to pass by the Plomb du Cantal, it's such an unassuming little place not far from the theatres on the rue de la Gaité. But if you miss it, you will not have experienced a very characteristic Auvergnat restaurant of Paris. There's an air of great friendliness here, and although there is no set menu, prices are low and servings large. Our friend who knows her way around the Auvergnat and Breton world of Paris, says that she can make a meal from one dish. The gratinéed 'Bougnat' soup is topped with bread and cheese, 32F. A potato casserole from the Auvergne is made with potatoes, garlic, cream and tome cheese. Their main-course salads, such as the one with duck livers, croutons, eggs and *frisée* lettuce, are 50F. After that, if you can face it, try the chestnut *flan*, 30F. Wine is pricey, stick to mineral water or a carafe of water. Sometimes you hear Auvergne bagpipes moaning and wailing in the cellar where musicians practise. Crowded, popular, either book, go early, or brace yourself to wait for a table. Open noon to 3:00 p.m., 7:00 p.m. to midnight. Closed Sundays and August. Open most holidays unless they are on a Sunday, but as usual it's safest to phone first.

15E ARRONDISSEMENT

Bistrot Bourdelle

12 rue Antoine Bourdelle, 15e
Tel: 01 45 48 57 01
Métro: Montparnasse (use the Bienvenue exit)

A simple restaurant, with its own circle of habitués, oil-cloth covered tables, posters on the walls, a couple of tables outside in good weather, a cordial patron, and excellent, imaginative food. The two-course menu of 74F includes a number of salads to start (mushroom and cabbage, lentil salad, cucumbers in cream, salad with warm chicken livers, *fromage de tête*), followed by a *plat du jour*, or *andouillette* in mustard sauce, *quenelles de brochet* in Nantua sauce, steak in a choice of sauces, *boeuf bourguignon*. Desserts are extra at 26F, among them *îles flottantes* and chocolate mousse. There's a good house Côtes du Rhône, 12–15F. Open noon to 2:00 p.m., 8:00 to 10:00 p.m. weekdays. Saturday dinner only. Closed Sundays, and an unspecified three weeks in August.

17E ARRONDISSEMENT

Formula Uno

28 rue de Vernier, 17e
Tel: 01 40 54 05 39
Métro: Porte de Champerret

This tiny neighbourhood restaurant specialises in Moroccan food and is always packed with locals and people from other neighbourhoods who come to choose from one of the eight excellent kinds of couscous or *tagines*, the North African casseroles of chicken with prunes and almonds, or chicken with olives and preserved lemons. The menu at 76F includes service and Moroccan wine, and is served at lunch and dinner – four plates daily to choose from. We liked the *aubergine purée* as a starter, and the spicy but not over-hot *brochette*; another choice was ratatouille with spiced merguez sausage. A fresh fruit cup was a cool finish to a highly-flavoured meal. *A la carte*, the *tagines* and immense servings of couscous with chicken (garnished with chick peas and raisins in a flavoursome broth with fiercely hot harina sauce served alongside) begin at 84F. Home-made almond and fresh fruit pastries are are 23F. Service is included. Open noon to 2:30 p.m., 7:00 to 11:30 p.m. Closed Sundays, one week in May for Ascension, and August. Open 'some' holidays. Service is really slow, so be prepared for a long lunch or to sit around most of the evening.

18E ARRONDISSEMENT

Les Chauffeurs
11 rue des Portes Blanches, 18e
Tel: 01 42 64 04 17
Métro: Marcardet-Poissonières

Our latest visit found this restaurant as appealing as ever. The owner is chatty and friendly, his wife is still the chef, the only waitress is still helpful. The *à la carte* menu is well-priced and a good meal could cost as little as 63F, including service and a quarter-litre of wine. The dishes change every day, often using fresh produce from the family farm in the Touraine. Our first courses included *confit de porc* or smoked pork fillet, both 12F, rabbit *terrine*, 16F, asparagus vinaigrette, and a large plate of paper-thin slices of Auvergne country ham, the most expensive starter at 42F. Main courses that day were *pot au feu* with leeks, turnips, potatoes and carrots – a real country dish, big and hearty, for 38F, *sole meunière* and roast chicken. The profiteroles are special; *choux* pastry shells made at the restaurant are filled with rich ice-cream and swamped with hot, bittersweet chocolate sauce, 25F. The 25F ice-cream sundaes with fresh fruit, liqueurs, sauces and whipped cream are topped with ridiculous campy little paper umbrellas and figurines. Open noon to 2:30 p.m. and 7:30 to 11:00 p.m. Closed Wednesdays and Thursdays, and July, August and most holidays.

Le Fait Tout
4 rue Dancourt, 18e
Tel: 01 42 23 93 66
Métro: Anvers, Pigalle

The rue Dancourt is a short street leading into the peaceful and pretty place Charles-Dullin, and it has several little restaurants. Le Fait Tout (full name: A Napoli ... On Fait tout) looks from the outside to be a run-of-the-mill pizzeria; inside it's simple, clean and pretty, with wooden tables and benches, flowers on tables. You can have a salad with walnuts, or *pâté*, or onion tart to begin, then grilled *châteaubriand* steak, or pork with black peppercorns, followed by cheese or a *tarte*. The 49F and 64F menus include salads with crisp bacon slivers, and onion soup, then steak with mustard sauce, fish, veal escalope normande (in a rich cidery sauce). The sweets run to richness too, with pastry puffs filled with good ice-cream and topped with dark chocolate sauce. Everyone says the same thing about this little place – quiet and convivial, the cooking simple but not undistinguished. And everyone likes the low price and its closeness to Pigalle. Service is included; the house wine is 17F a quarter litre. Open noon to 2:30 p.m., 6:00 to 11:00 p.m. No weekly or annual closing, and open holidays.

L'Homme Tranquille
81 rue des Martyrs, 18e
Tel: 01 42 54 56 28
Métro: Abbesses

New to us, and very welcome in this neighbourhood where so much is overpriced AND overcrowded. It is well named, with a calm and beautifully soothing feeling, very welcome after a long day of sightseeing. At 118F for three courses, service included but wine (moderate-priced) extra, it's crowding the top of our price range, but worth every franc. The small room seats only about thirty people. Table linens are really linen, napkins are big, music is soft and classical. When we were there, the waiter was relaxed, efficient and unhurried; when he wasn't serving, he sat with a glass of Bordeaux and a salad – now that's style. The food is inventive, beautifully cooked, the menu changes every day, everything is obviously *fait à la maison* and fresh. The *terrine* of tuna as a starter was faultless, with salad and a tangy dressing – other choices were vegetable *terrine* with a creamy herb dressing, and a salad of warm St-Marcellin cheese on a plate of assorted lettuces. As main courses, there's chicken with basil in a cream sauce (great), lamb chops poached with fresh thyme (ditto), or trout with smoked bacon, and pork chop with honey and curry. Desserts range from very rich – red currant crumble with thick Normandy cream – to simple, pure lemon sorbet with a twist of lemon rind. Booking is imperative; people were being turned away on a Sunday evening. Open only for dinner, 7:00 to 11:30 p.m. Closed Mondays, August, and Christmas Day. Open Easter, New Year's Day and 14 July.

19E ARRONDISSEMENT

Au Rendez-vous de la Marine
14 quai de la Loire, 19e
Tel: 01 42 49 33 40
Métro: Jaurès, Stalingrad

Don't come without a reservation. The Rendez-vous is always full – a very good sign indeed. In fact, you may want to book a few days ahead. It's on the Bassin de la Villette, in a neighbourhood which is rapidly going up in the world. The utterly absorbing river traffic is seen through the big glass windows. But the real reason for coming here is dishes like scallops in a heavily garlicked sauce, salmon steaks, *magret de canard*, steak with various sauces – everything wonderfully cooked, and served with a green salad, rice pilaff and fresh vegetables. There's no *prix-fixe* menu, but you could eat and drink well for about 100F (120F with wine), including service. Main dishes cost 40–60F, starters are 26–40F, and include monkfish in green peppercorn sauce, snails, leeks vinaigrette, or duck *pâté*. Dessert choices are good, but after two courses you may not have room for any more food. The restaurant is always busy. Service is friendly but on the leisurely side of slow, so spend time on your meal. Drink is extra: wine 28F a quarter-litre, mineral water a reasonable 16F. Open noon to 2:00 p.m.,

8:00 to 9:45 p.m. when last orders are taken. Closed Sundays, Mondays and August; open holidays unless they fall on a Sunday or Monday.

Duthil (*pâtisserie/traiteur*)
4 rue de Meaux, 19e
Tel: 01 42 02 11 13
Métro: Laumière, Bolivar, Jaurés

It is worth travelling up to this very, very French and fascinating neighbourhood to find Duthil, one of the most interesting *pâtissiers/ traiteurs/épiciers* of Paris – and to our taste, far better than many of the more highly publicized ones in central Paris. It combines a super pastry shop, great take-away prepared dishes, and even some very fancy groceries. A beautiful shop, staffed by remarkable people who treat a customer buying a single portion of lemon cake with the same friendly, helpful, interested demeanor as the one ordering a complete banquet. 'The cakes explode with cream,' reports one of our more gluttonous Paris eaters. Ice-cream is home-made and perfect. Pastries cost from 15F to 28F. On a sunny day, you might choose something from their ready-cooked foods, plus some crusty *petit pains*, a raspberry tart, a half-bottle of wine, and take off for the little-known park of Buttes Chaumont (see page 148) for the picnic of the world. Afterwards, check out the fascinating Marché Sécretan street market nearby. The *pâtisserie* specializes in organizing dinners, so if you are looking for a caterer, they can give you a hand. Duthil is open Tuesday through Saturday from 8:30 a.m. to 7:30 p.m., Sunday mornings, and on 'some' holidays.

20E ARRONDISSMENT

Crèperie La Rozelle
4 place Martin-Nadaud, 20e
Tel: 01 47 97 26 04
Métro: Gambetta, Père Lachaise

If you've ever tried to find a good place to eat after dropping in to call on Chopin, Collette, Piaf and company at Père Lachaise, you'll know that this isn't an easy neighbourhood to find special food. But now a Breton *crêperie* has escaped the traditional location of the 14e arrondissement, and is almost at the Gambetta *Métro* stop. Must-haves: buckwheat *crêpes* – *galettes* – filled with asparagus, mushrooms, ham, cheese, eggs, hamburger, sausage, smoked salmon (the most costly at 58F), or just plain melted butter for 12F and with sugar 15F. *Crêpes* with jam run about 20F; dessert *crêpes* are about 30F, rolled around chocolate, honey and walnuts, various jams, and a big swirl of chocolate chantilly (whipped cream) for the foolhardy. This is a good place to take children as *crêpes* range from simple to epicurean. *A la carte*, you can have a two-course meal, plus Breton cider, for about 90F. Open 11:30 a.m. to 2:30 p.m., 6:30 to 10:00 p.m. and Fridays and Saturdays until 11:00 p.m. Closed Sundays and holidays, and from 15 July to 15 August.

'LE SELF' – YES OR NO?

As the pace of Paris life becomes faster, self-service restaurants are proliferating, and they're a very good bet if you want to eat *à la carte*, inexpensively, and without the usual hour and a half over lunch. The great advantage of '*Les Selfs*' is that if you have a fancy for making a meal of starters instead of a main dish, it's easy and cheap: ideal for vegetarians. The disadvantage is that if you let yourself go among the rather dazzling choices you can spend as much in a '*Self*' as in a prettier, more comfortable restaurant with some character.

The best-known '*Selfs*' in such fashionable venues as the rue de Rivoli and around the Louvre are distinctly not good value for money. They are over-praised, over-crowded and over-priced, and especially at lunchtime can be more of an ordeal than a pleasure.

However, there are some lesser-known '*Selfs*' which can be an agreeable surprise to anyone whose idea of a self-service place is based on McDonald's. Can you believe a meal that begins with salad of *frisée* lettuce with *chèvre* 18F, goes on to beef in a rich red wine sauce, 46F, a cool plain yogurt 4F, or real ice-cream with fresh fruit and whipped cream 12F? A quarter-litre of drinkable wine will be about 8F. The quality was higher than many neighbourhood restaurants could have provided on *prix-fixe* menus. In another '*Self*', a complete meal – starter, main course, salad, bread, dessert and wine, beer or mineral water – was about 50F, in a clean, bright, air-conditioned room.

'*Les Selfs*' are, on the whole, quite attractive. At lunchtime, they are lively with chatter and laughter; not so much so in the evening when those who eat there tend to be, as in any big city, people who haven't much else to do. But they are well worth considering, when you want a good meal or a hearty snack without spending the whole afternoon eating, or when you're planning a splurge on museums, perfumes, gifts.

La Samaritaine

19 rue de la Monnaie, 1er
Métro: Louvre, Pont-Neuf

For lunch, dinner or snacks in the big department store, go early and get a table near the window or on the terrace, for the astounding view across the river and over the city. The food is fairly standard; don't expect a gastronomic miracle. The setting is the thing. Mushrooms in a spicy tomato sauce for a starter, a beefsteak hamburger with *frites*, and a fruit pie with whipped cream made for a satisfying and inexpensive meal at 69F for an English student studying 'and trying not to starve' in Paris last spring. *A la carte* salads are 30F, cold main courses 45F, hot dishes are 49F and salmon is 55F, sandwiches and desserts are 25F. There are two menus of three courses each, at 49F and 69F. Open 9:30 a.m. to 7:00 p.m., Thursdays until 10:00 p.m. The earlier the better at lunchtime as it gets very crowded and the best choices go early.

Take-away

all of rue de la Huchette, rue de la Harpe, 5e
Métro: St-Michel

The centre of take-away food: almost every restaurant or storefront along these streets will treat you to delicious charcoal-grilled *souvlakia* (skewered lamb an vegetables) or *shawarma* (barbecued, thinly sliced spiced lamb), both in pita pockets. Walk a little further, and you find sweet Mid-East pastries to eat from the hand. At various times we've enjoyed sandwich *tunisien*, with tuna, olives, tomatoes, peppers, lettuce drenched in a hot sauce and overstuffed into a hard roll, at El Hammamet; and a giant *pan bagna*, a huge roll crammed with *salade niçoise*, at Au Gargantua. They'll cost between 18F and 22F wherever you find them. The names change constantly in these streets but it's still a pocket of the Mediterranean world, charcoal fumes drifting from every door. The crowds are good-natured, enjoying life in the open air. Even in dark or rainy weather, a spicy hot sandwich and a mug of beer is very herring. Food is available all day long, from 10:00 a.m. or even earlier. Nothing doing on Christmas or New Year's Day, as far as we know.

The Belleville area
boulevard de Belleville, near rue Ramponeau, 20e
Métro: Belleville

Food in the extraordinary quarter called Belleville – the Arab and old Jewish Paris – is dealt with at greater length in 'Getting around', (page 31). At any of these take-aways, tell the cashier whether you want a *sandwich tunisien,* about 20F, or an *assiette tunisienne*, about 24F: take the ticket to the counter, where your order is slapped together at speed. You will get a big thick roll or pita bread, crammed with olives, tuna, capers, cucumber, tomato, with a fiery sauce, in a paper napkin or a plastic bag, or the same thing on a plate, with crisp lettuce and a hunk of baguette. Or have *brik àl'oeuf*, a delicious crumbly Tunisian pastry enclosing a fried egg, and get crumbs all over you and your clothes as you eat it, for about 20F. You can, of course, have a sandwich to take away and eat from the hand, sloppy and delicious, as you watch all Belleville sauntering by. Also available: twelve kinds of olives, capers, hot peppers, many other highly spiced foods, sold by weight in plastic bags, to take away for a picnic lunch or supper with some thick crusted North African bread. The restaurants are open about 10:00 a.m. to 9:30 p.m. Closed Friday evenings from sundown until sundown Saturday. Open all day Sundays.

OUVERT LE DIMANCHE (open on Sundays)

1er arrondissement
Le Galtouse
Le Stado

2E ARRONDISSEMENT
Anadolu
Le Drouot
Restaurant Kurde Dôlan

4E ARRONDISSEMENT
Galerie 88 (all day)
La Canaille (evenings)

5E ARRONDISSEMENT
La Maison de Verlaine
All the take-aways of the rue de la Huchette, rue de la Harpe

6E ARRONDISSEMENT
Le Bistro de la Grille
Marco Polo (evenings)
Le Polidor

8E ARRONDISSEMENT
L'Assiette Lyonnaise

9E ARRONDISSEMENT
Chartier
Xavier Gourmet

11E ARRONDISSEMENT
Palais de la Femme
Cannibale Café (all day)

13E ARRONDISSEMENT
L'Espérance
Hawaï

14E ARRONDISSEMENT
Crèperie de St-Malo

18E ARRONDISSEMENT
Les Chauffeurs
Le Fait Tout
L'Homme Tranquille (evenings)

19E ARRONDISSEMENT
Most of Belleville

OUVERT EN AOÛT (open in August)

1ER ARRONDISSEMENT
Auberge du Palais Royal
Le Galtouse (for two weeks)
L'Incroyable
Le Palet
Au Petit Ramoneur (1st two weeks)
Le Stado

2E ARRONDISSEMENT
Anadolu
Le Drouot
Restaurant Kurde Dîlan

4E ARRONDISSEMENT
Galerie 88
La Canaille
Le Chateaubriand
La Comète (two weeks)
Le Cristal
Le P'tit Comic
Le Petit Gavroche (dinner only)

5E ARRONDISSEMENT
Le Baptiste
Le Blé d'Or (two weeks)
Le Bouche Trou
La Maison de Verlaine
All the take-aways of rue de la Huchette, rue de la Harpe

6E ARRONDISSEMENT

Bistro de la Grille
La Bolée (1st two weeks)
Orestias
Osteria del Passe Partout
Le Polidor
Restaurant des Beaux Arts
All of rue de la Huchette, rue de la Harpe

8E ARRONDISSEMENT

L'Assiette Lyonnaise
Hyotan (three weeks)

9E ARRONDISSEMENT

Chartier
Duhau
Xavier Gourmet

11E ARRONDISSEMENT

Cannibale Café
Palais de la Femme

13E ARRONDISSEMENT

Hawaï

14E ARRONDISSEMENT

Crèperie de St-Malo
Midi-Trente (three weeks)

15E ARRONDISSEMENT

Bistrot Bourdelle (open one week)

18E ARRONDISSEMENT

Le Fait Tout

19E ARRONDISSEMENT

Duthil
Most of Belleville

20E ARRONDISSEMENT

Crèperie La Rozelle (open last two weeks)

Les spectacles (Sights and sounds)

The number one attraction in Paris is Paris. A little footwork can provide all the entertainment you need. Parisians have always relied on their feet for diversion – there's a Parisian art of strolling – the city is inexhaustibly explorable. For a few possibilities, see the chapter on 'Getting around' (page 31).

For incomparable theatre, there are the Parisians themselves. They dress distinctively, and carry themselves with a certain air: they have a highly developed vocabulary of gesture; their voices range from a croak to a twitter to an operatic singsong; they love to see and be seen. Almost any place will do for Paris and Parisian-watching: park benches, Métro stations, the *zincs* in local cafés, outdoor markets. It's up to you to be receptive.

Should street-life pall, there are other, more organized entertainments – a surprising number of them free, or very cheap.

PARIS PARKS

There are dozens of parks scattered through the city: tiny, intimate parks in the shadow of churches; parks that are 'wild' and rambling in a curiously artificial and very French way; vast, arid, formal parks consisting of gravel and neoclassical sculpture. All are meticulously kept. Here are a few (you'll find many more yourself):

Jardin des Plantes
bounded by the Seine and the rue Geoffrey-St-Hilaire, 5e
Métro: Jussieu, Gare d'Austerlitz, Monge

Part formal garden – minimal grass – part botanical station, with some lush peripheral areas. Contains the Natural History Museum and the Ménagerie. The latter, like every other 'caged' zoo in the world, is dismal, smelly and to be avoided.

Parc Monceau
boulevard de Courcelles, 8e
Métro: Monceau

Large, full of artificial waterfalls and ponds, glades, romantic statuary. Like most upper-echelon Paris parks, good nanny territory. Two steps away, at 63 rue de Monceau (southern edge of the park), is the Musée Nissim de Camondo: an eighteenth-century mansion, preserved inside and out (see page 167).

Park André-Citroën
bordered by rue Balard, rue Leblanc and rue de la Montagne-de-la-Fage, 15e.
Métro: Balard, Javel

A masterpiece by the landscape artists Alain Provost and Gilles Clément. This new park is composed of three principal sections: *le jardin blanc*, a light, clear area for promenades and play; *le jardin noir*, dense with foliage and sombre vegetation; and *le grand parc central* which descends in graceful waves.

Square des Batignolles
directly behind Église Ste-Marie des Batignolles, 17e
Métro: Brochant, and a fair walk

A charming, unpretentious park in a quiet neighbourhood, with duckponds and a population of elderly park-sitters. The low iron fencing along the paths resembles a lattice of bent twigs – a reminder of the French love for 'natural' artifice.

Parc des Buttes-Chaumont
bounded by the rue Manin and the rue Botzaris, 19e
Métro: Buttes-Chaumont

This is a park which most tourists miss because it is so out of the way – a pity, because it is charming. Set on a hillside in the not very fashionable 19e, it was created by Baron Haussmann in response to his monarch's love for anything English. It was once a much more sinister place, where corpses blackened on the gibbet of Montfaucon in the Middle Ages; later a slaughterhouse for horses, finally a general rubbish heap. Haussmann had the idea of making rock gardens *à l'anglaise*, and there it is, a perfect and peaceful park.

It's rich in waterfalls, grottoes, rustic chalets, a fake-Greek temple, even fishponds (to fish, you need a permit from the *gendarmerie*). It's sixty acres of lovely strolling and picnicking ground, with a fresh breeze always blowing. If you have been in Belleville in the neighbouring 20e, and have collected a sandwich and a bottle of beer for lunch, get on the No. 26 bus heading towards St-Lazare, step off at the Botzaris-Buttes-Chaumont stop, and find a sheltered grotto for lunch. Even the local dogs, which run to neatly clipped poodles and brushed spaniels, have good manners, and despite the English look of the park, people walk lightly, if at all, on the tidy grass.

Bois de Boulogne
from Porte d'Auteuil to Porte Maillot, 16e
Métro: Porte de Neuilly, Porte Dauphine, Les Sablons

When Parisians say 'Le Bois', they are referring to this park. It's a nineteenth-century creation, roughly modelled on Hyde Park, at the suggestion of that passionate Anglophile Napoleon III. Its history as a green wooded space dates back centuries, to the days when it stood just inside the fortified boundary of Paris. It was a favourite duelling-ground until, and even after, that sport of the court was outlawed by Louis XIV. Now it is 2,000 acres of beautiful, varied, country-like terrain: with one museum, two world-famous race courses, a small zoo, a rose garden, a polo ground, a 'Shakespeare Garden' where grow all the plants mentioned in his plays, two lakes, broad avenues for riding, paths for biking. One can literally live in the Bois – there are camping grounds for tents and caravans.

Of the Métros which serve the Bois, Les Sablons takes you closest to the charming Jardin d'Acclimatation with its little zoo and playground. And one of the most delightful of Paris museums is nearby: the Musée des Arts et Traditions Populaires. This is great for a rainy day; a compendium of everything from country crafts (butter moulds, bee-keeping) to games (*boules*, royal tennis) to bagpipes, Breton head-dresses, lace sixteenth-century toys – the list is endless.

Boats in the Bois can be hired by the hour, at an office near the Lac Inférieur, and the pretty little man-made islands can be visited. Take a picnic: and stay away from the restaurants, which are calculated for the rich.

The exquisite park of Bagatelle, within the Bois, is nearly sixty acres surrounding a fairy-tale palace, and in June it is a paradise of roses. Sir Richard Wallace, said to have been the illegitimate son of the Marquis of Hertford (and a passionate lover of Paris), lived here.

At Night In the daytime the Bois is peopled with strollers, dog-walkers, kite-flyers, riders, cyclists, lovers and dreamers. But at night it's a different story. Stay away. It's not romantic even in moonlight, and it's very, very dangerous. For years it was the pickup place for certain kinds of Paris prostitutes, and at least some of *les girls* are South American transvestites. Vandalism and violent crime have taken over the Bois at night.

BATEAUX-MOUCHES

Glass-enclosed excursion boats glide up and down the Seine for about an hour and a half, under various names but generically called Bâteaux Mouches. There are also excursions for lunch, tea or dinner but these are obviously much more expensive and the food is very poor. If you plan to go in the evening, make reservations in advance.

BATEAUX-MOUCHES: from the Pont de l'Alma, right bank (*Métro*: Alma-Marceau), every 30 minutes. From 10:00 a.m. to noon, then 1:30 p.m. to 8:30 p.m., 40F; under 14s, 20F. Reservations, tel: 01 42 25 96 10.

BATEAUX-VEDETTES PONT NEUF: from the Square du Vert-Galant on the Île de la Cité, 1er (*Métro*: Pont Neuf): 10:30 a.m., 11:15 a.m. and noon, then every 30 minutes from 1:30 to 6:30 p.m. Evening cruises 9:00 to 10:30 p.m. in the summer, 45F and under 10 years ride for 20F. Reservations, tel: 01 46 33 98 38.

CEMETERIES

A taste for these is not as macabre as you may think (but it does help to go on a rainy day. If you're depressed, they're great places to wallow in despair). There are at least thirteen within the city limits. The best known, and the best for browsing, is **Père Lachaise** (you could win bets as to its real name, which is Cimetière de l'Est).

Bounded on two sides by the avenue Gambetta and the boulevard de Ménilmontant (*Métro*: Père Lachaise) it consists of nineteenth- and twentieth-century tombs and sepulchres: some mouldering and decrepit; some sprucely cared for; some distinctly spooky; others – shiny granite and plastic photographs – very sentimental. Here lie Colette, Proust, Wilde, Chopin, Hugo, Balzac, Piaf, Gertrude Stein. And Jim Morrison. On sunny days the cats come out to bask on the *tombeaux*. A map of the cemetery can be purchased for a few francs from the *gendarme* at the gate.

If you haven't exhausted your taste for the illustrious dead, your next stop should be the **Cimetière de Montmartre** in rue Caulaincourt, 18e; *Métro*: Place de Clichy or La Fourche. Contents: Dumas *père* (where is *fils?*), Stendhal, Berlioz, Fragonard, Baudelaire.

MARKETS

As you must have gathered by now, food is an object of worship in Paris. It's appreciated on the plate, and almost as much on the hoof. Paris abounds with open-air and covered markets where everything is displayed to perfection: fruits and vegetables placed just so; incredible conglomerations of fish and shellfish; poultry and game hung disconcertingly at eye level. There's nothing antiseptic about the markets, and nothing haphazard – the stall proprietors are there to sell (voices that can be heard streets away), and those who come to buy are determined to get the best. It's hard to know whether to look at the sellers, the clients, or the merchandise.

The 'moving markets' of Paris are almost unknown to the casual visitor. But they are essential to understanding Parisians, from elegant matrons of the 8e *arrondissement* to the women in *djellabas* of the 11e.

OPEN AIR: Try these, 8:00 a.m. to noon only:
Carmes, 5e: At Maubert-Mutualité Métro. Tuesdays, Thursdays, Saturdays.

Boulevard Raspail, 6e: between rue de Cherche-Midi and rue de Rennes. Upper-class food (including 'biologique' or chemically untreated fresh foods), beautiful people. Tuesdays, Fridays.

Belleville, 11e: rue Oberkampf to Belleville Métro. Huge, mainly run by North African French – everything from wild strawberries to Bleu d'Auvergne cheese to plastic sandals. Tuesdays, Fridays.

Père Lachaise, 11e: begins at the Ménilmontant Métro and runs east along boulevard Ménilmontant to rue des Panoyaux. Next to Belleville, but completely different – very French, very classy, beautiful fish, cheese and the best olives and dried fruits at Pierre Blanc's English-speaking stand.

Avenue du Président Wilson, 16e: between rue Debrousse and place d'Iéna. Even more BCBG than boulevard Raspail. Wednesdays, Saturdays.

COVERED MARKETS (*Marchés Couverts*): Weekdays, 8:30 a.m. to 1:00 p.m., 2:00 to 7:30 p.m. Sundays, 8:00 a.m. to 1:00 p.m. (Schedule may vary according to season.)

Saint Honoré, 1e: place du Marché St-Honoré
Saint Germain, 6e: 3 bis rue Mabillon
Saint Martin, 10e: rue René Boulanger
St-Quentin, 10e: 95 bis boulevard Magenta
Marché Couvert de Paris, 12e: place Aligre
Passy, 16e: corner of the rue Bois-le-Vent and rue Duban
Batignolles, 17e: rue Brochant
La Chapelle, 18e: 10 rue d'Olive
Sécretan, 19e: 33 avenue Sécretan
Europe Asie, 19e: 36 rue Joinville.

WINDOW-SHOPPING

FOOD

For museum-quality displays, go to Fauchon, *the* de luxe shop which faces two sides of the place de la Madeleine, 8e (*Métro*: Madeleine).

Early morning is best, when the *terrines* and *pâtés* are arranged in the window, the crayfish and lobsters set out. Unbelievable *gelées*, *pâtisseries*, arrangements of bread, displays of wine, cheeses you never dreamed of. On the opposite side of the Madeleine is Hédiard – smaller, more compact, and just as expensive.

Exquisite *pâtisseries* and *charcuteries* can be found all over Paris, in the most surprising *quartiers*, some that are nearly slums. No one hesitates to spend five minutes or more peering in the window, choosing one pastry or a *tranche* of a wild boar *terrine*. One wonders how all this intricately decorated food ever gets eaten, never mind prepared from day to day. A partial answer is the restaurant trade: the thousands of restaurants large and small rely on the shops of their *quartier* for the day's *terrines* and *tartes*. Somehow, Parisians have overlooked the idea of mass-marketed, prefabricated victuals, and they do seem to be happy in their ignorance.

CLOTHES

As you know, they are of vital importance to the French sense of self-esteem and to their economy. The couturiers' windows are accordingly magnificent. Whether sedate or outrageous, they display their wares beautifully, imaginatively, both inside and in the windows of the great houses. The smaller boutiques, too, have a fresh and lively approach to display. The department stores, however, in comparison to almost any American store and some English ones, are a dead loss – frozen in the display techniques of the 1950s. The only worthwhile window among them is the dome of stained glass in the Galeries Lafayette, and that's spectacular.

Walk up the rue Royale, along the rue du Faubourg-St-Honoré, along the side streets and avenues of St-Germain-des-Prés, along the avenue Matignon, the avenue du Pierre-Premier-de-Serbie, the rue Boissy d'Anglas, and you come away reeling with the great inventive talent and daring of Hermès, Cardin, Chanel, Dior, St Laurent, Givenchy. It costs nothing to look in the windows of Cartier, Bulgari, van Cleef and Arpels, and unconsciously you are absorbing what makes for elegance, quality and flair.

ANTIQUE SHOPPING

The pleasure of 'antiqueing' in Paris, too, is for the eye only. Prices are high and rising, as the rich take their panic money out of gold and put it into irreplaceable objects of beauty and luxury. So consider the time you dally in front of windows or in shops as part of your education in what constitutes value in craftsmanship and materials.

If you love antiques and want to see an incredible collection all under one roof, an obvious but good answer is Le Louvre des Antiquaires, in the place Palais Royal, 1er. This three-storey building is a mass of showrooms run by some of the best-known dealers of Paris. Unless you are conspicuously well dressed, don't expect much attention or friendliness from the dealers: they know their customers, and are fairly sure as soon as they set eyes on you that you're not a prospect.

The back streets of the Marais, around the rue des Francs-Bourgeois, are beginning to be lined with elegant small antique shops, but here again you will find few if any bargains. Look, too, at the Village St-Paul, in the rue St-Paul near the Seine (4e), a beautifully reconstructed cluster of grey stone mansions now housing some lovely shops. Then cross to the Left Bank, and wander around the side streets that make up the St-Germain-des-Prés area: rue Jacob, rue Furstenberg, rue du Bac, rue des Beaux Arts, rue de l'Université.

In the more rarefied reaches of the 7e, you'll find the Village Suisse – a collection of rather expensive dealers – at 78 avenue de Suffren (*Métro*: La Motte-Picquet), open Thursdays through Mondays, 10:30 a.m. to 7:00 p.m.

What is conspicuously missing in Paris is fine antique silver: much of the best table silver and decorative pieces owned by the aristocracy and the rich bourgeoisie were melted down to pay for the wars of Louis XIV, and most of what remained went into the fires of the Revolution. The few pieces that escaped are now in museums. You will now find that the best silver on offer is elaborate late-nineteenth-century work, a few fine Art Nouveau pieces and – more available – some of the chic, stark creations of the 1930s, at prices about one-third *more* than a London or New York dealer would charge. You may be lucky in a flea market or a small semi-junk shop, but don't count on it.

Again, all this comes under the general heading of education. Remember, too, that if you find anything you like and can afford, and it's too big to go in your luggage, you will have to deal with shipping, insurance, customs and collection at the other end, which can easily double the original price.

THE FLOWER MARKETS

If it's not food, clothes and paintings that separate Parisians from the rest of the world, maybe it's their intoxication with flowers. The flower shops and stalls are fantasies of scent, colour, life, and the sort of instinctive flair for arrangement of even quite humble flowers that is absolutely French. The markets are found on the Île de la Cité, at the back of the Madeleine (8e, *Métro*: Madeleine) and at the place des Ternes (17e, *Métro*: Ternes). The first two are thick with tourists in high summer, but don't let that deter you. The place des Ternes is well off the tourist beat and has flower stalls as well as the charming street market Marché Poncelet. A few blossoms in a water glass or Perrier bottle will cheer up your hotel room.

PLANTS: walk along the quai de la Mégisserie, 1er (*Métro*: Pont Neuf), if you want to see how the French approach the whole question of gardening, with an emphasis on window-box plants, kitchen and herb gardens, small-scale city adornment. One of the great seedsmen of Europe, Vilmorin, has a big shop here. A packet of real French basil grown from their seed seems to have a special flavour which may be more in the imagination than in reality (but check to see if your country allows you to import seeds). Open every day.

DUCKS, DEER, SWANS: also on the quai de la Mégisserie are the caged animals, birds, tortoises, domestic and wild fowls – which can break your heart. Two swans in a cage; a miniature deer for some rich child's private zoo; even the chickens are pitiable. Don't look.

MONUMENTS

We know you'll find these without our help (you'll probably see one or two outside your hotel window), but here's a very brief list of the typical tourist must-sees to give you a head start in filling out your own list:

L'Arc de Triomphe
Métro: Étoile
Hours: Tuesday to Saturday, 9:30 a.m.–10:30 p.m.; Monday, to 6:30 p.m.
Admission: 32F adults; 21F reduced price; 15F for 12–17-year-olds.

Notre-Dame de Paris
(Cathedral/Archaeological Crypt)
Métro: Cité
Hours: Everyday 9:30 a.m. to 5:45 p.m.
Admission: 28F adult; 18F reduced tariff; 15F for 12–17-year-olds.

Sacré-Cœur
Métro: Anvers
Hours: Everyday from 7:00 a.m. to 11:00 p.m.
Admission: Free.

For the Dome and Crypt the hours are: Everyday from 7:00 a.m.–7:00 p.m.
Admission: 15F and 10F reduced tariff.

Eiffel Tower
Métro: Bir-Hakeim
Hours (access to the 1st, 2nd and 3rd levels): Everyday from 9 a.m. to 11 p.m.
Fee (elevator): 20F to the 1st level, 40F to the 2nd, 56F to the 3rd.
Fee (stairs): More befitting to a pauper, the price is 12F to the 1st and 2nd levels . . .
The rest is up to you and your pauper's pocket . . .

MUSEUMS

Paris glories in the existence of nearly a hundred museums: from the largest in the world (the Louvre) to one of the most specialized which displays only the crystal of Baccarat. Many are in the area of central

Paris (see museum map, pages 268–9), others within half an hour's travel on the Métro, bus or RER express lines. Some are small, exquisite and so highly specialized that in their best week they get no more than a dozen visitors. Some are great private houses now open to the public, worth seeing even if you didn't look at the contents. One of the most extraordinary, the Musée Nissim de Camondo, is a frozen slice of eighteenth-century France, created by the grieving parents of a First World War hero. Still another has an enticing collection of mechanical toys and clockwork gadgets. There are not one but *two* modern museums in Paris, while poor London struggles on without any.

Many of the major Paris museums are free or half price on Sunday. Some give discounts to students (an International Student Identity Card helps) and to those under or over a certain age. Details are given under each museum mentioned. If you're under 18 or over 60 (women) or 65 (men), show your passport and ask for *demi-tarif* which cuts museum charges in half. Two elderly friends of ours were admitted free to the Petit Palais on production of passports.

It's true that almost every museum charges an admission fee, and if you are a conscientious pauper used to the generous free museums of Britain, this comes as a shock. Brace yourself, do without lunch if you must, but either pay the sum asked or wear yourself out on Sundays. You will be rewarded in every sense by the thrill of the beautiful, the odd, the heart-warming or the blood-chilling.

Most museums close on Tuesdays, a few on Mondays, some both days. A few are open on public holidays but most are closed. All are near a Métro stop or within five minutes' walk. All have free cloakrooms (obligatory) for carrier bags, umbrellas, briefcases, but they won't take anything that holds money, jewellery, passport or camera. Some let you take photographs, some forbid flash equipment. Check for rules when you go, as they change from time to time.

Most Paris museums, as one would expect from the general French attitude towards civilized comfort, have benches or chairs on which to fall when your feet, eyes and mind give out. The attendants on the whole give good directions as to what's where, and will do their best to answer questions in English. They have eyes in the backs of their heads and voices that when raised can cut like a laser beam. Don't touch, don't breathe on, don't put a finger near the surface of a painting or a sculpture unless you are prepared for a loud metallic French shout.

Be prepared to queue for admission to the Louvre, to the Musée d'Orsay (Impressionists, Post-Impressionists) and to any major exhibitions which may be open. For these, take along a thermos of coffee and sandwiches to sustain you. Sellers of hot coffee and croissants from heated carts make a good franc or two. One couple we spotted were sharing a small bottle of wine and a bag of sandwiches at 8:00 a.m. Waiting so long in hot weather, or cold rain, can leave you too exhausted to enjoy what you came to see. Sometimes queues are shorter at lunchtime, or when an exhibition has just opened, or during the last ten days when crowds are minimal.

One way to beat the queues is the fairly new *Carte Musées et Monuments* which gives you free entry to the dozens of museums and historical sites in Paris (with the exception of temporary exhibitions and guided visits). It costs 70F for one day, 140F for three consecutive days, 200F for five consecutive days. You'd get your money's worth if you are a real museum buff and can cope with three or four a day: and it allows you to bypass queues, enter by 'group admission' doors, and sail past the ticket offices. At the Louvre, for example, you don't stand in the endless line inching towards the new Pyramid, but go to the escalator in the arcade leading from the Palais-Royal Métro, normally reserved for groups. Work it out for yourself if the convenience is worth the money. We think the three- or five-day investment is a better buy than the one-day pass. Our thanks to Howard Rye of London, who used the *Carte Musées et Monuments* with pleasure and profit. This expensive but useful admission card can be obtained in the UK from Voyages Vacances, tel: 0171 287 3171, as well as at museums, monuments, major Paris Métro and rail stations and the Office de Tourisme (127 avenue des Champs-Élysées).

The museums listed and described in this section include our own personal guide to the lesser-known ones as well as the more popular leaders.

1ER ARRONDISSEMENT

The Louvre
Métro: Palais-Royal, Louvre
Bus: 21, 24, 27, 39, 48, 69, 72, 76, 81, 95

HOURS: Thursday, Friday, Saturday, Sunday from 9:00 a.m. to 6:00 p.m. Mondays and Wednesdays to 9:45 p.m. Closed Tuesdays.

ADMISSION: 45F; Sundays and after 3:00 p.m. weekdays it's 26F. Reduced rates for students, free if you're under 18.

The Pyramid! It's been called 'an architect's megalomania', 'a magical machine', 'violation of the historic Louvre', 'a triumph of the imagination', and a litany of phrases ranging from violent denunciation to ecstatic praise. Go and see for yourself. It is the main entrance to the museum, and is attracting queues of the curious. This elegant airy structure is 71 feet high and surrounded by three baby likenesses. It has freed many of the superb rooms from the clutter of ticket-windows, postcard racks, gift shops and whatnot. Access to the museum's unbelievable treasures is now astonishingly easy, and you could spend half a day playing with the computerized information service below the Pyramid.

Perhaps the best thing is that, as you move out of the high-tech underground entrance hall, you find the great crypt, revealed during the excavations, which now displays the original walls of places of past centuries. Beyond that, the Louvre stretches for ever. It's continually in the process of transformation and in years to come more rooms will be opened, more wonders revealed. At the moment, so many things are going on in what Mary Blume of the *International Herald Tribune* once called 'the uncomfortable, dingy, distinctly user-unfriendly Louvre' that it's almost impossible to sum it up here.

Obviously, if you had but one day in Paris (or one lifetime), the Louvre would be the one indispensable museum. The Big Three (*Winged Victory of Samothrace*, *Venus de Milo*, *Mona Lisa*) may have been overexposed, but you must see them, at least on your first visit. A guided tour, booked in the entrance hall, could be a good way to learn your way around: after that you'll find your own personal treasures, the Poussins, the Chardins, the Rembrandts, the Egyptian hoard, the Italian primitives.

A sophisticated Parisian recommends sauntering around the Pyramid, hoping to see the daring Alpinistes who abseil around it to clean its glittering panes (apparently little account was taken in the planning for the ravages of rain, dirt, city pollution and seagulls); the best time, really, is on a still, moonlit night when reflections dance and shimmer in the triangular reflecting pool. After your first visit to see the Pyramid, she says that if you are in a hurry to get into the Louvre, make for the Pavillon de Flore, westward of the main block (*Métro*: Tuileries). Be wary of a very hot or very cold day at the Pyramid: there is neither shade nor shelter as you wait for security checks and single-filing into the entrance, and in summer the sun beats down relentlessly on the entry-level platform before you descend to the gloriously lit *sous-sol*. Apparently, the great central pillar in the Pyramid was meant as a base for the Winged Victory, but cooler heads prevailed.

The Louvre itself is set on the site of royal palaces that date back to the twelfth century and stretches over acres along the Seine. Much of the present structure is 'new', as things Parisian go. Both the great Napoleon and the later, lesser Louis-Napoleon had a hand in building or reconstructing. François I was the first royal collector – or looter – in the sixteenth century. He picked up trifles like Giottos, Leonardos, Veroneses on his way through Italy and Spain.

The incredible Egyptian collections owe their existence to the Napoleonic campaigns. Louis XIV housed most of his 'finds' at Versailles, but after his death they were dispersed, some to the Luxembourg Palace but most to the royal palace of the Louvre. After 1789, the Louvre became the Central Museum of the Arts of the infant republic, and was almost at once opened to the public.

This is a sketchy description of what may be the world's greatest museum: to do it justice, the rest of this book would have to be dropped. Go early in the morning, go often, leave before you develop visual fatigue. Remember that if you are lucky you will return to it many times in the future.

The Jeu de Paume
place de la Concorde, 1er
Métro: Concorde, Tuileries

HOURS: Schedule varies from exhibition to exhibition, as the museum is open only when there is an *exposition*. The present schedule is Wednesday to Friday from noon to 7:00 p.m.; Tuesdays from noon to 9:30 p.m.; Saturday and Sunday from 10:00 a.m. to 7:00 p.m.

ADMISSION: Prices will vary for each exhibition, from 35F, with 25F concessionary rates and under-13s admitted free.

The lovely little Jeu de Paume, whose treasures crossed the Seine to new and airier premises in the Musée d'Orsay some years ago, has been redecorated and opened as a showcase for major temporary exhibitions. It has a beautiful small art bookshop, and great windows letting light in from the Tuileries gardens, a dramatic long staircase and a lift. In 1991, it launched its new career with a big show of work by Dubuffet. The usual queues ensued. Check for the current exhibition and the cost of admission in *L'Officiel des Spectacles* or in *What's On in France* (see Periodicals, page 245), or watch for posters in the Métro. And be prepared to queue for quite long stretches, as security checks and ticket-taking is necessarily slow.

The Orangerie
place de la Concorde, 1er
Métro: Concorde

HOURS: 9:45 a.m. to 5:00 p.m., every day except Thursdays and major holidays.

ADMISSION: 28F; reduced rate of 18F for students under 26, and over-60s. Free for under-18s.

A hundred yards closer to the Seine from the Jeu de Paume, this is a museum with (so far) no queues. It houses the Walter Guillaume collection, mostly early twentieth-century paintings, reflecting the highly personal choices of Mme Walter and her two husbands (Paul Guillaume and Jean Walter). There are fourteen ravishing Cézannes, some fine Picassos, many Derains and Soutines, some unusual

Douanier Rousseaus – and areas of creamy, satiny, plushy Renoirs. Certainly worth seeing – many critics hated it; those who find out about it seem to love it. The great Monet water-lily paintings in the Salle des Nymphéas are not to be missed.

The Museum of Decorative Arts
107 rue de Rivoli, 1er
Métro: Palais-Royal

HOURS: Currently closed for building work, check for the new schedule in *Pariscope* (3F) or *L'Officiel des Spectacles* (2F).

ADMISSION: 25F; 16F reduced price for students and over-60s.

A magnificent collection of furniture, tapestries, arts and crafts, books about the decorative arts. It often has fine special exhibitions such as the show called 'Poupées d'hier, créations d'aujourd'hui' (Dolls of bygone days, creations of today) which had 300 dolls from all parts of the world, some almost 200 years old, plus work by contemporary fashion designers and artists from Japan, the United States, and all of Europe. In addition, there has been a startling show of furniture of the decade 1980–90 from Italy's avant-garde designers. Permanent collection includes the Renaissance Galleries and seventeenth-, eighteenth- and nineteenth-century collections.

Musée de la Publicité
107 rue de Rivoli, 1er
In the Museum of Decorative Arts, 3rd fl.
Métro: Palais-Royal

HOURS: 12:30 to 6:00 p.m. Closed Mondays and Tuesdays.

ADMISSION: 25F; 16F for the unemployed, for students and *Carte Vermeil* holders or over-65s with passport. The ticket admits you to their little *cinémathèque*.

The poster and advertising museum has moved from its beautiful old Art Nouveau building in the 10e *arrondissement* to a more modern space in the Museum of Decorative Arts. It shows every form of advertising, including signs, prints, cinema posters and ads, and always has an interesting special exhibition to do with advertising. The museum's own *affiche* is well worth buying for the pleasure of the graphic design. The French have been doing this with wit, flair and irony for a hundred years. Look at the postcard reproduction of the original posters advertising the great French liner *Normandie*, queen of the Atlantic before the Second World War.

3E ARRONDISSEMENT

Musée Carnavalet
23 rue de Sévigné, 3e
Métro: St-Paul, Chemin-Vert

HOURS: 10:00 a.m. to 5:40 p.m. Closed Mondays and holidays.

ADMISSION: 27F; 14F50 for reduced price tickets.

The Bicentenary year of 1989 saw a long-overdue renovation of this exquisite seventeenth-century building which houses the museum of the City of Paris. Once the home of Madame de Sévigné, it has been extended and joined to its next-door neighbour, the Hôtel Le Peletier de St-Fargeau. All the history and beauty of Paris right back to Roman times are beautifully displayed here – with a most remarkable feeling that it has all been assembled by one ardent collector. A fantastic collection of revolutionary artefacts is in the Le Peletier house – fans, buckles, proclamations, warrants for arrests and executions; drums, flags, Louis XVI's razors, Napoleon's travelling *toilette* set, the little notebooks of the imprisoned Dauphin. Beautiful period rooms have been reconstructed throughout both buildings; don't miss the Art Nouveau room for the old Café de Paris, and a 1920s ballroom.

Musée Picasso
5 rue de Thorigny, 3e
Métro: Chemin-Vert, St-Paul

HOURS: 9:30 a.m. to 6:00 p.m. weekdays, Saturdays and Sundays from April to September. Until 5:30 p.m. from October to March. Closed Tuesdays.

ADMISSION: 28F; 18F reduced price tickets, free for under-18s.

All we can say is Picasso, Picassissimo: if you are a fan, go. If not, skip it. In addition to Picasso *in excelsis*, it includes work by other painters which he owned, treasured, and kept all his life. Great photographs of himself at work, on the beach, with friends; and usually a film in the little cinema high up under the roof of this beautiful and historic palace on the edge of the Marais.

4E ARRONDISSEMENT

The Conciergerie
1 quai de l'Horloge, 4e
Métro: Cité, Châtelet

HOURS: 10:00 a.m. to 5:00 p.m., Mondays through Fridays. Closed holidays.

ADMISSION: 28F; 18F reduced price tickets. Free for under-12s.

Don't go unless you feel fairly strong. Deep in the huge and pretty formidable Palais de Justice, the Conciergerie puts the Terror of 1789 right at your throat. No matter how you feel about the pre-revolutionary aristos, the sight of Marie Antoinette's cell, and the rooms where philosophers, writers, artists and the nobility waited for death, cannot leave you unaffected.

Beaubourg: Musée National d'Art Moderne
Centre National de l'Art et de Culture Georges Pompidou, 4e (this mouth-filling title is usually shortened to *Beaubourg*)
Métro: Hôtel de Ville, Rambuteau

HOURS: Noon to 10:00 p.m. weekdays, 10:00 a.m. to 10:00 p.m. Saturdays, Sundays and holidays. Closed Tuesdays.

ADMISSION: 35F; 24F reduced price tickets. Free for under-18s.

A dazzling collection of every important modern painter and sculptor of the twentieth century. Sit down from time to time to rest and stare, because this art is not meant to soothe the eye or the spirit.

Beaubourg itself is like a great museum on its own, and much of it is free, including the escalator that snakes up the front of the building and gives you an unmatchable view of the city from the roof. But the small escalator that leads to the big one is narrow, short, and often jammed with queues that even crowd the huge entrance courtyard.

N.B.: It will be closed from September 1997 for at least a year for renovation, but will be open only for temporary exhibitions.

5E ARRONDISSEMENT

Musée de Cluny
6 place Paul-Painlevé, 5e
Métro: St-Michel, Odéon

HOURS: 9:15 a.m. to 5:45 p.m. Closed Tuesdays.

ADMISSION: 28F; 18F on Sunday and reduced price tickets. Under-18s free.

Utterly fascinating medieval monastery buildings which now house one of the world's great collections of arts and crafts of the Middle Ages. Spurs, chastity belts, sculpture, ivories, bronzes – and, except in the high summer months, almost empty of visitors. Often you find yourself in a small dark room staring at some endearing little object that no one has bothered to document or catalogue. And of course, the high point is the haunting tapestry series called, collectively, *La Dame Aux Licornes*. Bonus: when your feet finally give out, you can hobble a hundred yards to an inexpensive good restaurant near the boulevard St-Michel . . . L'Osteria del Passe Partout (see page 116).

L'Institut du Monde Arabe
1 rue des Fossés St-Bernard, 5e
Métro: Jussieu, Cardinal Lemoine

HOURS: 10:00 a.m. to 6:00 p.m. every day except Mondays.

ADMISSION: 35F.

The price is high, the building is spectacular inside and out. It's a treasure-store of archaeology, history, calligraphy, decoration, books and photographs of the world of Islam. There's a cafeteria, a restaurant, a *salle image et son* for films, music. At the very least, go and see the exquisite façade, even if you'd rather have an inexpensive lunch than pay the 35F admission fee.

7E ARRONDISSEMENT

The Invalides
Esplanade des Invalides, 7e
Métro: Invalides, Latour-Maubourg, Varenne

HOURS: 10:00 a.m. to 6:00 p.m. in summer, until 5:00 p.m. in winter.

ADMISSION: 35F; 25F for students and *Carte Vermeil* holders. This ticket entitles you to all three of the museums and to Napoleon's tomb, and can be used on two consecutive days.

The Invalides is a catch-all name for the complex of museums which deal primarily with Napoleon, but also with everything to do with French armies from the shot-torn battle flags of Louis XIV to more modern armour. Napoleon's tomb, under the dome of the Invalides, is majestic, solemn and always surrounded by a silent, circling group.

Musée d'Orsay
1 rue Bellechasse, 7e (at the quai Anatole France)
Métro: Solférino

HOURS: 10:00 a.m. to 6:00 p.m. every day except Thursdays, when it is open to 9:45 p.m. Open at 9:00 a.m. on Sundays. Closed Mondays.

ADMISSION: 36F; 24F reduced price tickets. Under-18s free.

Built for the Great Exhibition of 1990, the old, derelict Gare d'Orsay has been joyously transformed into a palace of nineteenth- and early twentieth-century French art: Ingres and Delacroix, Daumier, Moreau and Degas; Manet, Monet, Renoir; Seurat, Redon, Toulouse-Lautrec; Bonnard, Vuillard and Vallotton ... the entire contents of the Jeu de Paume, with generous helpings of the Louvre and the Palais de Tokyo, are ranged among three floors of galleries and halls. The light is for the most part natural – filtered through the glass roof – and the internal architecture has a curious King Tut's Tomb effect – at once airy and monumental, in muted tones of grey. It's a stunning success. As well as its permanent collections, it usually has a special show of interest; in 1996: 'The Life and Work of Jacques Offenbach'; 'The Family Halévy: Between Theatre and History (1760–1960)'; and an exhibition of Adolph Menzel's work spanning his seventy-year career.

Hang on to your ticket: you can go in and out of the museum as often as you like in the course of one day.

Musée Rodin
77 rue de Varenne, 7e
Métro: Varenne.

HOURS: 9:30 a.m. to 5.45 p.m. Closed Mondays and major holidays.

ADMISSION: 28F; 18F reduced price tickets.

This old and beautiful house in a rather pompous part of Paris holds many of Rodin's superb works – their power and vigour fairly burst the walls. More sculpture in the remarkably beautiful garden. And a place to eat in the museum. A nice Paris touch: on the Métro platform at Varenne, life-size reproductions of the greatest Rodins, and some small ones in a dramatic spotlit glass cage.

8E ARRONDISSEMENT

Musée Nissim de Camondo
63 rue de Monceau, 8e
Métro: Villiers

HOURS: 10:00 a.m. to 5:00 p.m. Closed Mondays, Tuesdays and holidays.

ADMISSION: 27F; 18F reduced price tickets.

Very quiet: most tourists pass it by, which is their loss. A museum dedicated to the memory of a young aviator shot down in the First World War, which sounds both dull and depressing. Not so. His father, a wealthy art collector, re-created the interior of a house as it would have been done by an eighteenth-century tycoon. French furniture, *objets d'art*, then were of a luxury and perfection seen nowhere else in the world, and there they are, gleaming with care, love and polishing, and waiting for the minuet to begin.

Musée du Petit Palais
avenue Winston-Churchill, 8e
Métro: Champs-Élysées-Clemenceau

HOURS: 10:00 a.m. to 5:40 p.m. Closed Mondays and holidays.

ADMISSION: 27F; 14F50 reduced price tickets. Free for under-18s and over-60s.

This museum, also often neglected by Paris visitors, has some fine works bequeathed by private collectors – beautiful Manet pastels, Berthe Morisot, Mary Cassatt, Toulouse-Lautrec pastels, Bonnard, Vuillard, Cézanne – and historic French furniture, *bibelots*, clocks, and so forth. The peaceful, flowering circular garden is usually deserted; a good place to rest, read, meditate. However, they courteously discourage picnicking, so don't try it. Often there are fine temporary exhibitions: check *What's On in France* or street posters.

12E ARRONDISSEMENT

Musée des Arts d'Afrique et d'Océanie
293 avenue Daumesnil, 12e
Métro: Porte Dorée

HOURS: 10:00 a.m. to 12:00 p.m., 1:30 to 5:30 p.m. weekdays. Saturday and Sunday from 12:20 to 6:30 p.m. Closed Tuesdays.

ADMISSION: 23F; 13F Sundays; free for under-18s.

It's worth trailing all the way out to this fairly remote part of Paris to find an almost unknown treasure. The arts of black Africa – bold statements in wood, bone, leather, brass – the delicate beauty of carvings and leather from Muslim North Africa – and some gemlike artefacts from the Pacific islands colonized by the French. Poster collectors: don't miss the museum's own magnificent *affiche*.

16E ARRONDISSEMENT

Musée Guimet
19 avenue d'Iéna, 16e
Métro: Iéna

HOURS: 9:45 a.m. to 6:00 p.m. Closed Tuesdays and holidays.

ADMISSION: 15F; 10F reduced price, under-18s admitted free.

The exact opposite of the Beaubourg Modern Museum: calm, soothing Far Eastern art. This is the Asiatic Art Collection of the Louvre, and worth return visits if you can afford it – save money with picnic lunches. Japanese and Chinese masterworks, irreplaceable sculpture from parts of Cambodia that have vanished for ever in wars, art of India and Pakistan, and an important exhibition on Japanese Buddhism.

Musée Marmottan
2 rue Louis-Boilly, 16e
Métro: La Muette, then about 10 minutes' walk through a park

HOURS: 10:00 a.m. to 5:30 p.m. Closed Mondays and holidays.

ADMISSION: 35F; 15F for students and over-60s.

Rejoice! The stolen Monets which have been missing for several years have been found and are now back where they belong, on the walls of the renovated Marmottan. One, *Impression at Daybreak*, is the painting that gave Impressionism its name. For many years the Marmottan was little visited – now you can expect a queue down the ten steps and into the street. Be patient and you'll get in. For the less mobile, there's a narrow lift to take you down to the beautifully lit underground room with everything from a cool Scandinavian farm scene to the dazzling and baffling water-lily paintings that became the nucleus of the famous Nymphéas collection in the Orangerie (page 161). There are many other works by friends and contemporaries, and some treasures from the Renaissance. Don't miss the touching exhibition of Monet's letters and postcards to friends: a haunting record of difficulties, illness, lack of money and broken promises from patrons and dealers.

Musée d'Art Moderne de la Ville de Paris
11 avenue du Président-Wilson, 16e
Métro: Iéna

HOURS: 10:00 a.m. to 6:45 p.m. on Saturdays and Sundays; until 5:30 p.m. from Tuesday to Friday. Closed Mondays and holidays.

ADMISSION: 27F; 19F reduced price tickets.

Much of the Musée d'Art Moderne's contents have been moved to the Musée d'Orsay, across the river on the quai Anatole France, and to Beaubourg – but there is still an impressive permanent collection on exhibit, and it installs great temporary shows: retrospectives, private collections and thematic exhibits. This is the place to find Cubist, Fauve and École de Paris paintings. Check *What's On in France* for current events.

18E ARRONDISSEMENT

Musée de Montmartre
12 rue Cortot, 18e
Métro: Lamarck, Anvers
Bus: Montmartrobus

HOURS: 11:00 a.m. to 6:00 p.m. every day except Mondays (closed).

ADMISSION: 25F; 20F reduced price tickets.

An eighteenth-century house crammed with souvenirs of the legendary artists' quarter. The Toulouse-Lautrec posters may have been reproduced on cheap paper a million times, but the originals can still stop you in your tracks. Many drawings, relics and costumes of the days when Montmartre was a place to be enjoyed, not where one is ripped off as at present.

This list of museums, of course, is the merest scratching of the surface. We have missed out (but you don't have to) such esoteric delights as the Musée Bricard (locks and keys from Roman times to the 1950s, some as fine and intricate as jewellery), the Delacroix and Balzac houses, the Victor Hugo Museum in the place des Vosges, the Grévin (waxworks to make Madame Tussaud melt with envy), and a great crazy one devoted entirely to the art of the counterfeiter. Would you believe a Rock 'n' Roll Hall of Fame? Go to the Forum des Halles, Porte du Louvre. A Musée de la Vie romantique, with souvenirs of George Sand? A Hunting Museum, at the Hôtel Guénegaud at 60 rue des Archives? If you can read French and want details of every museum in Paris and the surrounding area, get the brochure *Musées, Expositions, Monuments de Paris et de l'Île de France*, published every two months by CNMHS (Caisse Nationale des Monuments Historiques et des Sites), Hôtel de Sully, 62 rue St-Antoine, 4e (*Métro*: St-Paul) and often available from the Tourist Office at 127 avenue des Champs-Élysées.

GALLERIES

Welcoming and forbidding, worthwhile and not to be bothered with – for a century or more galleries have been a keystone of Paris life. For the visitor, they are the best way we know to let you see the world through other eyes, without paying entrance fees to museums, or scrambling to see as many as you can in one, three, or five consecutive days with the good but fairly expensive *Carte Musées et Monuments* (see page 158).

Paris is lavish with art for paupers, from inexpensive art posters available in bookshops, to postcards given away in bars and tourist offices. The galleries are scattered all over the city, from the luxurious 15e and 16e *arrondissements* to the small streets leading to the Gare de Lyon in the plebeian 12e *arrondissement*. Since they tend to cluster by kind, here's an *arrondissement* by *arrondissement* guide.

The 8e *arrondissement* has 'Establishment art'. Work by the famous dead, Boudin, Jongkind, Pissaro, Dufy, Redon, Seurat and by the million-dollar living artists, is at home all the way down the avenue Matignon, rue Miromesnil, rue de la Boëtie, rue St-Honoré.

The Left Bank, in the 5e, 6e and 7e *arrondissements*, is where you'll find Picasso – mostly sculpture, ceramics, etchings, lithographs – Braque, Mirò, the greats from before the First World War – until well into the 1970s. A good art-walk is along the quais from St-Michel, westward to the Musée d'Orsay. Smaller galleries range around St-Germain and St-Michel in the narrow streets to the Seine.

Across the river, in the burgeoning 3e and 4e *arrondissements*, there are interesting, sometimes controversial, young rising stars in galleries centred on the place des Vosges, rue du Pont Louis-Phillippe, around Beaubourg.

Newest of all is found in the vital and fascinating 11e *arrondissement*, and the 12e from the Bastille *quartier*, a web of streets going north and east – rue de Charonne, rue de la Roquette, rue Keller, rue du Faubourg St-Antoine. Where furniture-makers, framers, joiners, junk shops once stood, galleries are popping up.

Many galleries, especially the grand ones around the rue de Seine, St-Germain-des-Prés, Latour-Maubourg, avenue Matignon, and the rue St-Honoré, aestivate in August – that means they're closed. Galleries often open only Tuesdays through Saturdays, or Mondays through Fridays. Some in the newer art areas have Sunday morning openings, or *vernissages* the night before a show is to begin, when the doors may be open for the passing art-prowler to walk in, meet the artist, have a glass of wine and try to see the pictures. The grander ones are by invitation only, but around the 3e, 4e, 6e and 11e *arrondissements*, try your luck. Check *Pariscope* (3F), *L'Officiel des Spectacles* (2F), *Figaro* (7F) and all handouts from the Champs-Élysées Tourist Office, for specific shows.

The galleries listed here are a sampling: many established for thirty, forty, even fifty years; with others, the printing-ink is almost still wet on their posters.

Note: we have not listed the really world-famous galleries – such as Louise Leiris, Galerie Maeght, the Galerie des Naïfs et Primitifs, the Galerie du Chat en Majesté – because you can't miss their posters, displayed like works of art themselves in shop windows all over Paris.

1ER ARRONDISSEMENT
Galerie du Jour Agnés B.
6 rue de Jour. Work of new, young, promising artists.

Schmitt
396 rue St-Honoré. Nineteenth- and twentieth-century masterpieces – Vuillard, Delacroix, Manet, Bonnard, Rouault and others,

3E ARRONDISSEMENT
Daniel Templon
30 rue Beaubourg. Top-ranking, top-price American and international, Roy Lichtenstein *et al.*

4E ARRONDISSEMENT
ADAC Galerie-Atelier
21 rue St-Paul. Youngish, progressive artists' group.

Baudoin-Lebon
38 rue Ste-Croix de la Bretonnerie. Avant-garde paintings, photos.

Zabriskie
37 rue Quincampoix. Many famous magic-realists and surrealists and twentieth-century photographer 'names'.

6E ARRONDISSEMENT
Nicole Ferry
57 quai des Grands Augustins. Collective shows, some modern Eastern European work.

Galerie Claude Bernard
5 rue des Beaux Arts. Always fine and famous artists on show.

Callu-Mérite
17 rue des Beaux Arts. Very modern, interesting gallery.

Galerie 1990–2000
8 rue Bonaparte. The great surrealists, including photographers – Man Ray, Masson, Mirò, Picabia.

8E ARRONDISSEMENT
Alain Daune
14 avenue Matignon. Well-known artists, velvety atmosphere.

Artcurial
9 avenue Matignon. Big group shows, established artists, kind welcome to wandering visitors.

Daniel Malingue
20 avenue Matignon. Very famous artists of the twentieth-century.

11E ARRONDISSEMENT
J. and J. Donguy
57 rue de la Roquette. Near the new Opéra, in a street that is a living, walking, talking art display of its own.

12E ARRONDISSEMENT
Michel Vidal
56 rue du Faubourg St-Antoine. Artists under thirty, very provocative work. Vidal is one of the first to open in this interesting and blossoming area.

CULTURAL CENTRES

You can take advantage of nationalistic self-promotion by attending free, or almost free, events at various cultural centres. Some are dull beyond belief; others – among them the ones listed here – are full of life, even explosive.

Centre Culturel Grande Bretagne
9–11 rue de Constantine, 7e
Tel: 01 49 55 73 00
Métro: Invalides

Centre Culturel Canadien
35 avenue Montaigne, 8e
Tel: 01 44 43 29 88
Métro: Franklin-D.-Roosevelt

Centre Culturel Indo-Français
12 rue Notre-Dame de Nazareth, 3e
Tel: 01 42 78 80 53
Métro: République

Centre Culturel Suédois
11 rue Payenne, 3e
Tel: 01 44 78 80 20
Métro: St-Paul

Centre Culturel Italien
4 rue Prêtres St-Séverin, 5e
Tel: 01 46 34 27 00
Métro: St-Michel

Centre Culturel Franco-Japonais: Espace Turquetil
8 passage Turquetil, 11e
Tel: 01 43 48 83 64
Métro: Boulets-Montreuil

Goethe-Institut
17 avenue d'Iéna, 16e
Tel: 01 47 43 92 30
Métro: Iéna

Check also (if your interests run in these directions) the *centres culturels* of Yugoslavia, Egypt, Russia, Greece (*Hellenique*) and Algeria. They're all in the phone book.

CONCERTS

The French are not the most musical nation on earth, and the dearth of classical music in Paris seems to be worrying quite a lot of people. Compared to London, New York, Manchester, Chicago, Cleveland, it's a bit of a desert. The 'major' composers rank as minor compared to Germans, Austrians and Italians. French popular music is unoriginal, not even a good copy of American or English. But there is music to be found, and more of it every year. Much of it is vastly overpriced, but we've tracked down a number of concerts that are either free or very nearly so. For current listings, check the magazine *What's On in France* or *L'Officiel des Spectacles*.

IN CHURCHES
You can hear some of the finest organ music in the world, played in the incomparable settings of Paris churches, often on Sunday afternoons, and it's free.

MAISON DE LA RADIO
An orchestra organized by the French National Radio Service often gives free, or very inexpensive, concerts. For details, send a self-addressed stamped envelope to Radio France, 116 avenue du Président-Kennedy, 16e. Or drop in and see what you can find out. *Métro*: Ranelagh, Passy.

GRANDE HALLE DE LA VILLETTE
place de la Fontaine aux Lions, 19e
Métro: porte de Pantin

Free 'pre-concerts', two hours before big Jazz Festivals. Impromptu music, shows, etc. Check 'Jazz-Pop-Rock' listings in *Pariscope* or *L'Officiel des Spectacles* and the free English-language newspapers (page 229).

MÉTRO MUSIC

Classical music students at the Conservatoire National are encouraged by their teachers to learn to perform, not just to practise, and a very good way for them to do so is to pick a spot in a Métro corridor and play for the passers-by. It's a neat way to pick up some change, too. The quality is often exceptionally good, although the acoustics may leave something to be desired. Some fairly good Irish bands, accordionists, provincial flute-and-drum ensembles, and even expatriate American blues and jazz singers also make use of the Métro, and are not to be sneezed at (they're impossible to ignore, anyway).

BEAUBOURG

The cobblestoned vastness in front of the Georges Pompidou Centre, 3e (*Métro*: Hôtel de Ville, Rambuteau) often plays host to musicians of a very good standard, mixed in with the mimes and fire-eaters.

RUE DE PROVENCE, 9E

Of all unlikely places, a pedestrian square near Printemps frequently has chamber groups, soloists or blues or pop singers performing to people sitting on the steps of the nearby church. *Métro*: Havre-Caumartin.

DISCOUNTS

Student discounts: reduction in ticket prices for classical music in the big concert halls is usually available. Check listings in *What's On in France* or *L'Officiel des Spectacles*.

Senior citizens: with the *Carte Vermeil*, which the French generously provide for women over 60 and men over 65 *of any nationality*, discounts for musical events are given. See page 224 for details of this marvellous card. Look for the initials 'CV' in the price listing of any event. Or show your passport at the box office.

FREE MUSIC – a typical week's offerings*

The Paris International Quartet: Vivaldi, Brahms, Massenet at the Chapelle St-Bernard.

Classique au Vert: An afternoon concert in the Parc Floral de Paris with works by Ravel and Vivaldi.

Guy Morancon: Organ pieces by Mendelssohn, Rheinberger, Schumann, Mozart and Vierne at the Église Notre Dame du Val du Grâce.

Choir music: Music of Bach, Mozart, Rossini at the Église St-Martin.

Ensemble Intercontemporain: At the Cité de la Musique.

Solo-Ensemble Bruno Wyzuj: 'Three Centuries of Vocal Music' at the Église Italienne.

Jonas Vitaud: Piano and organ music at the Chapelle Sainte-Clotilde.

*Pariscope and *L'Officiel des Spectacles de Paris*, out every Wednesday, list all the musical events of the week. Look for the words *Entrée Libre* or *Gratuit* in the listings, which mean you get in free.

SPECTATOR SPORTS

RACING

If you can resist betting, a day at a French track with the sun shining, the crowd shrieking and stamping on losing tickets, is an experience not to be missed. You'll also see some very classy animals, hot competition, and a mix of people from working-class to the truly elegant racehorse owners and followers.

The two racecourses at the southern end of the Bois de Boulogne are enchanting. **Longchamp** is by all odds the smartest and most modern. It's the world's longest track, and said by horsey people to be one of the most difficult. The Prix de l'Arc de Triomphe and the Grand Prix are the great social events – go very early if you hope to get in. However, on other days, go for the fun, and the beauty, and try to refrain from betting as, unless you really understand the monumentally complicated French system, you may find that in the end you didn't have your money on the horse you chose at all.

To get to Longchamp, take the Métro to Porte d'Auteil, then a special bus which costs 7F50 (*Carte Paris Visite* and RATP tickets not valid). Inside the Bois, on the bus route, you will see several gates marked *Pelouse*: entrance here is to the infield, standing among the crowd, and costs least. If you chose the gate marked *Pesage*, you enter the grandstand which costs more for unreserved seats on wide bare stone steps. Take a newspaper to sit on, they're dirty.

Here, we recommend splurging on the higher-priced entrance fee, as the surroundings are beautiful and comfortable, and you can follow the knowledgeable to watch the horses from above the saddling enclosure behind the stands. Take the lift to one of the towers marked 'Restaurant Panoramique' for a most lovely view over the course and the park. And some extremely posh lavatories, free.

Racing at Longchamp goes on from early April to October.

Auteuil, the other racecourse in the Bois, is for steeplechasing, and gets a very mixed crowd (i.e. pickpockets). If you can get there for the Prix des Drags in early summer, it's one of the best almost-free sights of the world. Again, admission to the *pelouse* is cheap, to the grandstand more expensive.

Vincennes, in the Bois de Vincennes at the other end of Paris, is another city track, this time for trotters, which looks like something out of a Degas painting. There's daytime racing all year round; night racing from the end of March to the first week in December – a great way to spend a spring or summer evening. Don't believe anyone who tells you it is a ten-minute walk from the Château; it's fifty minutes' dusty or muddy foot-slogging. Get there by RER to Joinville-le-Pont (free with your *Carte Paris Visite* or a ticket), then about fifteen minutes' walk.

The **Hippodrome** at St-Cloud is reachable in either of two ways: quickly by RER to Rueil station, then by bus No. 431 to the stop 'Laboratoire Débat' for the *pesage* or 'Champ des Courses' for the *pelouse*; more slowly, the Métro to Pont de Sèvres, then bus No. 431 to the stops as above. St-Cloud is the place for flat-racing, a lovely track which attracts lots of fashionable people and famous horses at certain classic races. Last week in February to end of July, then from late September to the end of November.

TENNIS

Tennis generates immense interest in Paris, where quite a lot of tournaments with some of the world's great players competing are held. The scene changes so fast that it is impossible to make an accurate listing here, so check the newspapers if you're a fan. The Stade Roland-Garros (*Métro*: Porte d'Auteuil, then – during major tournaments – special buses to the stadium) is world famous, but the prices are high, especially for big events, so don't say you weren't warned.

CINEMA

For many film buffs, France leads the world in appreciation of the cinema, and Paris leads France. No matter what your taste in films – recent release, art-house, cult movie, retrospectives, Third World – some cinema in Paris will be showing it. *What's On in France* has reviews in English; *Pariscope* and *L'Officiel des Spectacles* have complete listings. 'V.O.' means the film is shown with its original soundtrack (and so its original language). 'V.F.' means a French soundtrack has been dubbed in.

CIRCUS

The circus is having something of a revival in Paris – a great place to take the kids when walking around Paris palls. One of them actually offers a whole day with the circus artists who will show you rehearsals in the morning, then sit with you at lunch, and perform the full spectacle in the afternoon.

You may see posters up while strolling or check with *Pariscope* or *Le Figaro* for up-to-date listings. Fortunately, you don't need to understand or speak French to enjoy these spectacles.

Cirque de Paris
Parc Départemental des Chanteraines
115 boulevard Charles-de-Gaulle
Villeneuve la Garenne, 92 (the suburbs)
Bus: 37

HOURS: 9:00 a.m. to 6:30 p.m. Performances Wednesdays, Sundays and holidays, 3:00 p.m.

ADMISSION: 45–95F children, 70–155F adults; 195F children, 235F adults for a full day, reserved in advance.

Here's where you can spend the whole day with the circus people, if you telephone first. Reservations, tel: 01 47 99 40 40.

Circus Alexandra Franconi
Square Séverine, 20e
Métro: Porte de Bagnolet

HOURS: Wednesday, Saturday, Sunday and school holidays at 3:00 p.m.

ADMISSION: 40F children, 60F adults.

PUPPETS

Marionnetterie, if there is such a word, is a very old French art, and although the shows are nominally for *les jeunes*, parents and hangers-on love them too. They are seasonal; the ones noted here are among the old favourites, others will be performing during your visit. Have a look at *Pariscope* for up-to-the-minute listings.

Marionnettes des Champs-Élysées
rond-point des Champs-Élysées, at the corner of avenue Gabriel and avenue Matignon, 8e.
Métro: Champs-Élysées-Clémenceau, Franklin-D.-Roosevelt

The *guignol* horror show that has entranced kids for ever. Wednesdays, Saturdays, Sundays, holidays, 3:00, 4:00 and 5:00 p.m.

Marionnettes du Champs-de-Mars
Champs-de-Mars, 7e
Métro: École Militaire

During school holidays, every day at 3:15, 4:15 p.m. Otherwise Wednesdays, Saturdays and Sundays only, same times.

Marionnettes de Montsouris
avenue Reilles-rue Gazan, near the lake, 14e
Métro: Cité-Universitaire, Glacière

Mondays, Tuesdays, Wednesdays, Saturdays, Sundays, 2:30, 3:30 and 4:30 p.m.

Théâtre Guignol Anatole
parc des Buttes-Chamont, 19e
Métro: Laumière

Wednesdays, 3:00 and 4:00 p.m.; Saturdays, Sundays and holidays, 3:00, 4:00 and 5:00 p.m.

Children's Theatre   Paris is extremely rich in children's theatres which do magic shows, straight plays and pageants. Often there are extra performances during Christmas and Easter holidays. Some theatres close for five to eight weeks during the period mid-July to mid-September, so it's best to refer to the current *Pariscope* or *L'Officiel des Spectacles* for last-minute information.

Two of the best which usually have something going the whole year:

Cité des Sciences et de l'Industrie
30 avenue Corentin-Cariou, 19e
Métro: Porte de la Villette

HOURS: 10:00 a.m. to 6:00 p.m., 7:00 p.m. on Sundays. Closed Mondays.

ADMISSION: 45F, 35F reduced, under-7 free.

Musée en Herbe: Jardin d'Acclimatation
Bois de Boulogne, 16e
Métro: Sablons, Pont de Neuilly

HOURS: Every day from 10:00 a.m. to 6:00 p.m., Saturdays from 2:00 to 6:00 p.m. Tickets give you entry to a theatre performance and the museum.

ADMISSION: 25F, 16F reduced.

TELEVISION

French TV is *very* French. If your hotel has a set in the office, breakfast-room or lobby, linger and look. When a big soccer match, race or (best of all) the Tour de France is on, make for the nearest TV dealer and join the crowd which will stand there for ever with boos, whistles, groans and some racy French language. The TV news 'speakerines' are chosen for intelligence and wit; they sparkle – eyes, teeth, lipstick and intellect – in the hard, brilliant studio lights.

PARIS, PLUS

VERSAILLES

Some of the most alluring places to visit are within an hour or two of Paris by public transport or by fast train. It would be almost illegal to be in Paris and not see Versailles. This vast complex of parks, palace, and pavilions known as Les Trianons, is almost impossible to comprehend when you are on the spot. It's wise to collect and study a good small guidebook before you go. The *Blue Guide* (see page 228) has a very good, succinct and easily followed section on the Château, the park and gardens, and if you have already invested in it you really won't need another book. Versailles is easy to reach, and if you have the time to do it, go for a few hours three or four times, rather than wearing yourself out mentally and physically by one long visit.

You can reach Versailles free with your *Carte Paris Visite* (Zones 1 and 4). Métro to Pont de Sèvres, then bus No. 171, but it takes about an hour, or RER C train to Versailles: Rive Gauche. SNCF trains from Saint Lazare and Montparnasse stations take about half an hour, but be prepared for long queues at the ticket windows; buy an *aller-retour* ticket and make sure you go to Versailles Rive Gauche (RG), nowhere else.

Half-day all-inclusive tours, by coach, including transport, entrance to major attractions and guide are between 220–270F from many ticket agencies, but in our view to be avoided. You are shoved through at a brisk trot, told where to look, never allowed to lag or sit down, and returned to Paris more dead than alive. You can do the whole thing at your own pace for half the price.

The main treasures of Versailles – the Chapel, the State Apartments of the King and Queen, and the Hall of Mirrors – must be seen by every visitor. The fee for them is 45F, reduced to 35F if you are between 18 and 25 or over 60.

The King's Private Bedroom and the royal Opera, the Queen's Rooms, and Madame Du Barry's Rooms, can be seen only by guided tours, lasting an hour and a quarter, and require a supplement to the 45F fee.

The Grand Trianon costs 25F, the Petit Trianon 15F.

The Le Nôtre gardens carved out of the swamp, and the Mansart fountains, a marvel of hydraulic engineering, are 'musts'. If you can visit more than once, don't miss two of the smaller delights: the Musée des Voitures, with its perfectly preserved state coaches, wedding carriages and hunting *calèches*; and the extraordinary Hameau, the rustic village where Marie-Antoinette went on playing at being a country wife up to 1789.

Guided tours of the Versailles park and grounds are available; information from the Versailles Tourist Office, tel: 01 30 84 76 18 or 30 84 74 00.

The Château is open from 9:00 a.m. to 5:30 p.m. and to 6:30 from May to September; the Grand and Petit Trianon are open Tuesday to

Friday, 10:00 a.m. to 12:30 p.m. and 2:00 to 5:30 p.m. Everything is closed on Mondays and public holidays.

CHARTRES

Again, it can be done by taking a tour bus, which gives you cosy but costly shepherding; or, cheaper, more fun, and infinitely more flexible, take the train from Gare de Montparnasse as early as you can and wander round on your own. Trains run about every 45 minutes from 6:26 in the morning, with the last train back at 10:53 at night. Return fare is free with Eurailpass.

After visiting the Musée des Beaux-Arts at 29 cloître Notre-Dame (10F entrance), wander round the delightful town and absorb the miracle of the cathedral by yourself at your own pace, unblurred by tour-guide patter. Then find a small neighbourhood restaurant, which will be half the price and twice the pleasure of any suggested by an organized group, and eat what you want at a price you want to pay. Or take a picnic. Get a small, good guidebook to Chartres before you leave Paris, and read it on the train. Henry Adams, the nineteenth-century American writer, did rather a good job on both Chartres and Mont-St-Michel.

A coach tour to Chartres costs around 265F, takes five hours (and since it's eighty-eight miles from Paris, travelling time eats into Chartres time); it gives you a view of Rambouillet and Maintenon châteaux on the way, and a guided tour of the cathedral. Various companies do tours on different days, so check with a travel agent for details or pick up a pamphlet at the Office de Tourisme at 127 Champs-Élysées.

THE MONET GARDENS – GIVERNY

A coach tour to the famous water-lily gardens of Monet now costs from 330F for half a day from Paris – don't do it, as the bus trip out is intensely boring and the commentary more so, with piped music all the way back. Instead, take the train from St-Lazare to Vernon for 104F, and bus to Giverny, pay about 35F for admission to the house and gardens, wander freely, picnic, and come back when you choose. The ponds and bridges and flowers are exactly as they were painted. Closed 31 October–1 April.

MONT-ST-MICHEL

Don't take a coach tour, they are very expensive. If you don't mind a little navigating, take public transportation. Take the train from Paris Montparnasse to Rennes at 8:20 a.m.; at Rennes (about two hours later) follow the sign *Sortie Nord* to the *Gare Routière* (bus station, just next door), buy a return coach fare to Mont-St-Michel for 116F, leaving at 10:50 a.m., board the bus and you'll be there by 12:05 p.m. Buses leave Mont-St-Michel at 4:10 p.m.; ask for the return schedule at the *Gare Routière* ticket counter. This trip is recommended, it's not very expensive, it's all in French and it's an experience you'll never forget.

MALMAISON

These two châteaux are curiously neglected by visitors to Paris, unless they are passionate about Napoleon. Take the RER from Charles de Gaulle-Étoile to la Défense, five minutes away, then the No. 158A bus to the Malmaison-Château stop. Buses run about every 15 minutes and take about 25 minutes to the bus stop nearest the Château, then it's about an eight-minute walk.

The RER station at the Charles de Gaulle-Étoile Métro stop is huge, eerie, depopulated, and if you get lost you'll find yourself asking directions from a weary flower-seller. If you have a *Carte Paris Visite*, travel on the RER and the suburban bus line is free. Otherwise, take a ticket from the automatic dispenser (one way). Follow signs marked 'St-Germain-en-Laye' for trains to La Défense. On the No. 158A bus, if you're travelling without a *Carte Paris Visite*, the fare is one ticket.

Malmaison is the Château bought and furnished by Napoleon for Josephine, set in most lovely grounds. Across the park is the Bois-Preau *petit château* which has souvenirs of Napoleon's final exile at St-Helena, and the Church at Reuil-Malmaison has the tombs of Josephine and Queen Hortense. You can't wander around: when a little group has collected, a guide appears. The tour takes about an hour and a quarter, it's all in French, so if you are a true Napoleon fan, read the very good entry in the *Blue Guide* (page 228). At the end of the tour (which tells you more than you want to know about the history of the porcelain plates and the very banal paintings), give the guide one or two francs. The Château is unexpectedly small for such a great man (and the beds are tiny);

but for those who expect Napoleon to rise from the dead and take over France, it's very touching. Open 10:00 a.m. to 12:30 p.m., 1:30 to 5:30 p.m. (last visits noon and 5:00 p.m.). Closed Tuesdays, public holidays.

Au bon marché (The shops)

What are paupers doing shopping anyhow? Generally speaking, you've got a much better chance of picking up bargains on your home territory. Still, there are things that the French and French shops do better than almost anyone else. And if we have to put a label on what that *je ne sais quoi* is, we'd say it was attention to details. You'll find it in the cut of clothes, the choice and display of foods, and in accessories for you or your home. With space and the weight of your luggage in mind, we'd suggest small things that show individuality: if you wear specs, look at French frames; or replace your watch, buy a new fountain pen, find just the right piece of jewellery, tie or belt. If you're a seamstress, look at the vast range of fabrics and buttons. If you're houseproud, this could be your chance to buy the doorknobs or finger-plates that will make the difference to your home.

Shopping is distinct from window-shopping, though you can combine the two. What you crave in Lanvin or Kenzo can be duplicated or approximated elsewhere at a discount; or found 'once-worn' at a *dépôt-vente*. You can use Paris to stock up on outlandish items of food: pickles and conserves that would cost a mint in Soho, available for next to nothing at the Prisunic. Second-hand books, museum prints and every kind of flea-market hand-me-down. But remember, you've got to fit it all into your luggage and get it home.

Manners: as everywhere, you can go farther and faster on a few elements of *la politesse* and a smile. In some situations, however, no amount of manners will do you the least bit of good. Sales-people in large establishments tend to be more abrupt and less willing to help than in small ones. Solution: know what you're looking for; find out the correct French terms (the name of the article, the colour, the size, the brand); do not be browbeaten into buying something you don't want; if one person won't tell you where to find it, try another.

If you can, pay for everything in cash. A bank will always give you a better exchange rate than a shop (or for that matter, a hotel or restaurant) for traveller's cheques or foreign currency. However, even really small shops take VISA and Mastercard cards, which are a considerable convenience if cash is low and you've *got* to shop.

BARGAINS

Here we include cheap shops – not resale. Paris is a mine of good clothes at less than Parisian prices if you know where to look. The rue St-Placide in the 6e is lined with shops plastered with signs: 'Dégriffes', 'Soldes Permanents', 'Les Prix Dingues'. The rue St-Dominique, in the 7e, is a magnet for bargain hunters. However, be warned that shops in both these streets have a mushroom growth and disappear just as fast. A big vacant shop can be stocked up with clothes for men, women and children, from various sources, do a roaring trade and vanish in six months or less. La Clef des Soldes was a biggish place in the rue St-Dominique a few years ago, specializing in de luxe ready-to-wear for men and women (Cardin, Hechter, etc.). Then it went completely over to sports and ski-wear, the next year it was gone, and then it was back again, full of racks and bins . . .

While you're out and about, look for *dépôt-ventes* and signs for *braderies de mode*. At the former you can find the almost new musthaves of yesterday left by wealthy women with active closet turnover, and at the latter you might find last season's line of Kryzia, Esprit, Tehen and Lolita Lempicka . . .

These shops can be fun to fish around in. They often have bins of oddments, or racks of clothes that can be just what you are looking for (equally good chance of nothing but monster coats and dwarf dresses). With patience you can turn something up.

This listing is the current 1996 crop of good cheapies all over Paris. Don't write us a letter of reprimand if they've disappeared. We would rather have a letter from you telling us of *your* discoveries, so that we can look them over ourselves and possibly include them in a future edition.

1ER ARRONDISSEMENT

La Clef des Marques
20 place du Marché-St-Honoré
Tel: 01 47 03 90 40
Métro: Tuileries

This is a great big bargain hunting-ground – just opened in 1996 – where everything is a quarter of the original price. 'Everything' ranges from designer prêt-à-porter pieces to street and sportswear, lingerie, children's clothing and shoes. (See page 222.)

2E ARRONDISSEMENT

Kookai Le Stock
82 rue Réaumur
Tel: 01 45 08 93 69
Métro: Sentier, Réaumur

An immense Kookai outlet in a stylishly decorated loft space. Really inexpensive, categorized and priced by colour. Check out the swingy printed sundresses priced between 60F and 100F. Open Monday to Saturday from 10:00 a.m. to 7:00 p.m.

4E ARRONDISSEMENT

rue Vieille du Temple
Métro: St-Paul or Hôtel de Ville

This is one of many streets running through the Marais where you'll find great restaurants, bars, cafés and quirky shops. Down towards the rue de Rivoli there are three or four small boutiques that specialize in *fin-de-séries*, quality brand names sold at temptingly low prices. These aren't *haute couture* catwalk cast-offs but chic French (everyday) clothing. Often the brand tag has been cut off, but everything else is still intact and rarely more than a season old.

MOUTON A CINQ PATTES: No. 15

Directly translated as 'sheep with five feet'. A large selection of men's and women's clothing. You won't find a whole line of seasonal coordinates on a rack here as you might at Stock Griffes, but there are some *haute couture*-ish pieces that look like they're catwalk material as well as a big open crate of T-shirts, scarves and accessories at rock-bottom prices. Shoes, too. Tel: 42 71 86 30.

Also:

130 avenue Victor Hugo, 16e

19 rue Gregoire de Tours, 6e

STOCK GRIFFES: No. 17

Fine brands – with the back section of the store, in 1996, devoted exclusively to Tehen – sold at a substantial discount. Here the racks are packed solid with quality goodies including original pieces by up-and-coming designers, so take your time. Tel: 48 04 82 34.

Also:

25 rue Dauphine, 6e

166 rue du Faubourg St-Antoine, 12e

1 rue des Trois Frères, 18e

ZADIG ET VOLTAIRE: No. 25

Zadig, Voltaire and others. End of the season pieces, coordinated and moderately priced. Great batik sarong skirts and dresses for under 200F. Tel: 01 42 72 84 83.

6E ARRONDISSEMENT

rue St-Placide

Métro: St-Placide, Sèvres-Babylone

Bus: No. 96

HOURS: mostly Mondays through Saturdays, 10:00 a.m. to 7:00 p.m.

The whole of this street is lined with shops which offer either a) fine value at average prices, or b) real cheaperinos varying from a silk scarf at 20F to a designer T-shirt for around 75F. We have concentrated on just one length of the street, after which point our *meute des magasins* – which roughly translates as shop-hound – gave up and fell into a very expensive tearoom for restoratives. There are many more shops to be discovered. These she found in a single day:

DU PAREIL AU MÊME: No. 7
Simon Benharrous has never publicly revealed his secret: how Du Pareil au Même puts beautiful, well-made children's clothes on sale for so little. This is a chain of small stores that offer typical French designs for children at remarkably low prices. A cotton cardigan costs 44F, a summer dress in sunflower print costs 65F.

BOUTIQUE STOCK: Nos. 26, 30 and 51
Jumpers – some angora – for 100F. Also, three shirts for 100F and some more finely tailored pieces from 170F to 470F – the latter for a swishy short-sleeved, silk jacket.

PHILOMÈNE: No. 34
A favourite shopping place of ours for about eight years, very good stock, mainly raincoats. They have good winter coats, sometimes handsome tailored shirts for women, classic styles, beginning at 100F.

BRADERIE: Nos. 36, 46 and 56
Very good prices for some famous names, like Versace's Versus jeans, in silk for 399F. Also less famous makes at proportionately cheaper prices.

BOBA: No. 37
Very *House and Garden* gifty things – gadgets for 25F to such novel items as a porcelain lemon dish for 59F, oversized heavy glass stemmed 'sundae' dishes, 29F; a magnificent chrome-and-wood fish-shaped tray, 195F, and silk flowers, pot-pourri, little flowered boxes, telephone pads, wicker, porcelain, glass, crystal, wooden things at all prices. Major credit cards accepted.

DISCOUNT R: No. 37A
Lots and lots of dresses, two-piece summery-type suits, all for less than 100F.

VU D'ICI: No. 42
Sportswear for men and women, and very smart too – look for well-made T-shirts (59F), jogging outfits, trainers, sweatshirts.

DEXTER: next door to Vu d'Ici
More elegant sportswear at half the prices you'd pay at Galeries Lafayette or Au Printemps.

RETOUCHES: No. 43
If you're prepared to spend 250F for a single beautifully styled floral dress or skirt, make for Rétouches, and hope it is still there.

MODA: No. 45
A shoe shop that has stayed at the same address for several years, featuring Sonia Rykiel women's shoes for around 430F, other brands begin at 350F.

BARGAINS DE MANSFIELD: No. 47
End-of-range shoes for men and women, elegantly conservative styles, about half the original price of this expensive brand.

L'ANNEXE: No. 48
Inexpensive and for the most part fairly well-made men's casual clothes. VISA, Mastercard and American Express cards accepted. Open Mondays through Saturdays, 10:00 a.m. to 7:30 p.m. but sometimes inexplicably closed.

LE TRAIN BLEU: No. 55
A big shop with several floors of toys and games and models, and the only place our shopper has come across that sold a hexagonal chess set (three sets of chessmen play on a hexagonal board).

LARA ET LES GARÇONS: No. 60
Formerly Magic Kids, this shop caters for children 0 to 16, and the prices are remarkable value for jeans, shirts, trainers, some little girls' dresses; a few boxes and racks for the young mothers of their primary customers. A size 8 (American) friend bought a small wardrobe of cotton trousers, shirts, dungarees, straight off the teenage racks.

7E ARRONDISSEMENT

rue St-Dominique
Métro: Latour-Maubourg

We've seen the street of bargain shops go up-market and down in the ten years we've been shopping here. This year we had the help of our *meute des magasins* who has the flair of a truffle-hunter when it comes to smart buys. Now it seems to have settled into a good mix of gentrified and low-low priced shops. It's very busy, cheerful, full of people enjoying bargain-hunting. In between shops, you will be able to eat well, have superb coffee and pastries. Try **Choumieux**, at No. 79, **Au Petit Paname** in the rue Amélie, or **Le Malar** (good cheap salads) in the rue Malar for an inexpensive lunch. Most of the shops here take credit cards. They are usually open Mondays through Saturdays, about 10:00 or 11:00 a.m., until 6:30 or 7:00 p.m. Some are closed on Mondays.

MYC: No. 54
Upmarket, and rather expensive women's clothes, but compared to the rue St-Honoré, they are *not* high-priced. For example, a nice wool suit, with a finely detailed blouse, at 1500F, was less than half the price you would expect to pay. Major credit cards accepted.

MELI MELO: No. 60
Linens, pillows, duvets, duvet covers, Pierre Cardin bedlinens, 'Les Baux de Provence' designs for bed and table. A Ted Lapidus towelling dressing-gown was seen for 299F – you could pay more than that elsewhere for one much less stylish, commented our demon shopper. Also furnishing fabric, chairs, small gifts. Major credit cards accepted.

GISQUET: No. 62
One of Paris's great *boulangeries/pâtisseries*, with pastries in the window as exquisite as jewels. Gisquet is not cheap, but it will give you an idea of what Paris is all about. Presentation as well as taste matter, from paper-lace mats, to the smell of chocolate, vanilla, and the final flourish of the ribbon that ties up even the smallest package.

COUCOU C'NOUS: No. 80
Christian Dior, Valentino, Ungaro ... Big brands at lower, though not rock-bottom, prices.

FIL À FIL: No. 81
Beautiful shirts for men and women, beginning at 315F up, up, up. Some fine costume jewellery, links, studs, for about 250F. Prices are not low, but the quality is fine. Fil à Fil shirts seem to last the wearer a lifetime. French girls buy the men's shirts to wear as cover-ups on the beach.

SAFARI: No. 83
A shop which displays some of its wares in the window, and keeps many more in the back room. Great shoes at good prices, many with famous designers' names.

BOOKSHOP: No. 78
International books: French, German, Italian, English, all at cut prices, a rarity in Paris. This well-stocked shop sells postcards, guidebooks, art books, novels and best-sellers. Closed Mondays.

LA CLEF DES MARQUES: No. 99
A huge bargain bazaar crammed to the rafters with bins and racks for all ages and both sexes – brilliant bargains. At various times, our friends have bought: 'racing' maillots for serious swimming, 78F; Indian silk handkerchief-scarves, two for 10F; Dior fancy tights, 10F the pair; Ellesse cotton blouses, 59F; shoes for under 100F; furry-lined anoraks, 150F; huge down-padded ski jackets, 200F; packs of baby-pants, ten for 60F. Major credit cards accepted. Open Mondays, noon to 7:00 p.m.; Tuesdays through Fridays, 10:00 a.m. to 2:15 p.m., 3:15 to 7:00 p.m.; Saturdays, 10:00 a.m. to 1:15 p.m., 2:15 to 7:00 p.m. There's another shop at 20 rue du Marché-Saint-Honoré, 1er, tel: 01 47 03 90 40.

9E ARRONDISSEMENT

boulevard Haussmann
Métro: Havre-Caumartin
RER: Auber

If you're a serious shopper, here is where to start. Not as smart as the avenue de l'Opéra, it is still a Paris must. There are Galeries Lafayette, Printemps, Monoprix, Marks and Spencer – all within one fair-sized *endroit*. Dozens of discount and specialist shops are tucked away behind and between these giants.

AU PRINTEMPS: 64 boulevard Haussmann
Go on a Saturday to enjoy the fun of the stalls outside this elegant department store – but go inside as well, to admire the vast range of goods and the building's architecture. In Printemps-Maison, there are both chic and practical goods. In the Printemps main building, for clothes and fashion, you'll see a very good selection of what's in style. Men have their own shop, Brummel, just behind the main store.

PARALLÈLE: 68 rue de Caumartin
Behind Au Printemps, there's a pedestrian area facing the Église St-Louis. Parallèle is one of the long-stayers – a discount shop with casual clothes for women – racks outside, with Naf-Naf pullovers from 175F, suits and wool jackets for around 399F, and bright, cool summer clothes even in August.

JIGGER: No. 56 bis rue de la Chausée d'Antin
While you're wandering around here, listening to street musicians, see what's on offer at Jigger, you never know what you will find: T-shirts for 50F, shirts from 60F up. An ever-changing stock of inexpensive and fashionable clothes, dresses for about 150F. Open Monday through Saturday, 10:00 a.m. to 7:00 p.m.

PRISUNIC: 56 rue Caumartin
The enterprising Prisunic chain is the French – very French – equivalent of what Woolworths once was, but there the resemblance ends. You can buy a light-bulb, or saucepans in fashionable colours, food processors, lamps and waffle-makers in the household depart-

ment. And, year after year, smartly dressed Parisian girls shop early to find trendy accessories in the clothing department. In 1996: towelling cloth T-shirts, the latest in pastel linen pencil-pants and matching jackets, tennis dresses, bathing suits in every style, brightly coloured straw hand-bags, hats, school satchels, and printed espadrilles. A great women's lingerie department, too.

Check out the food department for herbs, mustards, wines, olive oil flavoured with rosemary or basil, a large selection of cheese, and the *pâtisserie*. Open Mondays through Saturdays, 9:00 a.m. to 8:30 p.m. Closed Sundays.

11E ARRONDISSEMENT

rue de la Roquette
Métro: Voltaire, Bastille

The maze of small ancient streets around the Bastille has been disrupted by the construction of the Opéra. But though the whole texture of the neighbourhood has changed, there is still one wonderful street, the rue de la Roquette, which retains its old character. (Most of the shops mentioned here are closed on Mondays.)

Start midway, at the Voltaire Métro and the sprawling shopping square shaded by big trees. Walk south towards the Bastille. The first shops sell handsome, inexpensive shoes – this was the *quartier* of the shoemakers. **El Indio Feliz**, at No. 69, has a Peruvian owner, who imports painted masks, toys, serapes, rugs, tapestries, reed pipes, and covetable handmade jewellery. Prices from 20F to about 150F.

On a side street to the east, **Tonkam** at 29 rue Keller has an incredible collection of *bandes dessinées*, 'BDs' to the French, and comic books, posters, fanzines, badges, pins.

Down a side street, at No. 21 rue Daval, is **Duelle** which sells jewellery miraculously made from wood, bronze, seashells, driftwood, tin, iron.

18E ARRONDISSEMENT

rue Séveste/rue de Steinkerque
Métro: Anvers, Barbès-Rochechouart

Between the boulevard Rochechouart and the Butte Montmartre there's a warren of streets given over to discount clothes, shoes, luggage and fabrics. Many of the goods are Third World imports, but if cheap and cheerful is what you want, the choice here is vast. The rue Séveste is a street market, with stalls outside, and some very inexpensive clothes indoors – perfect impulse shopping.

TATI 'LES PLUS BAS PRIX' 4–28 boulevard Rochechouart
At the Barbès-Rochechouart Métro stop, this complex of big, untidy and very cheap shops deserves a small book of its own. One of a chain, this Tati is paradise for those who have the time and the knack of picking through racks, shelves and bins of clothes despite being jostled and overheated. If you can manage this, you'll get smart clothes, often copies of rue Faubourg St-Honoré fashions at incredibly low prices. Alaïa, the fashion designer, has even designed huge canvas bags and beach towels using the pattern of Tati's carrier bags – a giant, pink hound's-tooth check.

Tati is divided into several shops: **Tati Hommes** for men, **Tati Femmes** for women, and especially good value, the children's shop. Most men won't go in. Most women, including some of the *richissimes* of Paris society, love to find silk-look dressing-gowns for 99F.

Also:
13 place République, 3e
140 rue de Rennes, 6e
106 Faubourg du Temple, 11e

CLUB ROCHECHOUART: 52 boulevard Rochechouart, 18e
A fashion editor told us about the Club a number of years ago – an unexpected shop in this very raffish street of cheaper-than-cheap shops. It has some very smart clothes for women, few of a kind, and you may have to go back several times to find what you want. A striking flowered print dress, probably a quick copy of one shown in

the summer Paris collections, was 280F – *'très Ascot'*, said the friendly manager. Summer suits in pastel linen for 399F. Open Mondays, noon to 7:00 p.m.; Tuesday to Saturday, 10:00 a.m. to 5:00 p.m. Open the year round, even in August. VISA cards accepted.

MARCHÉ ST-PIERRE, 18E
Open Monday afternoons, Tuesday-Saturday all day.

Fine fabric buys begin here. If you have the time and interest, work your way round the neighbourhood – rue d'Orsel, rue Briquet, rue Séveste, to find some of the most attractive, most French materials imaginable. Stock changes rapidly, but last time we saw linens at 99F a metre, all colours of stretch fabrics, crushed velours, shiny satins, beautiful lace, great prints for summer, tweeds and wool blends for winter. Look for upholstery and curtain fabrics capable of being transformed into spectacular clothes.

TISSUS REINE, 5 place St-Pierre
Great for *haute couture* fabrics, wools, printed cottons and blends, unrefined linens, silks and cottons; buttons, accessories and patterns are on the 2nd floor. Check the racks of material outside for bargains. This department store gets very crowded on Saturday, so try early afternoon on a weekday.

TISSUS DREYFUS, 20 rue Pierre Picard
Bargain boxes outside, several floors with exquisite velvets, animal prints, silks and the latest trendy fabrics inside . . .

TISSUS BUTTE MONTMARTRE, 5 rue Pierre Picard
A good example of the kind of fabric/material store you'll find while browsing in this area.

Almost all of the streets around the Marché St-Pierre have a view of the Sacré-Coeur, so when you're finished with your bargain-hunting you can slide into a chair at a café and contemplate the 'Taj of Paris', or climb up for a view of the city.

BIS! BIS! *Second-hand*

It's *encore, encore* for clothes, handbags, jewellery, scarves, shoes which rich people wear four or five times, then pass on to be resold. Paris abounds in shops featuring 'gently used', very good-quality stuff; this is how all the pretty Parisian girls who carry Vuitton bags and wear Charles Jourdan shoes manage to buy them on their salaries. It's one of the great features of city life.

You'll happen upon second-hand shops and *dépot-ventes* in all areas of the city. The clothes and shoes are generally high-quality, ready-to-wear pieces ranging from Naf Naf to Chanel, in recent or classic styles. If you're lucky, you can find a timeless black wool Chanel suit from the ready-to-wear collection of last year, for about 2000F–3000F, a fraction of its original price. The one we saw was buttoned in gilt, lined with silk, from hem to braided edge. Or a fine polished leather or reptile handbag, about 500F, instantly recognisable as one originally bought in a famous shop in the Palais Royal arcade.

More rarely, you can find superb men's clothes and beautiful, once-expensive children's clothes.

Some of these shops have been going for years, and have well-established connections not only with the elegant women of the *quartier*, but with the couturiers themselves. Often there are superbly finished, luxurious silk and brocade evening dresses, worn only in the seasonal collections, or shoes that have only walked on carpeted catwalks. They are almost always model sizes (for which read: tall and thin), and the shoes are apt to be narrow. If your taste runs to the extreme of fashion, these shops can be a joy. But it takes time and the patience to return several times if you don't find your little Yves St-Laurent treasure on the first visit. Most of the shops are closed on Mondays, and almost always in August. Usually they have a clearly posted sign (in French) about their policy on returns or exchanges, and some of them have salespeople who speak excellent English and are very helpful.

Most clothes are legibly labelled with the selling price (sometimes with the original price). In the few that we found where garments were shown without price tags, we had the feeling that the owner of the shop matched the price to the customer. In these cases, feel free to raise your eyebrows, say something like '*Un peu trop cher*' (a bit too expensive), and put the garment back on the rack. This tip was passed on by a friend who buys every year in one well-known shop, and never pays the asking price. Keep a steady nerve. Be prepared to leave the shop without buying anything. Check seams, hem, buttons, linings in men's suits and coats, the insides of shoes and handbags. Look for small spots, dust, or face powder on a luxury bag. Point out any defects which might bring the price down. In every resale shop we checked, however, the merchandise was in fine condition – having been cleaned, brushed or polished before being put on view.

These vendors of de luxe merchandise sometimes have a few rails of women's and men's clothes that come from the better French ready-to-wear manufacturers at the end of a season – special purchases in small quantities. They're often worth going through carefully, as what you take home – colours, fabrics, fine finish, the general air of Parisian smartness – will delight you when your Paris visit has become only a memory.

Some resale shops spring up hopefully in fashionable parts of Paris, buying fairly ephemeral clothes from the young and capricious. By their nature, these rather tentative shops may not be very long-lived. Their survival hangs on their supply of customers to bring in clothes, as well as those who come in to buy them.

It is hoped that all the addresses below will still be in business for a while: they are the best-established and most trusted by the more fashion-minded of our Paris friends. But don't lose your cool if you find they have moved or gone out of business. Most of the neighbour-hoods where they are located are worth a visit if only for local colour; and if one shop is gone, another one a hundred yards away may catch your eye. In summer 1996:

2E ARRONDISSEMENT

Rétro Activité
38 rue du Vertbois
Métro: Temple

In the wholesale-clothing district, a 'second-hand Rose' blossoms in a tiny crowded shop. Go! Great 1930s–1940s–1980s clothes, clean, smart and good quality – men's Burberrys sometimes; silk night-gowns at about 100F — the thing to wear to smart parties. Open Tuesdays through Saturdays, noon to 7:00 p.m.

4E ARRONDISSEMENT

Son et Image
8 rue Sainte-Croix de la Bretonnerie
Métro: Hôtel-de-Ville
Tel: 01 42 76 03 36

This recently opened Marais shop has racks of authentic 1950s–1970s clothes for men and women. In June 1996, short floral sundresses were under 200F, bold coloured men's short and long sleeved shirts were 35–50F. Very suited to 1990s clubbing fashions.

Also at Les Halles, 85 & 87 rue St-Denis, 1er *arrondissement* (*Métro*: Les Halles).

7E ARRONDISSEMENT

De Fil en Troc
1 avenue de La Motte-Picquet
Métro: La Motte-Picquet-Grenelle

Clothes and household objects in perfect condition. Big names spotted here include Sonia Rykiel, Apostrophe and Marella. Not dirt cheap, but less expensive than the freshly arrived series in department stores.

8E ARRONDISSEMENT

Anna Lowe
35 avenue Matignon
Métro: St-Philippe-du-Roule

Investment clothes, according to our Paris shop spy, sell for a fraction of the price they might command round the corner in the rue du Faubourg St-Honoré. Anna Lowe was a model and has connections with the couture houses, from which she gets end-of-season clothes. From the best ready-to-wear lines, she buys fashions only two months after they first appear. At various times, you'll find Yves St-Laurent Rive Gauche, Alaïa, Comme des Garçons, Karl Lagerfield, Kenzo, Guy Laroche, Hermès. Ms Lowe also has handsome clothes made especially for her shop, and to her taste which is perfect. Simple alterations are free! Open Mondays through Saturdays, 10:30 a.m. to 7:00 p.m. Closed the first two weeks in August.

Le Troc de Trucs
50 rue Colisée, 8e
Métro: St-Philippe-du-Roule

This is a *dépôt-vente* where well-heeled women leave their last season's clothes to be resold. You'll find superb-quality women's fashions for as little as one-quarter of their original price. Open Mondays through Saturdays, 3:00 to 7:30 p.m.

15E ARRONDISSEMENT

Troc-Ève
25 rue Violet, 15e
Tel: 01 45 79 38 36
Métro: Dupleix

Very small, very friendly, and packed with fashionable women's clothes. Some are new, end of range, all chosen with a fine hand; others are carefully maintained high-quality *encore* clothes. Also little antiques such as a toy-size, working carriage clock, and porcelain, crystal, jewellery, picture frames. Run by delightful women, it's open Tuesdays through Saturdays, 10:00 a.m. to 7:00 p.m. Closed August.

Trocanelle
35 rue de la Croix-Nivert, 15e
Tel: 01 43 06 34 15
Métro: Cambronne

Slightly worn, high-style clothes for women – not bargain prices but good buys. Also some new dresses, blouses, suits. Many superb-quality accessories, shoes, handbags, scarves. Open Tuesdays through Saturdays, 11:00 a.m. to 7:00 p.m. Closed August.

16E ARRONDISSEMENT

Réciproque
89, 92, 93, 95, 101 and 123 rue de la Pompe, 16e
Métro: rue de la Pompe

Huge and with a tremendously wide selection, worth spending a morning wandering around these shops. At No. 89 you'll find housewares; No. 93 women's evening-wear and accessories; No. 95 two floors of street and sportswear; at No. 101 menswear; and No. 123 coats and bags. You'll find well-arranged racks of good couture clothes worn a few times, by private clients or at fashion shows, jewellery, scarves and fine gloves and hats. Open Tuesdays through Saturdays, 11:00 a.m. to 7:30 p.m. Usually closed for the last week in August.

17E ARRONDISSEMENT

Trocade
5 and 9 avenue de Villiers
Tel: 01 42 67 80 14
Métro: Villiers

A fashionable neighbourhood, a beautiful, tree-shaded street, rich surroundings, and the clothes reflect this ambience. Prices are not low, but for *la haute couture* (both men and women) this is the place. For women, No. 9 has Chanel, Valentino and Lagerfield. Open

Mondays through Saturdays, 10:00 a.m. to 7:00 p.m., closed Monday mornings.

Trocissimo
18 rue Fourcroy
Métro: Ternes

The chic local women drop their outdated finery off at this *dépôt vente*. It's small, but wall-to-wall with prêt-à-porter suits, dresses, coats, shoes and accessories: one of everything and a wide variety.

18E ARRONDISSEMENT

Derrière les Fagots
8 rue des Abbesses
Métro: Abbesses

Really priceless clothes from 1890 to late 1960s – plus jewellery, mesh coin-purses, crocodile handbags, hatpins and fine shoes for women. For men, look at English tweed overcoats, grey Ascot-type toppers and walking sticks. Some of the best things are not on view, but Elaine will bring them out if you are a serious visitor. The windows are like jewel-cases, full of 1930s' and 1940s' costume jewellery worth a fortune, but gently priced here. Open Tuesdays through Saturdays, noon to 7:30 p.m. English is spoken.

GIFT SHOPPING

For a fairly light, inexpensive gift idea, take home a French book for francophile friends (or just to keep up on your French). There are 10F books known as The Thousand and One Nights that are attractively printed and come with a bibliography and a postscript. They arrived in France in 1994 and a better bargain couldn't be had. Others have followed: Librio, Maxi-Poche, the list goes on. See Bookstores in 'Staying afloat', page 219, or try the **Librairies Fontaine**, a chain of French bookstores in Paris which have very good sales –

'livres neufs à prix réduit' – and a large selection that includes French culture, art, philosophy, literature and beautifully illustrated French children's stories.

Librairies Fontaine
5 rue du 4 Septembre, 2e
88 rue de Sèvres, 7e
50 rue de Laborde, 8e
95 avenue Victor Hugo, 16e
69 avenue Kléber, 16e
48 rue de Lévis, 17e

Otherwise, if you want to shop till you drop, the shops of Paris are crammed with perfect gifts – at a price. Wander along the rue du Faubourg St-Honoré, or the rue de Rivoli, or rue Royale, or among the boutiques of the Left Bank, and you will begin to feel like a poor relation at a rich man's door. But once you get your eye in, you can with some perseverance find an enticing selection of small portable presents at a fraction of the big-name shop prices.

A good gift-shopping street in Paris is a very old one – rue de la Roquette, 11e, beginning at the Bastille. For full details, see page 196.
Note: many shops close during August for the annual holiday; and hours can change, from time to time. If a shop has closed, or even disappeared entirely, it's not a disaster; you'll wander the neighbourhood and find places of your own (let us know!).

MONOPRIX AND PRISUNIC

These have turned up frequently in these pages as perfect hunting grounds for food, clothes and household gadgets. Consider them for gifts, too. Make for the larger shops, near the Opéra, in the Marais, near Galeries Lafayette, in the more fashionable areas of the Right Bank, which quickly seize upon the year's fashionable ideas and copy them down. At 21 avenue de l'Opéra, 1er, *Métro:* Opéra, Monoprix usually has silk-look scarves in subtle colours for as little as 50–99F.

Look in Prisunic for traditional French earthenware plates and cups, handsome oven glassware, well-designed and colourful plastic for the *micro-ondes* oven, a range of handsome Italian glass refrigerator jugs and boxes: *really* inexpensive.

LES GRAND SURFACES SUPERMARKETS

Supermarkets such as Ed l'Épicier and GS-20 are a great and relatively untapped source of small, inexpensive and desirable household gadgets, speciality foods and good inexpensive wines on promotion.

Many supermarkets are open on Sundays until the early afternoon. During the week some, like Ed l'Épicier, close for lunch and then stay open until about 7:00 p.m. Often they stay open later in summer.

1ER ARRONDISSEMENT

FNAC
1 rue Pierre Lescot, Forum des Halles, 1er, *Métro:* Les Halles
136 rue de Rennes, 6e, *Métro:* Montparnasse
26 avenue Wagram, 8e, *Métro:* Étoile

These are big, well-stocked shops with books, magazines, cassettes, CDs, computers, cameras, and small gifts and gadgets. Great for last-minute buys. Open from 10:00 a.m. to 7:30 p.m., closed Sundays and Mondays.

Madame Bijoux
13 rue Jean-Jacques Rousseau, 1er
Tel: 01 42 36 98 68
Métro: Palais Royal, Louvre

A very small shop which specializes in 'retro' clothes and theatrical fantasies from the 1930s and 1940s. Masks, beads, 1920s shoes, costume jewellery, boas, buttons. Some junk, some gems. Open, usually, 11:00 a.m. to 7:00 p.m., Mondays to Saturdays, but phone first to make sure.

2E ARRONDISSEMENT

Centre Franco-Americain Parfumerie
49 rue d'Aboukir, 2e
Métro: Sentier
Tel: 01 42 36 77 46

As it now seems the duty-free shops at Paris airports are among the most expensive in Europe (after Frankfurt and Heathrow), you might do well to check out this small place where perfumes, etc., are tax-free, and 25 per cent off the marked prices. They offer Dior, Chanel, Cartier, Givenchy, Yves St-Laurent, Hermès scents, and hypo-allergenic skin and body treatment products and make-up. Open Mondays through Saturdays, 10:00 a.m. to 5:30 p.m., but closed on Saturdays in August. Prices are keener and the atmosphere more agreeable than in the very crowded shops of the rue de Rivoli, and it's strong on personal service. You can sniff around until you find exactly the scent that suits you, or to buy as a gift. VISA, Access, American Express cards accepted, and traveller's cheques.

Louis Chantilly
8 rue de Echelle, 2e
Tel: 01 40 20 91 79
Métro: Opéra

This quiet little shop is lined with international luxuries: jewellery from Van Cleef, handbags from Hermès, suits from Chanel, mink jackets from the haute couture houses, Dior, Rochas, Patou perfumes. That said, the entire ambience is Japanese – calligraphy, staff and customers. Yet despite the rich surroundings and the exquisite courtesy, the prices are discreetly discounted and much is affordable, from little pieces of porcelain to perfume at about 20 per cent less than airport prices.

Gil C.
36 avenue de l'Opéra, 2e
Tel: 01 47 52 40 65
Métro: Opéra

The small Gil C. is the nearest most people will get to being at the bottom of a rugby scrum. They discount perfume and skin-care products from 30 to 40 per cent, and at these prices, the shop is really crowded. The service is fast, expert, accurate, with no time for browsers, but if you know what you're looking for, hang in there. Our advice is to go early in the morning, and when the tourist season is over and the staff has time to advise the undecided. Open Mondays through Saturdays, 9:30 a.m. to 6:30 p.m. They take VISA, American Express, Diner's Club and traveller's cheques.

3E/4E ARRONDISSEMENTS

rue des Francs-Bourgeois (odd nos. are 4e, even 3e)
Métro: St-Paul

Jean-Pierre de Castro
17 rue des Francs-Bourgeois

Silver, silver, silver. Bracelets made from forks and spoons 70–90F, repro Art Deco frames from 60F, tea strainers 120F, elaborate candlesticks for 350F; old silver spoons, knives, forks sold by the kilo, about 15 pieces, for 450F! Open Mondays, 2:00 to 7:00 p.m.; Tuesdays through Saturdays, 10:30 a.m. to 7:00 p.m.; Sundays 11:00 a.m. to 7:30 p.m.

La Licorne
38 rue de Sévigné (near the rue des Francs-Bourgeois)
Tel: 01 48 87 84 43

The shops in the Marais change almost overnight, and if this is still here it's a delightful place to find not very expensive costume jewellery. VISA, Eurocheques. Open Mondays through Saturdays, 9:30 a.m. to 6:30 p.m.

La Maison Rouge
68 rue Vieille du Temple, 3e
Tel: 01 48 87 78 34
Métro: Hôtel-de-Ville

It's worth looking here for 1930s–1990s curios and trinkets, and sometimes you'll find some choice bit of jewellery. Open 10:00 a.m. to 7:00 p.m. Closed Tuesdays. Open Saturdays and Sundays from 2:30 to 7:00 p.m. Usually closed the last week in August but this can vary.

Izrael, Epicerie du Monde
30 rue François-Miron, 4e
Métro: St-Paul, Hôtel-de-Ville
Tel: 01 42 72 66 23

Spices, herbs, delicious goodies from all over the world in a very crowded neighbourhood shop. Try a few ounces of their olives with lime, coriander and sesame seeds. Open Tuesdays through Fridays, 9:30 a.m. to 1:00 p.m., and 2:30 to 7:00 p.m.; Saturdays, 9:00 a.m. to 7:00 p.m. Closed Sundays and August.

Robin des Bois
15 rue Ferdinand Duval
Métro: St-Paul
Tel: 01 48 04 09 36

Robin des Bois is famous in France for its activist work. The store is wall to wall with imaginative treasures like rubber-tyre coin purses for 35F, handmade blank pads and notebooks made with recycled books and maps from 5F to 35F, old-fashioned burlap teddy bears for 85F, bottles of jojoba oil (revitalizing!), and *'vegetal* ivory' figurines (no elephants needed). The appeal of this shop lies in its tastefully designed recycled products intended to promote conscientious shopping and living. 10:30 a.m. to 7:30 p.m., closed Sunday morning.

DOM
21 rue Saint-Croix de la Bretonnerie
Métro: Hôtel de Ville
Tel: 01 42 71 08 00

Clubbing housewares, a very 1990s idea. Fun, wacky stuff like cow figurine Christmas-lights, Jersey cow bowls and spoons 69F (the set), fake fur cow frames for 69F. Really kitschy, but very timely. Just opened in June 1996, so the hours weren't set out yet.

5E ARRONDISSEMENT

La Tuile à Loup
35 rue Daubenton, 5e
Métro: Censier-Daubenton

A shop scented with herbs, filled with beautifully designed, rather rustic gifts: wicker, wood, earthenware casseroles, basket and cookbooks (in French). Old-fashioned wicker heart-shaped *coeur à la crème* baskets, classic glazed earthenware wine pitchers, breadboards. Open Tuesdays through Saturdays, 10:30 a.m. to 7:30 p.m.; Sundays, 10:30 a.m. to 1:00 p.m. Open August.

7E ARRONDISSEMENT

Au Chat Dormant
31 rue de Bourgogne, 7e
Métro: Varenne

A minuscule paradise for cat lovers, with gifts ranging from postcards to antique silver boxes, everything saluting cats. Figures of cats in marble, metal, porcelain, plastic. Umbrellas whose handles are heads of cats. Paintings, prints, posters. Open Tuesdays through Saturdays, 11:00 a.m. to 7:00 p.m.

11E ARRONDISSEMENT

Miroiterie Brugnon
134 rue Amélot, 11e
corner of rue J.-P. Timbaud
Tel: 01 43 57 70 35
Métro: Filles du Calvaire

In a glazier's shop that does mirrors, double-glazing, picture framing, and security installations, there is a surprising collection of beautiful, small, portable and well-priced things. Baccarat-style paper-weights, from 50F, faux bamboo photograph frames, others in fine leather, chromium, fabric. Also crystal bowls and vases and pin trays, from 50F up to real money for the bigger items. Mondays through Fridays, 8:00 a.m. to 12:30 p.m., 1:30 to 7:00 p.m.

14E ARRONDISSEMENT

La Salle des Ventes
123 rue d'Alésia, 14e
Métro: Alésia
Tel: 01 45 45 54 54

In this lively, very untouristy area, a real discovery: one big salesroom which specializes in huge pieces of furniture, and another with old jewellery, china, glass, silver. A wonderful place to browse – and you might find some delightful, very French *objet* to take home: a crystal-and-gilt *compotière*, a 1920s' Jazz Age mesh coin-purse, a Victorian beaded cushion and a rope of spiky coral beads for 200F. A girl who regularly drops in here made a great find – a tortoiseshell and gilt piqué box that is perfect for stamps or earrings, for 195F. Open Mondays through Saturdays, 10:00 a.m. to 7:30 p.m. Closed holidays and August.

Brocante Montparnasse
62 boulevard Edgar Quinet, 14e
Tel: 01 43 20 79 91
Métro: Edgar-Quinet

An interesting shop in the rather touristy Montparnasse district, but so far unspoiled by antique and junk hunters. This brocante sells small pieces of fine real jewellery, but the best finds are authentic costume jewellery from the 1930s to 1950s, now beginning to fetch hundreds of pounds in the salesrooms of New York and London. Recently, there were also some 1990-ish porcelain bowls, silver picture frames, fans. And often, you will find bigger items such as an impressive walnut and marble mantel-clock topped with a bronze lion and a *'vendu'* (sold) sticker across the clock-face. Open every day: Mondays through Fridays, 10:30 a.m. to 7:30 p.m. We are told that if you speak French, or have a friend who is fluent, you might phone and arrange with the dealer (if he is there and not too busy) to go some morning. You can try bargaining, but prices won't come down more than about 10 per cent, if that.

FLEA MARKETS

Les Marchés aux Puces – one of those romantic conceptions of Paris, whose faded glamour lingers somewhat past its prime. As there are now 'flea markets' of sorts all over the world, your chance of finding a nice little precious object for almost nothing is not what it was some years ago. You could probably do as well in a Sunday morning sale in Salford, as in the most famous flea market in Paris. However, if you like the fun of scrabbling through bins and tables on a summer's day before a good lunch; or enjoy watching Parisians striking bargains in rapid-fire slangy French – and you still hope to find something everyone else has missed – so be it. Here is the latest, most realistic information.

THE FLEA MARKET AT CLIGNANCOURT
(Puces de Clignancourt)
Métro: Porte de Clignancourt and a fair walk

Even on our most recent visit to look the market over again, nothing had changed. We can only repeat our words of ten years ago: acres of sprawling market-stalls, crammed with people on the hunt for bargains or for 'the picturesque'. These days, this means German tourists photographing American tourists. It is the best-known market, and the most expensive. Much of the stuff you see is pure and simple junk, brought in to unload on the unwary. For the rest – the dealers know where the good buys are, and by the time you have reached here on a Saturday or Sunday morning, by public transport, they have come and gone. Most of the best-looking stalls are owned by merchants who also do business from glossier premises in the 1er, 8e and 16e *arrondissements*. The prices you see in the flea market will not be substantially lower than in the rue du Bac. However, it is an experience. If you are willing to make the longish journey, go for it – rummage, and enjoy the bargaining. It could be fun, it will be tiring. Open Saturdays, Sundays and Mondays from dawn to about 1:00 p.m. But do watch out for pickpockets!

Despite the apparent haphazardness of the market, it is actually laid out in a comprehensible and sensible fashion. Outside, on the fringe, are the inevitable stands and handcarts spilling over with second-hand clothing, leather jackets, brass bits-and-pieces like horns and knockers. Inside this sprawl, you will find a number of individual markets that range in speciality from buttons to beautiful antique clothing and furniture. Most interesting:

MARCHÉ VERNAISON, 136 avenue Michelet
Everything from gilt buttons off Napoleonic tunics, to small walnut prayer-stools, toys, jewellery, lamps, glassware. Forget about any Art Nouveau *trouvailles*, the Paris, London and New York dealers got there fifteen years ago. Go for the small pieces of the 1930s, 1940s, 1950s, even the 1970s. Fashion will catch up with you some day, and sooner than you think.

MARCHÉ MALIK, rue Jules-Vallès
Mostly old clothes, umbrellas, walking-sticks, tatty fake-sheepskin

coats, scratched records, bins of lace, 1920s-ish dresses, earthenware, glass, tin, perfume bottles – sometimes these are fun, smelling in a ghostly way of scents no longer made. The clothes will probably need washing, dry-cleaning, mending, new buttons.

MARCHÉ JULES-VALLÈS, rue Jules-Vallès
The most fun, and the most promising for finding something unusual and not too expensive, if you feel your stay in Paris isn't complete without something from the flea market. Look for small bisque-headed dolls, theatrical costumes, 1930s' shoes, decorative glassware, candlesticks, ashtrays, doll trunks. Bargain if you can. Most of the dealers speak a sort of English, and a little New York vernacular with some low German or Italian sometimes helps. Don't be disappointed if the final price is not really rock-bottom. No one forces you to buy.

THE OTHER FLEA MARKETS

These are where the knowledgeable Parisians find their bargains. As they become better known, the quality of merchandise brought to them goes up, and prices are rising fast. Some years ago, these were true junk stalls, set up along the edge of an established street market. Some still qualify for this status. But the dealers are moving in to buy, and smart young professionals are setting up their stands, so go now, if you can.

Place d'Aligre
11e
Métro: Ledru-Rollin

Six days a week, including Sunday – take the Métro, and follow signs to 'Marché Beauvau', one of the lesser-known and most delightful markets in Paris. In the square, about twenty tables, and many racks, are set up with odds and ends. Boxes of the most astounding old clothes – cracked leather shoes, a furry bowler hat, a pair of striped trousers, a stack of fourth-hand handbags. Keep looking. Old postcards, small pieces of silver or silver plate, glassware, crystal, beautiful 1990s' embroidered linen shifts, lace-and-lawn nightdresses, men's swallow-tail coats, cooking utensils of every age and condition, books, odd boxes of jewellery – mostly Woolworth stuff, but occasionally a fine and rare piece turns up. There's a table of buttons old and new that will send button-collectors wild. Everything is quite cheap, the atmosphere quiet, the dealers pleasant.

Don't miss our favourite 'Chineur' who sells astoundingly good blouses, shirts, sweaters, jogging trousers, for as little as 50F each (not there in August). The shops and stalls in the streets around the market are wonderful places to shop for fruit, flowers, North African olives and hot peppers, good breads, and the corkscrew you forgot to bring. Plenty of picnicking material, for a snack in the square bounded by rue Vollon and rue Trousseau. Open Tuesdays through Sundays, about 9:30 a.m. to about 1:00 p.m.

Puces de Vanves
avenue Marc Sangier, 14e
Métro: Porte de Vanves

A very good small flea market is held here on Saturday and Sunday mornings – mostly junk, but if you have a quick eye you can still spot some real bargains. Look for oldish dinky toys, copper jelly moulds, Art Deco compacts, empty 1930s scent bottles, old glass lamps, costume jewellery of the 1940s and 1950s, comics, postcards, pots, bottles. A few small (rather pricey) antiques. After lunch on Sunday it becomes a 'Marché aux Fripes' – real trash, lovely to pick through if you have a good eye, and can wash your hands after the rummage.

The grander end of this market in avenue Georges-Lefenestre, around the corner, is described below.

Marché aux Puces de la Porte Didot
Take the Métro to Porte de Vanves, walk through the tatty part, and in the avenue Georges-Lefenestre you find 'the real market of grandpapa'. This means delectable junk and little treasures, but not as cheap as at Clignancourt. You have to be able to bargain in French if you want to get prices down. Good for pretty china, glass, silver, ornate little picture frames, small antique furniture. Not many (foreign) tourists yet, but a lot of beady-eyed young French couples

and photographers hunting for props. On even the hottest summer weekend, it is agreeable to stroll under the trees and through the good-natured, ambling crowd. You can still find places to sit and have a picnic while your feet recover. Or find a café in nearby rue Raymond Losserand. Saturdays and Sundays, from 8:30 a.m. to about 6:00 p.m., but best before lunchtime, as by mid-afternoon most of the clients have peeled off for a rest, and the best stall-holders have begun to pack it in. Police show up regularly to chase away the unlicensed who spread their odds and ends on newspapers on the pavement. But the market still goes on.

Foire de la Brocante St-Paul
quai de l'Hôtel de Ville, quai des Célestins, 4e
Métro: St Paul
Bus: Nos. 69, 96

At various times during the year, there's a mammoth 'Brocante' Fair – second-hand goods from dining chairs missing their cane seats, to comic books, to small bits of fine jewellery, lots of good junk and plenty of portable small antiques – near the Seine in the Marais area. On a sunny day it's crowded with strollers, tourists, just-looking people – a lot of dealers from all over Paris hit this market every month. The stalls are manned with a mix of professional flea marketeers and amiable amateurs. The bargains aren't the greatest in Paris, but it's fun to have a wander round and who knows, you might find that missing Scalextric train engine. Try making an offer (in French if you can): prices are usually negotiable. Best buys are found in the winter months when only real Paris-lovers are willing to prowl in a grey, drizzly, bone-chilling morning. The Foire begins about 8:00 a.m. and goes on until early afternoon. Check *Pariscope* under the heading 'Fêtes Populaires' to see if it is happening when you are there. It's such a crowd-magnet that the local buses have to be re-routed around the area! Again, look out for pickpockets, don't carry a wallet in your back pocket, leave expensive cameras and handbags under lock and key at your hotel.

Paris pratique (Staying afloat)

The quality of your stay in Paris – reverie or nightmare – is going to depend on some very basic circumstances: the state of your digestion, your feet, your French. The amount of time you spend looking for a post office is stolen from the time you spend looking at paintings. The confusion you encounter when dealing with telephones, tipping and traffic detracts from your pleasure in everything else Parisian. The information that follows, alphabetically arranged, is simple and practical – it can make the difference between two weeks of fretting about mechanical details and ten minutes of dealing intelligently with them.

ANIMALS

Parisians are unsentimental about animals, but they like to have them around. Small dogs of peculiar breed on leads trail every other person – on the Métro, in restaurants, everywhere. The pavements are consequently treacherous. You can get entangled, or step in something, but you'll rarely be snapped or barked at.

Cats run wild in certain areas, notably the cemeteries, and are not to be petted. This goes for all animals in France, except those personally known to you. (See Animal bites, page 265.)

Live animals for food are closely caged and brusquely treated. If this puts you off your feed, avert your eyes.

BABYSITTERS

We recommend that you first ask your hotel if they can provide a *garde des enfants* service. If they can't, then look for advertisements in the English-language newspapers (page 242), or contact the American and English Churches in Paris who often have a roster of English-speaking sitters.

American Church
65 quai d'Orsay, 7e
Tel: 01 47 05 07 99

St George's English Church
7 rue Auguste Vacquerie, 16e
Tel: 01 47 20 22 51

Remember, if your babysitter travels to you, you must pay for his/her transport; late at night, this means a taxi-fare.

Other suggestions come from Paris friends. In most cases, you will find someone who speaks English at these places:

Alliance Française: Tel: 01 45 44 38 28. The sitters are students and usually multilingual. About 35F an hour, more after midnight.

Babysitting Service: Tel: 01 46 37 51 24. Agency fee of 50F, then 33F per hour for the sitter.

Kids' Service: Tel: 01 47 66 00 52. Trained nannies, young and expert: 48F an hour plus a 58F fee to the agency.

Institut Catholique: Tel: 01 44 39 52 00. A fee to the Institute, then around 35F an hour with a 3-hour minimum. After midnight, 39F an hour.

BATHS, PUBLIC

If your hotel doesn't provide a shower – or if it's too expensive – try the Bains-Douches Municipaux. Bring a towel, soap, shampoo and slippers (the flip-flop variety). Cost between 5F and 10F. Open

Thursdays, noon to 7:00 p.m.; Fridays and Saturdays, 7:00 a.m. to 7:00 p.m.; Sundays, 8:00 a.m. to noon.

8 rue des Deux-Ponts, 4e	5 place Paul Verlaine, 13e
18 rue Renard, 4e	34 rue Castagnary, 15e
50 rue Lacépède, 5e	18 rue de Meaux, 19e
42 rue du Rocher, 8e	place des Fêtes, 19e
42 rue Oberkampf, 11e	27 rue de la Bidassoa, 20e
188 rue de Charenton, 12e	296 rue des Pyrénées, 20e

There are also sixty-four fountains donated to Paris by Richard Wallace (he tried to give Paris his furniture collection, too; it was turned down and wound up in London). The fountains are scattered throughout the city, contain clean water, and are good for a *toilette de chat* ('a lick and a promise').

BOOKS (IN ENGLISH)

When French newspapers begin to give you indigestion, revert to English. Remember, though, that imported books are expensive – about double their home price. All stock *Paupers' Paris*, or can get it for you, if you've lost your copy or just need another one.

The Abbey Bookshop
29 rue de la Parcheminerie, 5e
Tel: 01 46 33 16 24
Métro: St-Michel

This Canadian bookshop says it is 'a quiet refuge for poet, scholar, pilgrim'. They have a children's reading hour on Saturdays from 11:00 a.m. to noon. And on Sundays they are open from lunchtime until late night. A very good place to look for new and second-hand books in English and other languages, after a leisurely Sunday lunch or dinner at one of the Rive Gauche restaurants. Open every day.

Brentano's
37 avenue de l'Opéra, 2e
Tel: 01 42 61 52 50
Métro: Opéra, Pyramides

Very big, efficient, friendly; the staff speak about a dozen languages. Brentano's often have English language paperbacks *en promotion*, another way of saying 'marked down'. Open from 10:00 a.m. to 7:00 p.m., Monday through Saturday.

Galignani
224 rue de Rivoli, 1er
Tel: 01 42 60 76 07
Métro: Tuileries

A well-stocked 'intellectual' bookshop long on art books, gorgeous postcards, superb guidebooks (mostly French); short on charm and helpfulness, we are told. Open from 10:00 a.m. to 7:00 p.m.

Nouveau Quartier Latin
78 boulevard St-Michel, 6e
Tel: 01 43 26 42 70
Métro: St-Michel

An eclectic international bookshop, with plenty of mixed fiction for the browser, and well-stocked academic bookshelves. Their true speciality, though, is in textbooks for foreign language teachers. Open 10:00 a.m. to 7:00 p.m. every day of the week.

Palacio de la Madeleine
11 rue Tronchet, 8e
Tel: 01 42 65 00 02
Métro: Madeleine

Beautiful new art books, great bargains – and knowledgeable people who speak good English.

Shakespeare and Company
37 rue de la Bûcherie, 5e
Tel: 01 43 26 96 50
Métro: St-Michel

This little shop has earned its place as one of the sights of Paris. It sells old and new paperback and hardcover English books, has chairs outside for browsers, is next to a charming little park, and has a splendid view of Notre-Dame. And there are notices of flats to let, poetry readings, places to stay, summer jobs, share-the-cost rides to the UK and all points south and east.

Tea and Tattered Pages
24 rue Mayet, 6e
Tel: 01 40 65 94 35
Métro: Duroc

We conquered our impulse to walk straight past a shop with such a twee name, and found a very useful place for books, browsing, looking over second-hand literature, and having tea and real American brownies. Open 7 days a week, 11:00 a.m. to 7:00 p.m. Closed August.

W. H. Smith & Son
248 rue de Rivoli, 1er
Tel: 01 44 77 88 99
Métro: Concorde

W.H.S. is familiar, comfortable, and staffed by kind and helpful people who will nanny you in the nicest way. Every English-language book you might need, or just want to buy and read, is stocked. From 9:30 a.m. to 7:00 p.m.

CLOTHING SIZES

WOMEN

DRESSES/SUITS

British	10	12	14	16	18	20
American	8	10	12	14	16	18
French	38	40	42	44	46	48

STOCKINGS/TIGHTS

British/American	small	medium	large
French	0 1	2 3	4 5

SHOES

British	4½	5½	6½	7½
American	6	7	8	9
French	37	38	40	41

MEN

SUITS/OVERCOATS

British/American	35	36	37	38	39	40
French	36	38	40	42	44	46

SHIRTS

British/American	15	16	17	18
French	38	40	42	44

SHOES

British	7	8	8½	9½	10½
American	7½	8½	9	10	11
French	41	42	43	44	45

DISCOUNTS – *FOR STUDENTS*

TRAIN TRAVEL: *CARTE CARISSIMO*

The *Carte Carissimo* is for the under-26s. Valid for a year, it entitles you to a 20 per cent discount on two return tickets, or four single tickets during the 'White' (most expensive) hours of train travel, and

50 per cent in the 'Blue' (off-peak) periods. It costs 195F from main railways or travel agents.

INTERNATIONAL STUDENT IDENTITY CARDS

For discounts on museum and film entrances, Eurail passes, and much more. You must have proof of full-time student status, a passport-sized photo and 60F.

Using the card: Look for prices under *'Tarif spécial pour Étudiants'*. You get the card from:

COUNCIL FOR INTERNATIONAL EDUCATIONAL EXCHANGE (CIEE)
49 rue Pierre-Charron, 8e
Tel: 01 44 55 55 44 or 01 44 41 74 74
Métro: Alma-Marceau

and from **Council Travel**, which is part of CIEE, at their 49 rue Pierre Charron, 8e, tel: 01 44 95 95 75; and 51 rue Dauphin, 6e, tel: 01 43 26 79 65 branches. Other branches may also issue the card by the time you read this: check the Paris phone book for addresses.

LIGUE FRANÇAISE DES AUBERGES DE JEUNESSE (LFAJ)
38 boulevard Raspail, 7e
Tel: 01 45 48 69 84
Métro: rue du Bac

For Youth Hostel card-holders. Hostels are cheap (80–100F per night) but offer little privacy. Not for long stays. See 'Au lit', page 55, for more information.

STUDENT RESTAURANTS (*LES RESTOS U*)
About 25F per meal. You must, however, have a student ticket, which you get by knowing someone enrolled in a Paris university. Crowded and noisy but plentiful and inexpensive.

Assas
92 rue d'Assas, 6e
Métro: Notre-Dame-des-Champs

Albert Châtelet
10 rue Jean-Calvin, 5e
Métro: Censier-Daubenton

Bullier
39 avenue Georges-Bernanos, 5e
Métro: Port-Royal

Censier
31 rue Geoffroy Saint Hilaire, 5e
Métro: Censier-Daubenton

Cuvier-Jussieu
8 bis rue Cuvier, 5e
Métro: Jussieu

Mabillon
3 rue Mabillon, 6e
Métro: Odéon

DISCOUNTS – *FOR THOSE OVER 60*

CARTE VERMEIL

With great generosity, the French provide this discount card for those of 'the third age' – a much nicer phrase than the unctuous Anglo-American 'senior citizens' – available to anyone, of any nationality, who is over 60 years of age (women) or 65 (men). It entitles you to discounts galore on entertainment, travel and many museums. But it costs 270F (valid one year), so if your stay in Paris is going to be a short one, the *Carte Vermeil* may not pay for itself. Showing your passport at cinemas, museums, theatres will often be enough to get you the reduced rate.

However, if you're staying for a while, or returning often, do consider investing in a *Carte*. Take proof of your age – your passport – to the *Abonnement* office in any major railway station, pay them the 270F, and get in return the *Carte Vermeil*, valid from 1 June to 31 May following.

The office at the Gare St-Lazare is an easy one to deal with, as the station is served by several Métro and many bus lines, and the office is not as crowded as the one at the big Gare du Nord. Don't expect anyone to speak English, but you won't need much French to communicate your wishes, as they are used to dealing with foreigners who have cottoned on to this very useful offer.

As you look through *Pariscope* for theatres, music, cinemas, etc., note the price reductions available for holders of the *CV*; it can be 40 per cent or more. Most museums and special exhibitions (such as those at the Grand Palais and Petit Palais) give half-price admission to holders of the *CV*.

Even without this card, production of a foreign passport will usually (but not always) get you into museums, movies, theatres or concerts at a reduced price.

Holders of the British Senior Citizen Railcard should note that they will need the Rail-Europ supplement card for discounts on rail/boat/hovercraft: check British Rail, in England (0171 353 5212), or in Paris, tel: 44 51 06 00, for details of specific offers. Dates and hours may be restricted; read the small print to make sure you can get back from your holiday when you want to.

DRY CLEANING

It's called *nettoyage à sec* or *le pressing*. Sample prices:

Trousers	40F
Jacket	50–70F
Dress	60–100F (for silk, cocktail, or even dresses, which no right-minded Pauper takes travelling)

Le pressing (your clothes are brushed and pressed) is also available everywhere for a touch-up – 15F up to 25F in 'good' neighbourhoods.

ELECTRICITY

Although the current in most modernized hotels is 220 volts, as in the UK (in a few older hotels it may still be 110 volts, so enquire before using any appliance), you must fit a *European* two-round-pin plug to the flex of electrical gadgets. Many hardware shops and ironmongers sell these (or get one in Paris). If you have an appliance with a three-cord flex, make sure the earth wire (green and yellow) is securely bound and covered with electrician's tape, so that it cannot touch the other wires or the wall socket. Or buy one of the pricey but safe adaptors sold in ironmongers. Also do be considerate: you might check with the *concierge* about using a hair-dryer, which draws a lot of current.

EMBASSIES

See 'Au secours', page 255.

EMERGENCIES

See 'Au secours', page 255.

ENTRANCES AND EXITS

French doors open inward. This takes a while to get used to.

Entrée = Entrance
Sortie = Exit
Tirez = Pull
Poussez = Push
Passage Interdit = No Admittance

FOR THE LESS MOBILE

Access in Paris by Gordon Couch and Ben Roberts is an English language guide available by post from RADAR, 25 Mortimer Street, London W1N 8AB. In France, there's the *Tourist Guide for People with Reduced Mobility (Guide Touristique pour les Personnes à Mobilité Reduite)*, published in French and English by Le Comité National Français de Liaison pour la Réadaptation des Handicapés (CNFLRH). It's available for 60F at the main Tourist Office on the avenue des Champs-Élysées, which always has the latest information.

To be perfectly plain about it, Paris isn't the ideal city for anyone in a wheelchair or with serious walking difficulties. Although RER lines A and B are accessible in parts, the Métro and the buses are only for those with a certain degree of mobility on their own two feet. Most museums, even the Louvre, are not user-friendly, although the new system of escalators and ramps in the Louvre itself does help to a certain extent. Remember, however, that you must be able to weather the unsheltered wait in the Pyramid courtyard to get in (see page 159).

The Musée d'Orsay (page 166) makes up for it: easy to get into, easy to get around, wide aisles, very short flights of steps, escalators, easy-access loos. And of course it is crammed and jammed with wonderful things to see. The Jeu de Paume (page 161), newly renovated and reopened, has only a few steps at the entrance to be negotiated, but it has several flights of internal stairs; there is said to be a lift for those in real need – ask at the cashier's desk.

The Marmottan, in Passy (page 169), is manageable if you yourself can manage a short flight of steps up to the entrance, and now has a narrow lift which takes you down to the room full of breath-taking Monets. Beaubourg (page 164) is reasonably accessible: it has a short escalator up to the main level, where you can transfer to a lift and go on to other floors (including the one with the Musée Moderne). There are platforms on each level, with all Paris spread out before you; and the Sculpture Terrace outside the museum is very visitor-friendly.

A French friend who walks with two sticks loves the Institut du Monde Arabe on the quai St-Bernard (page 165) for its easy access, elegant and soothing interiors, exciting architecture – and its mint tea and pastries!

For the less mobile, the best time for Paris is late autumn or winter, or spring up to about the middle of June. Then you avoid the crowds and can manoeuvre, gaze and enjoy at your own pace.

According to an article by Alison Walsh, in the *Telegraph* of 27 April 1991, driving in Paris with an automatic car is 'a doddle'. For holders of disabled badges, parking meter fees are waived, and charges in car parks are cut by 75 per cent. She also praises the facilities of the great science park at La Villette in the 19e *arrondissement* – everything accessible and pure enjoyment for children and adults alike.

Paris itself – its streets, beautiful parks like the Luxembourg and the Tuileries, tiny squares where you can watch the locals playing *boules*, pavement cafés, and its floodlit splendour at night – is infinitely accessible and always rewarding.

The official *Guide des Hôtels* indicates with a wheelchair symbol which hotels promise facilities for the less mobile, but in practice this is sometimes dicey. Many hotels with lifts are not as easy as they sound because there may be several steps to negotiate from street level to the reception room, or additional steps inside before the lifts are reached. Check the hotel descriptions in this book: we have tried to indicate those which are really easy of access.

GUIDEBOOKS

New guides to Paris come out every year, and you'd be wise to go to Brentano's, W. H. Smith, or the Abbey Bookshop and check out the current crop. These are the ones we like best, but remember that this is only an arbitrary opinion:

Blue Guide to Paris
In English, detailed information on museums and areas of historical interest, 121F or £10.00.

Michelin Green Guide
In English, good overview, and excellent maps, 60F or £5.45.

Gault-Millau: Le Nouveau Guide
In French, published monthly. An invaluable source of inside information on restaurants, wines, hotels, travel, holidays. Many of their restaurant recommendations are well above our price limits, but they often write about low- to medium-priced places too. Sometimes they make a find before we do, sometimes we get there first. They are utterly frank about the places they review, and they write wittily and often colloquially. One issue a few years ago had a feature on 'Restaurants to Flee From'. Restaurants weep with delight when Gault-Millau smiles on them, and start pulling down the shutters when the G-M score is 2/10 (meaning 'stay away'). 155F.

Le Nouveau Guide is a country-wide or even world-wide magazine, and may not be of much use to the casual visitor to Paris. So have a look at the cover of the current magazine on the newsstands; if there is a Paris feature, buy it. Even if the restaurants are too high-priced for you today, who knows – in a future life you may come back as a rich Parisian.

PARIS PAS CHER In French. Superb for household bargains, cars, fridges and consumer information, not as strong on more mundane things like hotels, restaurants, *'fripes'* and *'bis! bis!'*. For resident Parisians rather than tourists, but a good read.

Time Out A Free Guide to Paris: A helpful, trendy guide to Paris with sections on sightseeing, essential bars, arts and entertainment, music, theatre, sports and fitness, gay and lesbian info, accommodation and Disneyland. For information on weekly events. *Time Out* also publishes an eight-page insert in *Pariscope*.

What's On in France magazine: The most complete English guide to cultural events in Paris (as well as other parts of France) including monthly highlights; jazz, pop and classical concerts; theatre, dance and opera events; museums and exhibitions; a directory of addresses. On sale at W. H. Smith (see page 221) and leading French *kiosques*; or even better, pick one up before you leave home at major newsstands and newsagents throughout the UK; 3F or 40p.

COPING IN FRENCH

You'll want to get to grips with the French language, and now the choice of books, cassettes, even video, is vast. Decide if you want the simple ability to ask questions and understand the answers, or if you want to deliver a philosophy paper to the Académie Française, and pick the course that suits you. Here are a few that we've found useful:

Façon de Parler! *French for Beginners*

Hodder and Stoughton. A two-phase programme for beginners consisting of a 392-page course book, two 100-minute cassettes and an 80-page support book for £25.99 (198F); and, when you've graduated to the second beginner level, a 368-page course book, a 90-minute cassette and a 64-page course book for £22.99 (253F).

Restart French

BBC Enterprises. Two tapes based on the Radio 5 series to help you polish up your French for £15.50 (202F).

Routledge Colloquial French: A Complete Language Course by Alan Moys
Written and spoken French course consists of two 60-minute tapes, the book and everything you'll need to know for a week's stay, 110F.

HAIRDRESSERS

Le training – a first-class example of Franglais – offers you a chance to get a free or reduced-rate haircut or styling in some very good salons. These sessions are popular with the young and broke of Paris, so you may have to wait or return another day. For women only – as far as is known now, although the trendier unisex salons may by now have 'training' sessions, too. You are sure of getting something smart and professional, as the cutter who works on your hair is actually employed in the salon at normal times, not just a learner-driver, so to speak; and there is always one of the top stylists of the establishment hovering near to criticize, or comment, or direct. Don't mind if you are treated as an object rather than a client to be flattered and soothed. And you will probably find that your own wishes are not paramount. Don't go in with long straight hair and expect to come out with just a trim. Get an idea beforehand of the general attitude of the salon before you put your head in their hands.

Jean-Marc Maniatis
10 rue Poquelin, Forum des Halles, 1e
Tel: 01 40 39 90 95
Métro: Les Halles

and 35 rue de Sèvres, 6e
Tel: 01 45 44 16 39
Métro: Sèvres-Babylone

Maniatis is a famous hairdresser, known for styling the hair of many film and theatre stars. One day each month, one of his senior *coiffeurs* or *coiffeuses* demonstrates at low cost. And one evening a week, students working under supervision try their hands; then your treatment is free, but book well in advance.

École Jacques Dessange
37 avenue Franklin-D.-Roosevelt, 8e
Tel: 01 43 59 33 97 or 01 43 59 31 31
Métro: Franklin-D.-Roosevelt

Hair styling and make-up are done by the trainees of this famous
beauty academy. Free from Mondays through Wednesdays, but closed
during school holidays. Little English spoken, but try your luck.

École Jean-Louis David
5 rue Pierre-Charron, 8e
Tel: 01 43 59 82 08
Métro: Franklin-D.-Roosevelt

Jean-Louis David runs a chain of coiffeurs, and your hair will be cut
and styled by experienced people who work in one of their 300 shops.
Mondays to Fridays, from 10:30 a.m. to 7:00 p.m., and it's free – but
advance booking is necessary.

Note: For a non-training (paid) coiffure, expect to pay about 95F for a
cut, 50F for a shampoo, and blow-drying or setting, about 50–60F.
All prices in Paris salons include service (although many people do
tip).

HEALTH

See 'Au secours', page 255.

HOLIDAYS

1 January
Easter Sunday and Monday (Pâques)
1 May (French Labour Day)
Ascension Day
Whit Monday
14 July (Bastille Day)

15 August (Feast of the Assumption)
1 November (All Saints' Day – Toussaint)
11 November (Remembrance Day) and Christmas

The entire month of August is high season for tourists, low season for Parisians. The city trades in its population for a flock of provincials and foreigners. Stay out of town unless you don't mind being asked directions by passers-by. To us, Paris in August is close to paradise – empty, quiet, little traffic, hundreds of restaurants eager to feed you, museums open and not too crowded. We are 'Aoûtiens', happy to be in one of our most familiar bistros on a hot, drowsy day, where lunch with wine can cost as little as 50–65F, and the owners are free to sit down and gossip.

INFORMATION SOURCES

For basic information, consult the Office de Tourisme. The Hôtesses speak English, and will provide information on hotels, transportation, sight-seeing, travel in France and such.

OFFICE DE TOURISME
Main office: 127 avenue des Champs-Élysées, 8e
Tel: 01 49 52 53 54
Métro: George V

HOURS: Mondays through Saturdays, 9:00 a.m. to 8:00 p.m.; Sundays and holidays, 9:00 a.m. to 6:00 p.m.

Branch offices:

Gare de Lyon
Hours: Mondays through Saturdays, 8:00 a.m. to 1:00 p.m., 5:00 to 9:00 p.m., Easter to 1 November. Other months to 8:00 p.m.

Gare de l'Est
Hours: Mondays through Saturdays, 8:00 a.m. to 1:00 p.m., 5:00 to 9:00 p.m., Easter to 1 November. Other months to 8:00 p.m.

Gare d'Austerlitz
Hours: Mondays through Saturdays, 8:00 a.m. to 3:00 p.m.

The Yellow Pages
The Paris telephone directories for offices, goods and services are yellow-covered, available at most hotels and all post offices. Ask for *Le Professionel*.

LANGUAGE COURSES

Berlitz
35 avenue Franklin-D.-Roosevelt, 8e
Métro: Franklin-D.-Roosevelt
Tel: 01 40 74 00 17

Alliance Française
101 boulevard Raspail, 6e
Tel: 01 45 44 38 28
Métro: Notre-Dame-des-Champs

Institut de Langue Française
15 rue Arsène Houssaye, 8e
Tel: 01 42 27 14 77
Métro: Charles-de-Gaulle

La Sorbonne
47 rue des Écoles, 5e
Tel: 01 40 46 22 11
Métro: Cluny-Sorbonne, Luxembourg

LAVATORIES, PUBLIC

There are still one or two *vespasiennes* in Paris, but by the time you read this, there may be none. Métro stations frequently (but not always) have lavatories (marked WC-Dames, WC-Hommes); for once, correct vocabulary is *essential*. The attendant expects 1F in the saucer. Superb new automatic lavatories are sited on many street corners: a 2F piece gets you up to 10 minutes in an immaculate white cubicle.

Café and brasserie toilets offer various states of hygiene and civilization – about 25 per cent of the time, you'll find the *à la turque* variety, which can be very clean or very dirty, especially in the smaller out-of-the-way places. Most of our recommended restaurants, however, have clean, well-kept lavatories, usually well equipped. However, we still say *never* leave home without a pack of humane loo-paper.

If your need for a lavatory doesn't quite coincide with your desire for a cup of coffee, find a café or brasserie and ask politely to use the phone – '*Le téléphone, s'il vous plaît?*' Almost always, you will find the phone and lavatory next to each other. Don't use the phone. On your return to the *caisse*, smile politely and leave. Your party didn't answer.

LIBRARIES

If you expect to be able to use the great French Bibliothèque Nationale, quai François Mauriac, 13e, you will need some authoritative support: a letter from your university describing your research, or from your corporation. The more official the better. Count on bureaucratic resistance. Mitterrand's *pièce de résistance*, the new Bibliothèque Nationale at Bray, opened in December 1996. The Bibliothèque Ste-Geneviève, 8 place du Panthéon, 6e, however, will issue you with a library card, no questions asked, in about ten minutes, if you bring your passport.

LOST AND FOUND

We have found the Lost and Found charming and helpful, and they have at least one person who speaks good English.

Bureau des Objets Trouvés
36 rue des Morillons, 15e
Tel: 01 55 76 20 20
Métro: Convention

Open Mondays, Tuesdays, Wednesdays and Fridays, 8:30 a.m. to 5:00 p.m.; Thursdays, 8:30 a.m. to 8:00 p.m.

Lost or stolen passport: see 'Au secours', page 255.

MAPS

The best we know is the *Plan de Paris*, Edition A. Leconte, red cover, about 99F, and worth it. For details, see 'Aux alentours', page 31. You can also find free museum or shopping maps in the Maison de la France in Piccadilly, London, or in most three- and four-star hotels – the Galeries Lafayette and Printemps have free maps but apart from getting you to their stores they're not very useful.

MENTAL HEALTH

SOS AMITIÉ (IN ENGLISH)
Tel: 01 47 23 80 80
Hours: 3:00 p.m. to 11:00 p.m.

For pouring out your troubles by phone. No advice given, no sides taken, but they lend a sympathetic ear and can recommend other sources of specific help or refuge. They are very busy, and simply trying to get through might drive you to despair.

METRIC SYSTEM

To convert centimetres into inches, multiply by 0.39
To convert inches into centimetres, multiply by 2.54

1 cm = 0.39 in
1 m = 39.4 in = 3.28 ft = 1.09 yd

1 in = 2.54 cm
1 ft = 30.48 cm = 0.304 m
1 yd = 91.44 cm = 0.914 m

1 kilogram (kg) = 2.205 lb
2 kg = 4.409 lb
5 kg = 11.023 lb
10 kg = 22.046 lb

1 lb = 0.45 kg
2 lb = 0.90 kg
5 lb = 2.25 kg
10 lb = 4.50 kg

To convert degrees Centigrade into degrees Fahrenheit, multiply Centigrade by 1.8 and add 32.

To convert degrees Fahrenheit into degrees Centigrade, subtract 32 and divide by 1.8.

MONEY

See also 'Preliminaries', page 5, for an idea of how much to bring with you.

The denominations	**Will get you**
5 centimes	nothing
10 centimes	nothing
20 centimes	nothing
½F (50 centimes)	nothing
1F	tip for a lavatory attendant
2F	ten minutes in an automatic lavatory; one phone call
5F	coffee, drunk at the *zinc*
50F	a lunch with wine and service at one of our least expensive restaurants
100F	a light meal for two with a carafe of wine; or a real splurge meal for one

French paper currency is whimsical. The portraits on the bills are not of politicians but of artists: Berlioz (on the now defunct 10F note), De La Tour (50F), Delacroix (100F), Pascal (500F). This is conclusive proof that the French value philosophy above literature, and literature vastly above music.

If knowing exactly what you are spending is important to you, consider the X-Changer, a gadget that instantly computes foreign exchange rates. Around £7 from larger branches of Boots, Rymans, Debenhams in London. (However, there is such a thing as carrying too many gadgets and worrying too much about whether the meal cost £6.50 or £7.00 when you should be concentrating on the *ris de veau*.)

BUREAUX DE CHANGE

Despite our wise words about sleeping cheap and eating well, within certain sets of limits, money does seem to drip through the fingers in Paris. And when you need it most – on weekends, or just before dinner – where do you go to get it? Even during banking hours on weekdays you can find yourself walking miles, past bank after bank of busy money-changing citizens, but barred to you by the inflexible sign *no change, no wechsel*. Every guidebook lists the exchange facilities in the railway stations: but we can only say that they are a foretaste of hell. Fearsomely crowded, jostling with impatient travellers barging themselves and their rucksacks past you to get to ticket offices and trains. But fear nothing, here are the life-saving addresses:

BANQUE RIVAUD

93 boulevard St Germain, 6e, at the exit from the Métro.

No commission charged, good rates, unsmiling staff. It was impossible to get accurate information on hours and days, but as it is a very popular tourist area, they're probably open at hours convenient to you, especially in the four summer months.

CHEQUEPOINT

The English chain of *bureaux de change* now have about eighteen 'changes' in Paris, and in our experience give the best service, the best hours, and *smile* even at 3:00 a.m. And they cash personal cheques on English banks, backed by your cheque card! For up-to-the-minute information on their branches, etc., go to their main office, open 24 hours a day, every day, or telephone:

150 avenue des Champs-Élysées, 8e
Métro: Charles-de-Gaulle-Étoile
Tel: 01 49 53 02 51

Chequepoints open 7 days a week, 8:30 a.m. to 11:00 p.m.

> 134 rue de Rivoli, 1e, *Métro*: Louvre
> 36 avenue de l'Opéra, 2e, *Métro*: Opéra
> 9 boulevard des Capucines, 2e, *Métro*: Opéra
> 23 rue Aubry le Boucher, 4e, *Métro*: Châtelet-les-Halles

121 rue St-Martin, 4e, *Métro*: Châtelet-les-Halles
20 rue de Buci, 6e, *Métro*: Odéon

Chequepoints open Mondays through Saturdays, 8:30 a.m. to 11:00 p.m.

240 rue de Rivoli, 1e, *Métro*: Concorde
7 rue de la Cossonerie, 1e, *Métro*: Châtelet-les-Halles
274 rue St-Honoré, 2e, *Métro*: Palais-Royal
346 rue St-Honoré, 2e, *Métro*: Tuileries
19 boulevard St-Michel, 5e, *Métro*: Place St-Michel, Cluny
21 rue St-Severin, 5e, *Métro*: Place St-Michel
134 boulevard St-Germain, 6e, *Métro*: Odéon
1 rue Scribe, 9e, *Métro*: Opéra

CCF (CRÉDIT COMMERCIAL DE FRANCE)
103 avenue des Champs-Élysées, 8e
Métro: George V

HOURS: Mondays through Saturdays, 8:30 a.m. to 8:00 p.m., and in July, August and September on Sundays from 10:15 a.m. to 6:00 p.m.

CURRENCY EXCHANGE DU ROND-POINT
Inside the Galerie Élysées Rond-Point
47 avenue Franklin-D.-Roosevelt, 8e
Métro: Franklin-D.-Roosevelt, St-Philippe-du-Roule

HOURS: Open seven days a week in summer months (1 June to 30 September) 10:00 a.m. to 8:00 p.m.; off-season days and hours not posted as we write, so check on the spot.

No commission charge here, many languages spoken, notes and traveller's cheques, credit card advances, and the rates seem good.

BARCLAYS BANK
6 Rond-Point-des-Champs-Élysées, 8e
Métro: Champs-Élysées-Clemenceau
Hours: Mondays through Fridays, 9:30 to 4:00 p.m.

Barclay cheques only, and traveller's cheques.

BEAUBOURG
Centre Pompidou, 3e
Métro: Les Halles, Rambuteau

A *bureau de change* has been opened on the ground floor of Beaubourg – open during the Centre's daytime hours and on Saturdays and Sundays. The exchange rate is fairly standard, but note that a fee is charged on each transaction.

CITIBANK
30 avenue des Champs-Élysées, 8e
Métro: George V, Franklin-D.-Roosevelt

A small, busy bank in this very convenient location, with good exchange rates and useful opening hours: Mondays to Fridays, 9:00 a.m. to 6:45 p.m.; Saturdays 10:30 a.m. to 1:15 p.m., 2:30 to 6:30 p.m.

BUREAU DE CHANGE
9 rue Scribe, 9e
Métro: Opéra

HOURS: Mondays to Fridays, 9:00 a.m. to 5:15 p.m. No exchange fee charged.

MELIA TRAVEL AGENCY
31 avenue de l'Opéra, 1er
Métro: Opéra

HOURS: Mondays to Fridays 9:30 a.m. to 6:30 p.m., Saturdays 9:30 a.m. to 6:00 p.m. Days before holidays (e.g., 24 and 31 December): 9:00 a.m. to 4:00 p.m.

Banks and *bureaux de change* have varying charges for cashing traveller's cheques, or notes, so shop around. American Express traveller's cheques are best cashed (no fee) at their office, otherwise you pay at least 1 per cent. Barclays traveller's cheques cost you nothing to cash at their branches.

CHEQUES, CREDIT CARDS

TRAVELLER'S CHEQUES, of course, are the safest way to carry money; if lost or stolen they will be replaced with varying degrees of speed. However, you pay in advance, you pay a commission when you buy them and sometimes you pay when you cash them abroad. Most English banks, and major travel agencies like Thomas Cook, charge 1 per cent commission for sterling traveller's cheques, and 1.25 per cent for foreign currency traveller's cheques. Be a little wary of taking a lot of money in these last, as you'll lose on the exchange if you bring them back unspent and want to cash them. American Express and Barclays in Paris charge no fee for cashing their own traveller's cheques. Incidentally, keep a record of the cheque numbers, denominations, when and where cashed, separate from the cheques themselves – this is a chore to do, but if the cheques are pinched, at least you know what to tell the issuers.

EUROCHEQUES are, in our experience, more trouble than they're worth, at least in France. On the face of it, they seem a very good alternative to carrying cash, which is lost for ever if stolen or mislaid, or paying in advance for traveller's cheques. You pay your bank a yearly fee (£8 at Barclays), and get books of ten cheques each and a Eurocheque card, and write them out in local currency as needed. This saves you the petty annoyance of queuing at the banks or bureaux de change. BUT: many small hotels, restaurants and shops will either courteously refuse to accept Eurocheques, or will add on a fee which can range from 5 per cent to 10 per cent, because their banks levy a surcharge on Eurocheques from English banks. One French bank charges its account-holders a flat fee of 100F (more than £9) for every Eurocheque, no matter how small; in addition, you pay about 1.6 per cent of the sterling value of the cheque when it clears through your account here, plus about 30p handling charge for each. Is it all worth it? Less costly and time-consuming is to use your PIN number on your Eurocheque card at one of the many upgraded ATM systems throughout the city.

PERSONAL CHEQUES, backed by a bank card, or an Access or Visa card, can be cashed at Chequepoint offices throughout the city. Barclays at the Rond-Point des Champs-Élysées, will cash a Barclay cheque for up to £100 for a fee of 40F; other banks will ask you for two cheques of £50, and charge a fee for each. NatWest at 18 Place Vendôme will cash cheques for its account holders with the same fee as Barclays. French banks, which used to cash cheques drawn on English accounts, politely refuse.

NATIONAL GIRO will furnish its account holders with Post Cheques, which can be cashed at any post office in francs – and this can be a tremendous convenience for out-of-banking-hours emergencies. These Post Cheques must be ordered in advance, take about a week to ten days to get, and come in books of ten, each worth up to £50. And – a real plus – you keep the money in your account until you actually cash the cheque, unlike traveller's cheques which are bought in advance. However, no shops or hotels or restaurants will accept them, and French banks on the whole are baffled by them. A charge is added in the UK when the cheque clears.

CREDIT CARDS can be used to draw cash from French banks and their automated teller machines; the amount varies from year to year, but you will be charged interest at the current rate – at this writing, between 1.8 and 2 per cent per month – from the moment you get the money. No interest-free grace period here. And again, we have to warn that the exchange rate you will be charged will be the company's own rate.

American Express charge-card holders can cash personal cheques, backed by the AMEX card, for up to £350 every 21 days; American Express, tel: 01 47 77 70 00 (24 hours, 7 days a week). Diners Club will advance up to 8250F to its card-holders every two weeks, but as these are charge-cards, not credit cards, a sizeable interest charge will be added if the account is not settled promptly when the bill comes in.

When it comes to using credit cards to pay for meals, hotels and purchases, opinions differ. More and more shops, cafés and restaurants – even in such districts as Belleville, rue de Charonne, rue de la Roquette – will accept plastic. With VISA and Access, you'll have up to six weeks' free credit before you have to pay up. Diners Club and American Express like their accounts settled promptly. See our warnings above for full details.

Protect the Plastic: For around £8 a year, you can insure all your charge and credit cards against loss or theft. Sentinel (0181 691 2003) and Card Protection Plan CPP (0171 351 4400), run similar schemes. You report your loss with one phone call, they notify every organization you have specified and get replacement cards under way. Both have reverse-charge or toll-free facilities for overseas calls. Both plans will advance cash, subject to certain restrictions, interest free for a limited period, if your money has gone with your cards. If you call within 24 hours of discovering your loss, you're covered against any fraudster using your card (up to £1000): once the loss is reported, all fraudulent use is covered. But make sure you keep your PIN (personal identification number) separate from your cashpoint withdrawal card. Otherwise, if a thief cashes a cheque on your account before you notify the card protection company, you're out of the cash.

If you don't use insurance, then note down the numbers, expiration date, and loss-notification phone number of your credit card issuers. Call them right away and tell them exactly when you discovered the loss, so they can issue a stop-order which protects you against someone booking a round-the-world flight on your VISA card. Each company has a slightly different policy on covering losses on credit cards, so be sure you know your rights when you make your call. If you get an automatic answering service, at night, Sundays, or holidays, say your piece slowly, and include the phrase, 'As of this moment, X a.m. or Y p.m., of reporting the loss, I am no longer responsible for any charges incurred on this card number: 0000 0000 0000.'

NEWSPAPERS

In French: *Le Monde*, marginally left of centre, is the most serious and well informed; *Figaro* veers right. Either will give you a morning's occupation if your French is slow. *France-Soir* leans toward the sensational, a good source of crime and scandal stories; *Libération* (*Libé* for short) is for the young and branché; *Le Canard Enchaîné* is a sort of French *Private Eye*, and requires a firm grip on French politics and *argot* to make any sense at all; *Paris-Match* and *Gala* are France's weekly picture magazines. And there are a couple of hundred others, of all sorts and persuasions.

In English: The *International Herald Tribune* (daily) for comprehensive stock quotations, news, and American 'Op-Ed' features. Columnists syndicated from the *New York Times*, the *Washington Post* and elsewhere. *Guardian, The Times, Telegraph, Independent*, available daily near the Hôtel Crillon, Odéon, St-Michel, place de la Concorde, Palais Royal, Opéra, place de la République and other central news kiosks.

And see 'Periodicals', page 245.

NUISANCES

Noise: hotel regulations specify quiet before 10:00 a.m. and after 10:00 p.m. Bang on the wall or call the manager if you have noisy neighbours. Try *'Il y a du bruit'* (It's noisy), or *'C'est trop bruyant'* (too much noise).

OTHER COMPLAINTS

Mosquitoes: *Moustiques*
Fleas: *Puces*
Lice: *Poux* (don't complain, leave the hotel)
Inedible: (mild) *Cela ne me plaît pas*
      (strong) *C'est dégoûtant, ça*
Odour (extreme): *Ça pue!*
Unwelcome advances: *Laissez-moi tranquille. Fiche-moi le camp!*

Beggars: if you're unwilling or unable to give handouts, the best defence is not to understand what they want. *'Parle pas'* will do in most cases – but Parisian beggars have been known to beg in English!

Thieves: see page 264.

Smoking: Outside Barcelona, all but invisible in a cloud of blue cigarette smoke, Paris must be the 'smokiest' city of Europe. If the smell of strong tobacco bothers you, leave the country. It's true that smoking is forbidden in some post offices, all Métros, buses and certain other public places, but you can't spend all your time there. As Ian Irvine commented in *The Independent* in May 1990, the French treat the cigarette as a fashion accessory. Tobacco advertising has been banned from television, cinema, newspapers and magazines; but the tobacco companies get round that in many ways. For instance, they produce matchboxes and lighters identical to their cigarette packs and promote *them*. Classic advertising posters for cigarettes are reproduced on postcards, gift-wrapping paper, beach umbrellas, fabrics, anything which keeps the names alight. One clever ploy was an exhibition a few years ago: the world's greatest photographers were commissioned to take photographs of gypsies – their fees were paid, the show sponsored – to enthusiastic reviews – by Gitanes, whose bright-blue cigarette pack features a negligently lounging gypsy dancer.

NUMBERS

It's absolutely necessary to understand the difference between, say, *quatorze* and *quarante*; betweem *cinq* and *cent*. When you can tell in an instant what *quatre-vingt dix-neuf* means, you've arrived. Memorize the following:

1	un	14	quatorze	81	quatre-vingt-un		
2	deux	15	quinze	91	quatre-vingt-onze		
3	trois	16	seize	100	cent		
4	quatre	17	dix-sept	200	deux cent		
5	cinq	18	dix-huit	1000	mille		
6	six	19	dix-neuf				
7	sept	20	vingt				
8	huit	21	vingt-et-un				
9	neuf	31	trente-et-un	premier(ière)	first		
10	dix	41	quarante-et-un	deuxième	second		
11	onze	51	cinquante-et-un	troisième	third		
12	douze	61	soixante-et-un	quatrième	fourth		
13	treize	71	soixante-et-onze	cinquième	fifth		

Unless you understand the numbers, you won't be able to ask for information about bus routes; pay for a meal or a minor purchase without getting it in writing; figure out what the *gendarme* means when he says the Métro is *deux-cent cinquante* metres away.

OPEN AND CLOSED: ABBREVIATIONS

TLJ – every day (tous les jours)
Sauf lundi – except Monday
S, D & F – Saturdays, Sundays and holidays (samedis, dimanches et fêtes)

PERIODICALS

Pariscope, 3F, and *L'Officiel des Spectacles*, 2F: For weekly listings of cinemas, theatre, concerts, dance, music, cabaret, races and other sports and art galleries. In French.

France–USA Contacts (FUSAC): A fact-packed, lively, highly useful free sheet published every two weeks, distributed wherever English or American is spoken; or from their office, 3 rue Larochelle, 14e (*Métro*: Gaîté, Edgar-Quinet), tel: 45 38 56 57. It has a very American accent and slant, and an incredible amount of information about flats, sublets, hotels, restaurants, pubs, jobs, hairdressers, music, rides, flights, jumble sales, language courses, Fourth of July and Bastille Day parties – even therapy, health, AIDS and AA support groups.

Paris Free Voice: A newspaper something like the original *Village Voice* in New York. Ten issues a year, from 65 quai d'Orsay, 7e. Well-informed, rather serious-minded, strong on arts information including good new books, plays and films but not ignoring discos, jazz places; a range from mime festivals to the Paris–American Aids Committee. Good classified ads in their 'Bulletin Board' section; highlights of the most interesting cultural events in Paris. Free from selected restaurants, bars and book shops.

Boulevard France: A monthly for francophiles which includes *What's On in France*, the most complete guide to cultural events in Paris as well as other parts of France. Pick one up and enjoy the in-depth regional articles ('Wines of Provence', 'La Touraine'), or learn about the more local Parisian delights such as the Ile Saint-Louis and Ile de la Cité. Always packed with great business and shopping tips, the latest news in the Quoi de Neuf section, and interesting profile columns on people 'making it happen' in everything from politics to couture. On sale at W. H. Smith (see page 221) and leading French *kiosques*; or even better, pick one up before you leave home at major newsstands and newsagents throughout the UK. *What's On in France* is available separately, 3F.

Living in France: A practical guide for those who have started out as tourists and stayed on as residents. Published annually, it includes The Yellow Pages – eighteen pages of indispensable addresses – useful to residents and travelling paupers alike. The most recent edition includes invaluable information on schooling, health, banking, insurance, taxes and social security and investment and even having a baby in France.

POLICE (See also 'Au secours', page 255)

Paris police come in different guises. The everyday cop, the gendarme ('le flic'), travels on foot, usually in pairs. He is to be addressed thus: *'Pardon, Monsieur l'agent . . .'*

Any other means of getting his attention, short of falling in front of a bus, will get a chilly reception.

The CRS are a special anti-terrorist force who guard embassies, certain banks, some airline offices and the like. They wear blue windcheaters, carry guns, and look like thugs; do not ask them what time it is.

If you are a foreigner, and are asked, for whatever reason, to show your *papiers* – your passport – to a gendarme, do so. If you don't have it on you, it's a fast trip to the police station for you.

In general it would be unwise to break any laws while in Paris.

LA POLITESSE

Without which you might as well stay at home. Parisians – if you'll permit the generalization – are formal creatures. What they lack in rigid class distinctions they make up for in the personal carapace of manners that each carries around. While it is unlikely that any Parisian will adopt you into the bosom of his family, or spill his innermost secrets to you, Parisians can unbend to strangers. With the right approach you can at least penetrate the first line of defence.

The trick is to use the standard forms of politesse: *Excusez-moi, monsieur; s'il vous plaît, madame; pardon, mademoiselle* ... and use the honorific, never the *tu* form, unless a) you're a member of the family; b) you're a close friend or bitter enemy; or c) you're among the more casual student generation, who seem to have given up the second person plural. And say the polite words as if you mean them. As a rule, Parisians prefer to be spoken to directly; they are all for eye-contact; they enjoy shaking hands (brief – up and down only – but firm) on all occasions, once a relationship has been established.

And as a means of establishing relationships – even purely commercial ones – we suggest that you cultivate certain people and places throughout your stay. Even if you spend most of your days in the hinterland of the city, there should be a few characters – the *concierge* of your hotel, the owner of your neighbourhood café, the woman who sells you the newspaper, the staff of a restaurant or two where you return several times – who will come to recognize you, know you however slightly, welcome your appearance, bid you *bon appétit* (good appetite) or *bonjour* (good day). If you make the effort to communicate – in French, however stumbling – it will be appreciated. If you enjoy their food, their accommodation, their city, don't feel shy about showing it.

POST

Another exercise is bureaucracy: receiving parcels through the post office is said to be Kafkaesque.

Stamps (*timbres*) are available at post offices (*bureaux de poste*) and at tobacco shops (*tabacs*) for EC destinations only. Post-boxes are oblong, about 2 feet by 3 feet, a Dijon-mustard colour, generally attached to walls, and virtually invisible. In post offices you have a choice of three slots: *Paris, Avion* (airmail) and *département étrangers* (anywhere outside Paris).

The French produce some of the prettiest (and biggest) commemorative stamps in the world. They're called *timbres de collection*, and are available at a special window in the post office.

A 24-hour post office is open Mondays through Saturdays at 52 rue du Louvre, 1er (*Métro*: Louvre), but don't try it on a Saturday afternoon. Another 24-hour post office is at 71 avenue des Champs-Élysées, 8e, open seven days a week, but crowded on Sundays and holidays, for stamps, telephones and telegrams only – no other postal services.

LETTERS from Paris to the UK cost 3F for 20 grams (airmail envelope and two thin sheets of paper); postcards are a little less. Airmail letters to the US and Canada are 4F50 for 10 grams.

POSTCARDS sometimes take an abnormal length of time to reach the UK from France, which is so close to our shores. It is possible that you can speed up the process by putting your card in an envelope and addressing that. It costs a few centimes more but it might be worth it.

POST CODES: The postal code for Paris is 75, then 0, and then the number of the *arrondissement*. Most of the Marais is thus 75004. It's always written 75004 Paris, postal code first and town name second. The Bureau de Poste has even designed special envelopes with a box for the post code: decorative, sensible, available from most post offices.

TELEGRAMS: Via the telegram counter at any post office, or call (free) 05 33 44 11. Seven words minimum; the address counts as part of the message.

RAILWAY INFORMATION

The great source of all knowledge about how to get from anywhere to anywhere in France is in the Information Bureau at Gare St-Lazare, near the entrance closest to the rue de Rome. It takes a few minutes to crack the code of how to work the timetables, mounted on rollers behind glass. But once you've done that, you're in clover. Also available: a certain number of printed timetables from a central station in this office, each section labelled by the name of the station from which the train leaves. No one here speaks English, so equip yourself with your pocket dictionary to make sure you understand all the footnotes. And don't wait to do this planning until the last minute before a journey.

SLANG

The current *argot* runs to Franglais, which you should have no trouble with (although it does change: jogging, a few years ago, was known as *le footing*, now it's *le jogging*). Try, *très cool* for otherwise indescribable pleasures. And abbreviation: you can go to *un resto très sympa*, start off with *un coup de rouge* (a glass of wine), *bouffer* (eat) and possibly finish your meal with *un cogna*. If you've had a bit too much to drink you might wake up with *une gueule de bois*. Anyone in deep trouble is said to be *dans le chocolat* which is a delicate way to avoid saying *dans la merde*. *Vachement*, literally translated as 'cowly', is the most common way of saying 'very'.

Most slang covers the world of pop culture: thus *un group* is a group, *le leader* is a lead musician; *le rap* and *le hip-hop* will be played by *le Dee Jay* while bright young things do *le break-dance* and *le looking* (acrobatic dance based on the fighting dances of the Brazilian slaves). *Les trainers* or *les baskets* are trainers, *le tagger* spray-paints and scribbles on walls and the Métro, and *on est blacks* means 'we are (or I am) black'. And everybody eats *le hamburger* (pron. angboor-zhe), *les bagels* and *le cheesecake*.

TAXIS

Current prices in the City of Paris, as far as the Boulevard Périphérique:

From: 7:00 a.m. to 7:00 p.m. 'Tarif A'
Pick-up charge: 13F
Price per kilometre: 3F36

From 7:00 p.m. to 7:00 a.m., and Sundays and Bank Holidays. 'Tarif B'
Pick-up charge: 13F
Price per kilometre: 5F45
Fourth passenger: 9F
Baggage: 6F
Animals: 3F

and if you are on your way to the train station, that will be an extra 5F.

There are other rates for waiting time (*heure d'attente*: 30F an hour) or if the taxi is held up in traffic and can go at only 24 km per hour or less.

TELEPHONES

Run by France Telecom: public phones are widely visible, on streets, at airports, and always in post offices which are identified by big bright signs PTT (Poste, Téléphone). Otherwise, look for telephones in hotel lobbies, restaurants, bars, brasseries.

PAY PHONES: Public phones are *Télécarte*-operated although cafés tend to have coin-operated public phones. If you have a phone card, you have quite a good chance of finding a kiosk when and where you need one. Queues are shorter at *Télécarte* points. Cards can be purchased beginning at 50F (50 units) from post offices, *tabacs*, Métro stations and some stores, including Le Drugstore at Étoile.

After you have put in your *Télécarte*, or coin, and dialled the number, you will hear a jumble of noise and then a 'ring' tone which sounds like the British 'number engaged' sound. Don't hang up – this is the French 'number ringing' noise.

Some cafés, *tabacs*, and bars may have a notice over the bar telling you that telephones and toilets are reserved for the clientele. If you don't see such a sign, ask politely at the bar to use the phone. They will point it out, and you either feed in coins, or pay for the metered time at the end of your call. A few places still use the jeton system, with special tokens. Jetons are not transferable from café to café, so if your party doesn't answer, get your money back. Jeton phones require you to press a rectangular button to the right of the phone when your party answers.

Most luxury hotels have public telephones, and a place to sit down. Although they are courteous, they do not welcome callers with backpacks or shabby clothes.

LONG DISTANCE: outside the eight-digit area, time and distance come into play. In phone kiosks, there is a table listing the correct amount to pay for a call lasting a specified number of minutes.

Consult the table, dial, wait for an answer, insert the money. When your time is almost up you'll be warned by a tone. Put in more change then, not before the tone.

INTERNATIONAL: the cheapest way to call the UK is to use a *Télécarte*, or amass a pocketful of 1F and 2F coins and dial direct from any unvandalized coin-fed telephone kiosk. The instructions (in French) are clearly set out on a panel near the phone.

Don't, however, use British Telecom's BT-Direct service unless you are in dire need. The cost is astronomical. Here's how the system works:

From France you dial 00, wait for a second dial tone, then dial 44. This connects you to a London operator, who then makes a transfer charge call to any UK number, or on request will put the charge on your BT charge card.

This is all very swift and convenient, but calls of even the shortest duration ('Hello, I'll be home Thursday at lunchtime, how's the weather, goodbye') add up to be quite expensive. Each minute or part thereof is about 90p.

Travelling paupers should call home either through Paris PTT locations where an operator will put in the call for you and give you the charge when you're finished; or direct, with a handful of change.

International codes from France
UK: 00 44 1 (omitting the 0 for UK codes)
USA: 00 1
Canada: 00 1
Australia: 00 61
New Zealand: 00 64

All French numbers now have ten digits, rather than the 8 digits previously used. Paris and Ile-de-France numbers begin with 01, the rest of France is divided into four zones (02–05) and the present system of dialling 16 to the provinces no longer works. Free phone numbers change from 05 to 0800, international dialling codes start with 00.

Useful telephone services in Paris:
Operator assistance: 12
International directory: 00 33 12 followed by the country code; for the UK dial 00 44.

TIME

The French use the 12-hour clock, but run on 24-hour time. Hence, 5 p.m. is 17:00 (*dix-sept heures*); midnight is 24:00 (*minuit*); and so forth. It takes practice.

The days of the week, starting with Monday, are *lundi, mardi, mercredi, jeudi, vendredi, samedi* and *dimanche*. The months of the year are easier to deal with: *janvier, février, mars, avril, mai, juin, juillet, août, septembre, octobre, novembre* and *décembre*. We narrowly escaped Napoleon's idea of Germinal, Thermidor, Brumaire, which from 1793 to 1806 replaced the more familiar Gregorian Calendar.

France is one hour ahead of the UK; six hours later than the US (East Coast time). You should be aware of this before you call your friends in New York at 3:00 a.m., *their* time.

TIPPING

The rules are clear-cut. Try not to deviate if you want to stay on good terms with your hosts.

TAXIS: 10–15 per cent.

LAVATORY ATTENDANTS in public loos, where found: 1F or 1F50.

WAITERS: 15 per cent is almost always included (you'll note the words *service compris* on the menu). When service is *non-compris*, prices will be itemized, with 15 per cent (rounded off either way) tacked on at the bottom of your bill, and the whole thing totalled.

CAFÉS: 15 per cent is included (as for waiters) for table service. If you eat or drink at the bar, leave some small change – the light-weight coins that rattle around in your pocket – to make up 1F or 1F50.

HOTELS: Service is added onto the bill – but if the *concierge* or any other personnel have done you special favours (calling theatres, getting taxis), they should be rewarded. See page 58.

PORTERS AND LEFT LUGGAGE: Set price, 10F per piece of luggage. No tip needed.

HAIRDRESSERS: Service is included almost everywhere, but a few extra francs at the end won't break you, and it's a nice gesture.

THEATRE AND CINEMA USHERS: 1F for each person in your party.

TRAFFIC

Since we assume you're not suicidal, we won't deal with traffic regulations from a driver's viewpoint here. As a *piéton* – a pedestrian – you should know a few rules of the game.

If you're English, Scottish, Welsh, Irish or Japanese, you must never forget that traffic in France travels on the *right* and fast. Therefore, before you step off the kerb, do *not* look to your right. *Look left*. Then look right, left again, and in all directions as quickly as possible before you head out, or you'll be mown down. Many Paris streets, though not all, are one-way.

For pedestrians, GO is a little green man in the traffic signal; sometimes a pinpoint of green or white light; sometimes nothing at all. STOP is a little red man. In both cases, it's very difficult to see the lights in bright sunshine. Your best bet is to wait for all traffic to stop, and ride on someone else's coat-tails across the street. All traffic lights, red or green, are called *feux rouges*.

Zebra crossings exist, but are usually ignored by all concerned. Traffic tends to go straight ahead even if a pedestrian is clearly out on the white lines. Be very careful of mopeds and motorbikes, especially the great roaring Harleys and Hondas.

Paris streets are either incredibly wide (the *grands boulevards*) and hence impossible to cross without feeling totally naked; or incredibly narrow, with cars parked halfway up the kerb, pedestrians walking with one foot in the gutter, single file, or edging along the wall. Either way, it's risky, so watch your step.

WOMEN ON THEIR OWN

Word has it that women alone do just fine in Paris (the reverse has also been mentioned). Our sources say that women can eat alone in any restaurant (except around Pigalle and other obviously raffish neighbourhoods), drink alone at the counter or at a table in most bars, stay alone in hotels, walk alone in the daytime in parks, gardens and streets in almost every *quartier* without ever being disturbed or made to feel uncomfortable. None of this is true around Pigalle, boulevard de Clichy, or other disreputable areas: you must, in every case, use your head. Don't walk in parks or lonely streets at night – either alone or in company. You wouldn't do it in London, New York, Chicago; so don't do it in Paris. Some parts of Paris have had real trouble on the streets in the past few years, and the newspapers and television in Paris can keep you posted on where not to go in such cases. The woman (or man) who can't resist seeing what's going on is looking for trouble, and the Paris *flics* will toss you into the *panier de salade* (police van) no matter what gender you are, if you get in their way.

Any other advice applies all over the world. Don't be free with personal information, don't flash possessions or cash around, let the reception at your hotel know where you're going if you're going out with someone you don't know well, and keep your taxi fare back tucked up your sleeve.

Au secours (Emergencies)

Dealing with real trouble at home is bad enough. In a foreign country, and in a foreign language, it can be devastating. But there are resources.

MEDICAL EMERGENCIES

If it's more than a minor ailment, you need an English-speaking doctor or nurse, or a supply of medicine dispensed by someone who can understand you and your problem without the aid of faltering French or a translator. Here are the numbers to note. Write them down in your pocket notebook for the times (we hope rare) when you don't have this book in your hand.

SOS DENTISTS
87 boulevard Port-Royal, 13e
Tel: 01 43 37 51 00
RER: Port-Royal

An English-speaking dentist is almost always at hand. Ask for a receipt, as your form E-111 (page 23) covers only minimal repairs and real emergencies such as raging toothache or a lost filling. You should claim on your Travel Insurance Policy for anything above the amount deductible.

SOS MÉDECINS
87 boulevard Port-Royal, 13e
Tel: 01 47 07 77 77 or 01 47 37 77 77
RER: Port-Royal

As above.

24-Hour Ambulance (SAMU) dial: 15

HOSPITALS
British Hospital
3 rue Barbés, Levallois-Perret (in a suburb of Paris, reached by Métro, but a long ride)
Tel: 01 47 58 13 12
Métro: Anatole-France
Hours: 24 hours, 365 days a year.

In spite of its name, this is more or less a French hospital. Don't count on an English-speaking doctor or nurse, unless you make a special request. Telephone first for an appointment. Medical only; no dental facilities.

American Hospital
63 boulevard Victor-Hugo, Neuilly
Tel: 01 47 47 53 00
Métro: Porte-Maillot, then bus No. 82 to last stop.
Hours: Mondays through Saturdays, 9:00 a.m. to noon, 2:00 to 6:00 p.m.
Sundays, emergency treatment only, no fixed appointments. Dental as well as medical. Telephone first for an appointment.

This hospital is extremely expensive and, in the case of an emergency, you will have to leave your credit card at the reception desk before being admitted. Don't come here unless you are sure that it will be 100 per cent covered by your insurance policy.

Hôpital Hôtel Dieu
1 place Parvis Notre-Dame, 4e
Tel (consultations): 01 49 81 21 11
Tel (emergencies): 01 42 34 84 95

If you're not sure that you are fully covered, this hospital provides fine medical care at unbelievably low rates. We have a friend who tripped down some steps, broke her nose and was taken here by ambulance. She was given treatment within an hour of the accident and left, stitched, bandaged and on her way to full recovery. This, including the ambulance and a consultation to remove the stitches, left her only 350F poorer. The French-speaking staff was helpful, compassionate and efficient.

PHARMACISTS
Pharmacie Anglaise des Champs-Élysées
62 avenue des Champs-Élysées, 8e
Tel: 01 43 59 22 52
Métro: George V
Hours: Mondays through Saturdays, 8:30 a.m. to 10:30 p.m. Closed Sundays.

Stocked with familiar English and American brands of medicines, or their French equivalents, and attended by professional people – some of whom will speak English. They will fill a prescription from a doctor, or can give you advice about a proprietary product for minor ills (headache, diarrhoea, streaming colds, strains and sprains, rheumatic pain).

Pharmacie du Drugstore St-Germain
149 boulevard St-Germain, 6e
Tel: 01 42 22 80 00
Métro: St-Germain-des-Prés
Hours: Mondays through Saturdays, 8:00 a.m. to 2 a.m. Sundays, 9:00 a.m. to 2:00 a.m.

Pharmacie Derhy
84 avenue des Champs-Élysées, 8e
Tel: 01 45 62 02 41
Métro: Charles de Gaulle-Étoile
Hours: Mondays through Saturdays, 8:30 a.m. to 2:00 a.m.

British-American Pharmacy
1 rue Auber, 9e
Métro: Opéra
Hours: Mondays through Saturdays, 8:30 a.m. to 8:00 p.m. Closed Sundays.

Staffed with bright, multilingual people.

Pharmacie les Champs-Élysées
84 avenue des Champs-Élysées, 8e
Tel: 01 45 62 02 41
Métro: Franklin-D.-Roosevelt, George V

Open 24 hours a day, seven days a week – very small, but useful in any out-of-doors emergency. They speak about eighteen languages.

Allo SOS
Pharmacie Housecall Hotline, tel: 01 53 40 53 40

They really do make housecalls.

POISON CENTRE
Hôpital de l'Assistance Publique Fernand Widal
200 rue du Faubourg St-Denis, 10e
Tel: 01 40 37 04 04
Métro: La Chapelle

BURN CENTRE
Hôpital de l'Assistance Publique Trousseau
26 avenue Dr Arnold Netter, 12e
Tel: 01 43 46 13 90
Métro: Porte de Vincennes

or call the emergency hotline at Hôpital Cochin, tel: 01 42 34 12 12
at Hôpital Foch, tel: 01 46 25 20 20

DRUG CRISIS CENTRE
Hôpital Marmottan
19 rue d'Armaillé, 17e
Tel: 01 45 74 00 04
Métro: Argentine

or a free number 24 hours a day, 7/7: Tel: 0800 23 13 13

ALCOHOLICS ANONYMOUS IN ENGLISH
Tel: 01 48 06 43 68

OPTICIANS
Lissac Opticians
1 rue Auber, 9e
Tel: 01 47 42 57 80
Métro: Opéra

Lissac are said to be pricey, but good for emergency specs making or repairing, and they speak English. Most Paris opticians will refix a loose sidepiece (*une branche*) with courtesy and for free.

CHIROPODISTS: *PODOLOGUES*
Institut National de Podologie
7 rue du Marché-St-Honoré, 1er
Tel: 01 42 61 03 60
Métro: Pyramides
Hours: 2:00 to 5:30 p.m.; Friday mornings, 8:30 a.m. to noon. Closed during school holidays.

No appointments, you will have to wait, but if your foot trouble is minor, it's an inexpensive good thing. Students work under instruction, and you get your treatment and your feet soothingly massaged, for a moderate sum. A little English is spoken, but not much.

AIDS AND HIV POSITIVE COUNSELLING (FAACTS)
190 boulevard de Charonne, 20e
Hotline, tel: 01 44 93 16 69
For more information, tel: 01 44 93 16 32
Métro: Philippe Auguste

Monday, Wednesday, Friday, 6:00 to 10:00 p.m. Telephone for information or an appointment. For English and Americans in Paris, who have AIDS (SIDA) or are HIV-affected, and for their families, friends and lovers, this centre offers counselling, some therapies and referral to therapy services. Complete confidentiality assured.

VD CLINIC
Institut Arthur Venerien
36, rue des Assas, 6e
Tel: 01 44 39 53 23

FIRST AID
At night, Sundays, or holidays, your *concierge* or the hotel manager can telephone the nearest Commissariat de Police to get you the name of an emergency doctor. In case of a street accident or emergency, look for the automatic callbox marked *Services Médicaux*, at the nearest intersection of major streets.

MEDICAL BILLS AND INSURANCE
Medical: Don't assume that because you are a citizen of an EEC country, you'll get free medical care for the asking in France. Begin by getting the indispensable Form E-111 (see page 23) and hang on to it like grim death. This provides rather minimal cover, and you'll still have to pay at least 20 per cent of the total cost. If you're unlucky enough to need a private ambulance to a private hospital or clinic, you pay the full whack. If you are ill enough to need bringing home by an air ambulance, or by a regular flight with someone to care for you, this can cost up to £5000. So take out insurance (through your travel agent, if you like, but even then read through before paying for the policy). Don't buy the first policy you are offered, and *check for exclusions*.

House calls in Paris by a doctor will cost from 200F, depending on the neighbourhood. Office calls are about 150F.

EuropAssistance is one of the best-known *au secours* systems, offering emergency help 24 hours a day, every day of the year. Their Medical Emergency Service *plus* Personal Travel Insurance covers practically every contingency you can think of. For five days, it costs £13.66; for 12 days, £17.95; for 23 days, £21.12.

For this you are offered up to £5 million in medical expenses, unlimited cost of getting you home to the UK for urgent medical care, up to £1000 for accidents or if your journey is called off for reasons beyond your control, up to £1500 for luggage lost or stolen, £5000 for cancellation and so forth.

You pay the first £25 for any medical claim, for cancellation, or for loss of luggage or money. If you know there's a strike coming up on a certain day – as in the nerve-racking autumn of 1995 – if you're delayed by riot, war or civil commotion, your policy won't shell out. But if your travel plans are wrecked by an unforeseen wildcat strike, you are covered, which is a great comfort. Policies from travel agents, or direct from EuropAssistance, Sussex House, Perrymount Road, Haywards Heath, West Sussex RH16 1DN. Tel: 01444 442211. From Paris the Emergency Line telephone number is, 00 44 181 667 8667.

BUPA subscribers get up to £5 million in medical care, including the cost of bringing you home if necessary, and non-medical care which includes up to £3000 for cancellation or curtailment charges due to circumstances beyond your control, up to £5000 for loss of luggage, travel tickets, passports or whatever, and up to £500 allowance if you lose your money. These policies will cost you up to £28.85 for nine days and £32.95 for up to eighteen days. You pay the first £25 of any non-medical claim. There are no age limits on this policy of BUPA members. It is advised that you get your policy seven days before travelling. BUPA P.O. Box 155, Leicester, LE19G2. Tel: 0171–353 5212.

American Express has inexpensive, full cover policies to go with the travel tickets they sell: for ages between 18 and 65 their charge for 6 to 11 days is £21.90 and £23.10 for 12 to 17 days; half-price for under 18 years. Tel: 014442 39900.

VISA and Access card-holders are protected by free death and injury insurance if travel is charged on these cards. But if you've taken out one of the all-purpose policies mentioned above, remember that you can't claim on two different policies if anything goes wrong.

Fine print department: As it is almost impossible to find a policy that will give you instant money to replace clothes, camera, luggage, etc., or pay urgent medical bills, one veteran traveller advises charging everything on credit cards. Save the receipts, photocopy them, send the originals to your insurance company within 48 hours of returning home, and hope that the payout arrives before you have to fork over to the credit card company. If medical hospital bills are very high, the Emergency Number on your policy will guarantee payment.

Contact lens wearers must make sure their policy includes travel coverage.

TRAVEL INSURANCE

Everything you travel with – clothes, radio, watch, money, luggage, specs – can be covered by comprehensive travel insurance. This should, ideally, include cancellation insurance for plane, train or boat tickets that may not be usable because of illness or accident. Try to get the kind of policy that provides you with instant money to get replacement clothes, luggage, camera, etc., without waiting months for reimbursement; or follow the advice above in 'Fine print department'. Check the policy very carefully. One friend who thought her fur coat was covered by her household policy had it pinched in a restaurant, and too late found that the coat was only covered in the house – not while being worn. Ask your travel agent for the best deals going.

NB: Some credit cards include insurance, but check carefully to see exactly what.

ROBBERY, ATTACK, RAPE

Or any other crime of which you are a victim – use the automatic callbox, marked *Police Secours*. Ask for someone who speaks English. We are advised by feminist friends in Paris that the police are notably unsympathetic to anyone claiming rape, as they seem to take the attitude that women who wear anything more provocative than an anorak are asking for trouble.

LOST PASSPORT

Wise words from a travel adviser in Paris who has helped bail out the unlucky, the feckless, the forgetful: photocopy the first few pages of your passport which show your vital details, when and where the document was issued, the French visa (if necessary), and keep it either with your travel tickets or in your wallet. If you lose the passport, report at once to the nearest police station (ask a policeman or a *pervenche*, the blue-clad meter maid), then go to your embassy (addresses on page 265). They can issue you a new passport, or travel documents which will get you home or allow you to go on your way. In some parts of the Continent, this can mean at best a sour look and some questioning at immigration points; at worst a few hours of cooling your heels in airport or train station while they check up on you. Remember that your travel insurance policy will help pay the cost of replacing your passport (photos, embassy fees, etc.) which will at least ease the pain.

LOST MONEY

Report it to the police, as for passports, then forget it. See Travel insurance, opposite.

TRAVELLER'S CHEQUES

You *do* keep a record of those numbers in that notebook, don't you? Cross off each as you cash the cheques. If you lose the remaining ones, get in touch with the issuing company right away (their European addresses and telephone numbers are in the fine print that comes with the cheques). With varying degrees of speed, they will provide duplicate ones. Report this loss, too, to the Paris police.

LOST OR STOLEN JEWELLERY, CAMERA, CLOTHING, LUGGAGE

Report to the nearest police station (ask someone who speaks French, if you can't, to write out a brief description of the lost item in French). Last resort: the Lost and Found office (Bureau des Objets Trouvés), 36 rue des Morillons, 15e, *Métro*: Convention (see page 234). File a report of what you lost and where you think you lost it. The chances of recovering anything are almost nil, but in dealing with such an emergency you'll be surprised at how your French improves, and you'll get to see the inside of offices and police stations that are right out of Maigret. At the Objets Trouvés office, English is spoken, but in the *gendarmeries*, they are not really there to be linguists – it's not what they're paid for. So if you can chase up a French-speaking friend to go with you, it will help. And, of course, claim on your travel insurance.

THEFT

STREET THEFT

You can protect your serious money with an old-fashioned money belt, available from Youth Hostel and camping shops among others: or a more modern 'Hide-a-Pocket' in thin soft leather, on a short strap, to be looped over a belt and worn beneath trousers or skirt. It's about £5.95 from luggage shops and several mail-order houses; at 7 × 4 inches in size, it's big enough for passport, credit cards, traveller's cheques and cash. While this may sound fussy and grandmotherish, it is a neat, inconspicuous way to make sure that no alien hands are laid on your valuables.

THE CHILD THIEVES OF PARIS

If you find yourself surrounded by a posse of charming, laughing, appealing urchins, jumping, patting and pawing you, strike out with anything at hand: rolled-up newspaper, magazine, umbrella, your fists. These pretty little fiends are carefully trained by local Fagins to surround the unwary tourist, and with small lightning darts at jacket and handbag, take *everything*. Passports, money, credit cards and tickets go in a flash while you're wondering what hit you. Favourite venues are Notre-Dame, the Tuileries, the terrace outside Beaubourg, crowded Métro platforms, on the Left Bank, long queues at museums or anywhere else, for that matter. The kids race away laughing and jeering. Even if police pick them up, they cannot be held for more than an hour or two because of their ages, and in the meantime their *contrôleur* has received all the goodies. An American couple sat on a park bench to rest, and within two minutes were picked clean by kids who made a screen of newspapers around them. Two of the bandit band rifled pockets and handbag, and ended by snatching a gold chain from the woman's neck. If it happens to you, yell loud and harsh: *'Fiche-moi le camp! Voleurs! Va t'en!'* And lay about you with vigour. Forget about dignity. Get rid of these vicious kids.

ANIMAL BITES

Cat scratches, dog bites, a nip from a horse or a squirrel – don't shrug them off. The best we can advise is not to fool around with any animal on the Continent. Rabies is at large in Europe and coming closer to the big cities every year. No joke. The French call it *la rage*, and you will see warning posters in many places. If you are scratched or bitten, get a doctor at once, and report the incident to the police quickly. They will pick up the animal and hold it until it is proved to be either safe or rabid. And they will keep you under observation until the animal's condition has been thoroughly checked. At best, you will need an anti-tetanus shot and have a sore arm. If the animal is infected, you are in for a series of painful, costly and time-consuming injections that will save your life but wreck your holiday. So don't feed squirrels or stray cats, and unless you know an animal and its owner personally, keep your hands to yourself.

STRANDED

If you are without passport, money, traveller's cheques or transport because of loss, theft or other damage, call on your embassy. If they are convinced that you are a genuine victim without resources, they can arrange for your transportation home (the slowest and cheapest way). You have to pay them back as soon as you reach a source of funds. Each embassy has a different policy, so check with yours for the current rules. To get a temporary passport, remember you'll need photographs.

Claim on your insurance for all costs: photos, photocopies, transport, passport and visa fees, telephone calls. Keep every receipt and photocopy the lot before you send the originals to your insurers.

BRITISH EMBASSY
35 rue du Faubourg St-Honoré, 8e
Tel: 01 42 66 38 10
Métro: Concorde

It's a beautiful, historic house and worth taking a look at if you have legitimate reason to call. Nicer manners than at the American

Embassy, and not so many guns in evidence, but the same basic approach: cool, business-like, efficient, good in genuine emergencies.

BRITISH CONSULATE
rue Anjou, 8e
Tel: 01 42 66 38 10
Métro: Madeleine

AMERICAN EMBASSY
2 avenue Gabriel, 8e
Tel: 01 42 60 57 15
Métro: Concorde

Brusque but helpful. Don't expect much sympathy or offers of extra money, as they have had to deal with too many feckless tourists in the 1960s and 1970s who thought rich Uncle Sam was a soft touch. Take four real photos, not photo-machine pix, for a replacement passport, usually issued for six months only. (It's not a bad idea to carry a few extra prints of your original passport photo.)

AMERICAN CONSULATE
2 rue St-Florentin, 1er
Tel: 01 42 96 14 88
Métro: Concorde

The embassies and consulates listed below have the same basic requirements as the British and Americans. Always phone first and if possible make an appointment to see the right person to deal with your problem.

CANADIAN EMBASSY
35 avenue Montaigne, 8e
Tel: 01 44 43 29 00
Métro: Alma-Marceau

AUSTRALIAN EMBASSY AND CONSULATE
4 rue Jean-Rey, 15e
Tel: 01 40 59 33 00
Métro: Bir-Hakeim

NEW ZEALAND EMBASSY AND CONSULATE

7 rue Leonardo-da-Vinci, 16e
Tel: 01 45 00 24 11
Métro: Victor-Hugo

Bois de Boulogne

Racecourses

SEINE

8

14 7

13

● Museums

1 Musée de l'Affiche
2 Musée des Arts Africains et Océaniens
3 Musée Carnavalet
4 Musée de Cluny
5 Conciergerie
6 Museum of Decorative Art
7 Musée des Enfants
8 Musée Guimet
9 Les Invalides
10 Musée d'Orsay
11 Louvre
12 Musée de Luxembourg
13 Musée Marmottan
14 Musée Moderne de la Ville de Paris
15 Musée de Montmartre
16 Musée Nationale d'Art Moderne
17 Musée Nissim de Camondo
18 Orangerie
19 Musée Rodin

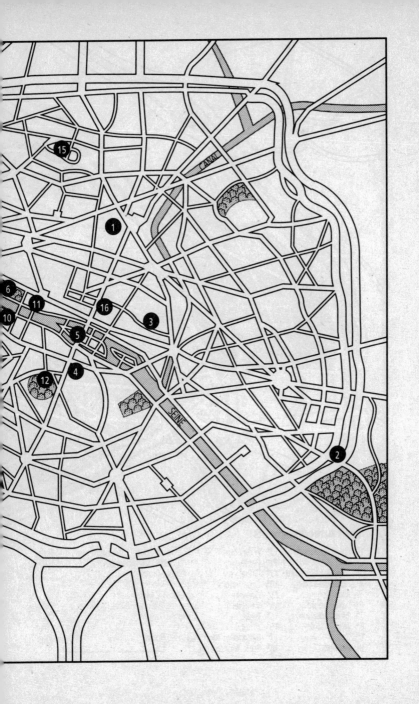

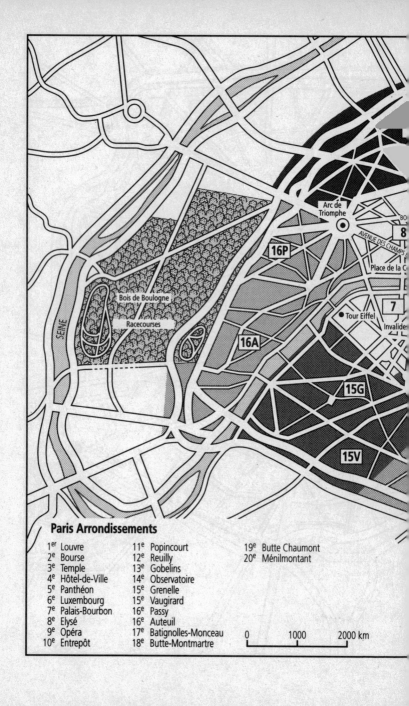

Arc de
Triomphe

16P

AVENUE DES CHAMPS

8

Place de la C

Bois de Boulogne

Racecourses

7

Tour Eiffel

Invalides

16A

SEINE

15G

15V

Paris Arrondissements

1er	Louvre	11e	Popincourt	19e	Butte Chaumont
2e	Bourse	12e	Reuilly	20e	Ménilmontant
3e	Temple	13e	Gobelins		
4e	Hôtel-de-Ville	14e	Observatoire		
5e	Panthéon	15e	Grenelle		
6e	Luxembourg	15e	Vaugirard		
7e	Palais-Bourbon	16e	Passy		
8e	Elysé	16e	Auteuil		
9e	Opéra	17e	Batignolles-Monceau		
10e	Entrepôt	18e	Butte-Montmartre		

0   1000   2000 km

Index

All Pan Books are available at your local bookshop or newsagent, or can be ordered direct from the publisher. Indicate the number of copies required and fill in the form below.

Send to: Macmillan General Books C.S.
              Book Service By Post
              PO Box 29, Douglas I-O-M
              IM99 1BQ

or phone: 01624 675137, quoting title, author and credit card number.

or fax: 01624 670923, quoting title, author, and credit card number.

or Internet: http://www.bookpost.co.uk

Please enclose a remittance* to the value of the cover price plus 75 pence per book for post and packing. Overseas customers please allow £1.00 per copy for post and packing.

*Payment may be made in sterling by UK personal cheque, Eurocheque, postal order, sterling draft or international money order, made payable to Book Service By Post.

Alternatively by Access/Visa/MasterCard

Card No.

Expiry Date

Signature

Applicable only in the UK and BFPO addresses.

While every effort is made to keep prices low, it is sometimes necessary to increase prices at short notice. Pan Books reserve the right to show on covers and charge new retail prices which may differ from those advertised in the text or elsewhere.

NAME AND ADDRESS IN BLOCK CAPITAL LETTERS PLEASE

Name

Address

8/95

Please allow 28 days for delivery.
Please tick box if you do not wish to receive any additional information. ☐